STUDIES IN HISTORICAL GEOGRAPHY

Planning the Past

STUDIES IN HISTORICAL GEOGRAPHY

Editors: Alan R. H. Baker and J. B. Harley

Also published in this series

Southern Africa
A. J. CHRISTOPHER

Finland
MICHAEL JONES

Rural Settlement in Britain
BRIAN K. ROBERTS

Mirrors of the New World
J. M. POWELL

English Towns 1500–1700
JOHN PATTEN

Climatic Change, Agriculture and Settlement
M. L. PARRY

STUDIES IN HISTORICAL GEOGRAPHY

Planning the Past
Historical Landscape
Resources and Recreation

ROBERT M. NEWCOMB

DAWSON · ARCHON BOOKS

First published in 1979

© Robert M. Newcomb 1979

Wm Dawson & Sons Ltd, Cannon House
Folkestone, Kent, England

Archon Books, The Shoe String Press, Inc
995 Sherman Avenue, Hamden, Connecticut 06514
USA

British Library Cataloguing in Publication Data

Newcomb. Robert M.
  Planning the past – (Studies in historical
  geography; 0308–6607)
  1. Landscape protection
  I. Title   II. Series
  719   QH75   78–40896

  ISBN 0 7129 0816 1
  ISBN 0308 6607

  Archon ISBN 0–208–01728–3

Film set in 10/12 point Times
Printed and bound in Great Britain
by W & J Mackay Limited

To those from the past who have gone ahead,
Carl T. Newcomb and Frits Hastrup,
and to the faith of
Karen, my wife, and Lillian, my mother.

Contents

Illustrations

Tables

Preface

Whenever he undertakes a prolonged visit to Old Europe an American historical geographer will find landscapes to stretch his time sense and colleagues to help educate him. Such has been my rewarding experience over the past twenty years, and from the beginning of this Old World connection I have developed an interest in the preservation of the patrimony of old landscapes and in the educating and entertaining ways in which they can be made to serve the present. My personal experience in three nations which have similar preservational goals but which have evolved quite different programmes has led me to share the information in this book. The visible past is all about us, but we must learn to appreciate it as our heritage and as a recreational resource.

Part I considers current, planned uses of the past as well as the techniques and programmes for expanding historic preservation and making the past more useful. The details and case studies upon which students of landscape history so depend – and in which they take such delight – follow in Part II which surveys rural and urban, industrial and political impacts, and examines relics detectable on the surface of the earth. Finally, the pioneer efforts invested in developing better and faster methods of landscape evaluation are considered for what they promise alike to the preservation planner and the layman on holiday.

No academic travels of this kind are made unaided, and I wish to acknowledge assistance received. In America, Joseph E. Spencer made the human experience in the distant past seem real to me and Donald W. Meinig sharpened my perceptive faculties. A dozen years spent on the staff at the Geographical Institute, Aarhus University, Denmark provided me with the opportunity to become

11

familiar with ancient landscapes and to profit from the scholarly friendship of Frits Hastrup, A. Krarup Mogensen and Adrian Randall, among others. Britain, with its landscape palimpsests and congenial colleagues, helped to round out my experience and I especially have Mich Aston, Alan Baker, Robin Butlin, H. C. Darby, Frank Emery, Brian Harley, William Mead, Hugh Prince and the late Harry Thorpe to thank for stimulation and guidance, past and present. In a more general methodological way Harry P. Bailey and William D. Pattison helped me to an appreciation of intellectual precision, and Barry J. Garner demonstrated how to make complicated concepts understandable.

Having now returned to the New World, it is appropriate to express my appreciation to the Geography Departments of the University of California, Los Angeles and California State University, Northridge for the shelter, support and stimulation which I have enjoyed beneath their respective roofs.

Finally, if Alan Baker and Brian Harley have been patient editors and the personnel of Dawson Publishing helpful guides, without the domestic steadfastness of my wife, Karen, my thoughts about the preserved past would still be lying unuttered amid the old fields of Mols.

R. M. Newcomb
Los Angeles, April 1978

Acknowledgements

One does not build either an historic park or a book without support and help from friends, colleagues and technical services. The diagrams and maps were produced by Nöel Diaz and his staff at the University of California, Los Angeles, and this artistic help is much appreciated. I am grateful for permission to use the following items: to Mich Aston for Fig. 6; to James Bond and the Birmingham and Warwickshire Archaeological Society for Fig. 26; Aerofilms Ltd for Figs. 24 and 36; Dept of Antiquities, Ashmolean Museum, Oxford for Fig. 3; D. D. Arreola for Fig. 29; the Australian Tourist Commission for Fig. 37; W. A. Bowen for Fig. 23; H. H. Deleuran for Figs. 19 and 39; Geographical Institute, Aarhus University, Denmark for Fig. 40; S. D. Hale for Fig. 32; M. Jones and V. Olsen for Fig. 31; E. B. Kallesøe for Fig. 35; Peder Kjaergaard for Fig. 8; Queen Mary Tour for Fig. 4; G. B. Peterson Photography for Figs. 1, 14 and 15; O. Simoner and the Austrian National Tourist Office for Fig. 30; Professor J. K. S. St Joseph and the University of Cambridge Committee for Aerial Photography for Fig. 25; Barbara Cohen typed the manuscript and Copy Mart did the duplication, and both receive my special thanks.

Introduction

1

The Visible Past

Introduction

In the summer of 1975 a field methods class from the Geographical
Institute, Aarhus University, Denmark was concluding an exercise
in the mapping of rural, vernacular buildings in the extreme northwest of Jutland when the day's route led to the isolated parish
church at Lerup. Across from the church, the old vicarage, a half-
timbered building, attracted the group's attention. According to the
resident owner, a date of 1638 was a reasonable estimate for the
structure. However, during his twelve years' residence here, he had
inspected the building thoroughly in his profession as an architectural historian, and in the fundament of the east wall he had discovered some historic revelations. He found that a portion of this
wall had been constructed of massive blocks of field stone in a style
characteristic of medieval building in Denmark. In the light of the
evidence he was inclined to date this portion of his home to the
thirteenth century. Appropriately enough, this man was an
architect employed by the North Jutland planning office to survey
the resources of historic buildings within the 6,000 sq. km (2,300 sq.
miles) of the county.

This homely example from a distant corner of a small country
illustrates the main themes to be developed in this book. An inventory of the past was the appropriate job held by the homeowner of
Lerup, and it was Danish preservation law which provided protection for his house as well as his job. New uses for the past were
represented by the comfortable adaption of an ancient vicarage into
a contemporary home, and the imprint of the state, through the
institution of the established church, was represented in visible
landscape form across the road by a Romanesque church nearly

17

eight centuries old. Lastly, the preserved and usable past was being experienced by students as part of a contemporary instructional and recreational course. In this case, not a single plan alone but rather the combination of many plans for the husbandry and use of the past coincided in a revealing way.

Historic Landscape Attractions

The past is all about us, the past has made us what we are and the legacy of the past is the foundation of the problems of the future. What we have inherited from the past can weigh us down or inspire us; we destroy the relics of the past in ignorance or out of spite or enjoy them as sources of diversion. Unique because it is past, yet actual in its meaning to the contemporary and prophetic of the future, the appreciation, use and conservation of this fragile resource present vital challenges to the contemporary world which shapes the past both in the present and for the future (Fig. 1).

There exist many dimensions of the past, ranging from the personal recollections of the individual to the collective traditions of the ethnic group (Fig. 2). The past in latent form would be the manuscript unread or the musical composition unperformed; the scenic past may lie unrecognized in the landscape or, if visible, be unappreciated for its full message. But the past can be a marketable commodity in the modern world, for it contributes to the peculiarities of a world region or nation as it colours the cultural milieu into which the visitor is immersed. The modern tourist brochure provides a spirited insight into the popular taste for the past as it may be enjoyed along with change of scene, wining and dining and more general experiences. The traditional approach to the visible past is through visits to historic buildings and to places and sites associated with famous people, battles or other epic happenings. Quaint local customs, many of which reflect an historic tradition, also rank highly as attractive to the tourist. An actual brochure designed to lure the British to the Continent, demonstrates the large amount of history which passes before one's eyes during the two days spent travelling from Venice to Rome. Landscapes like those in Renaissance paintings are framed by the bus window, giving one the feeling of perambulating through the backgrounds of works by Florentine masters. Within the city of Venice the panoply of ancient buildings laced by useful canals provides an attractive cityscape for anyone with an appreciation of history in stone. The strongly hedonistic sentiments which characterize travel

Fig. 1   Bridge at Llynogwen, Wales (SH 6561) represents the planned preservation of the visible past for our instruction and entertainment. Located in Caernarvonshire within the shadow of Snowdon and adjacent to the A5, this ancient foot and packhorse bridge is sheltered by its modern counterpart.

Fig. 2 The Danish Viking past from a thousand years ago is visible at Lindholm Høje near Aalborg in Northern Jutland. Within sight of the city's modern harbour and gigantic cement plants, this excavated and scheduled cemetery of the Northmen stimulates us to contemplate the past within the present. (Photo by the author.)

brochures and the significant time on tour devoted to the pursuit of the visible past suggest that it is considered to be a marketable experience which lives up to customer expectations. The old churches, battlefields and famous birthplaces fit nicely in with an effortless day's travel, a comfortable hotel and a delicious dinner.

An indication of what Americans expect from outdoor history is illustrated in *Visiting Our Past: America's Historylands* published by the National Geographic Society.[1] The nine million members of the Society are invited to travel the USA to discover that yesterday is still alive in their modern nation: battles of national significance, the historic homes of the Founding Fathers, the taming of the West, and the coming of the Industrial Age are themes selected from national history which can be illustrated by landscapes, old buildings and open-air museums. A patriotic interest in one's nation, the positive learning experience for both young and old and the actual participation in this rediscovery of the past are the values and gains which such travel will provide. The British equivalent would be the articles in *The Geographical Magazine* designed to reveal to the intelligent layman on holiday many of the visible remnants of historical change in the countryside and the cities of his land.[2] However purveyed, certain types of historical features become popular as tourist attractions, and this has been the case since the birth of the modern travel industry a scant century ago (Fig. 3). Today, with greater resources of time and money available, travellers are free to seek out an ever widening variety of historic relics and to enjoy reconstructions of the past, guided by the travel industry and professional writers from many disciplines. Scenic and interesting history is a regional resource which can easily be developed by the travel business for the entertainment and edification of its customers: for example, once you are in London, a free national treasure such as Westminster Abbey can provide convincing diversion sufficient for any tourist.

Planned Preservation of the Past

The forty-year career of the luxury ocean liner *Queen Mary* encapsulates many of the gains and losses characteristic of any attempt to save the past and make it useful in the present. She was built to provide mass transportation across the Atlantic in the 1930s and fulfilled her patriotic duty as a troopship in World War II. Her commercial day passed, however, and in 1967 the City of Long Beach bought the ship, thereby saving her from the wreckers, and docked her at Long Beach Harbour (Fig. 4). As a noble seagoing hotel, the *Queen Mary* flourished and inspired imitators. Looking back, many view the passing of the great days of luxury steamships with regret, and the nostalgia which such a ship ignites moved the City of Long Beach to spend twenty times the purchase price of three million dollars in an effort to turn the ship into a viable tourist attraction. Well preserved, if gutted of much of her machinery, the *Queen Mary* is today used as a combination maritime museum, aquarium, restaurant and hotel. Owned by the City of Long Beach and operated by lessees she currently operates at an annual loss of nearly a million pounds sterling. Only the rich petroleum income received by the city coffers have permitted such a degree of subsidization to continue for nearly a decade. Periodically the call goes out for bids on her purchase, and numerous suggestions are made for better, more profitable and more lively use of this marine relic.[3]

The general lessons provided by the case of the *Queen Mary* are

Fig. 3   The Prehistoric past surrounds the henge monument at Avebury, Wiltshire and its companion, Silbury Hill, in the upper portion of the photograph. Studied and scheduled, this complex landscape of the distant past welcomes the contemporary visitor. The photograph is itself an historic relic having been taken by Major George Allen, a pioneer of air archaeology, in June 1934.

that the preservation of the past is a very expensive undertaking, that it is an enterprise which seldom shows a profit, and that the use of the visible past for recreational purposes is a complicated undertaking. The technological accomplishments which the *Queen Mary* represents are difficult to display in an entertaining manner when the ship is today permanently moored at Long Beach and offers

Fig. 4 The *Queen Mary* lives on in Long Beach, California as a hotel, restaurant, museum and aquarium now that her forty-year career as a luxury ocean liner is ended. Afloat and carefully maintained, surrounded by the scenic expanses of the city harbour, attended by acres of parking space, and entered via a commercial approximation of a Tudor village, the ship has been converted to a theme park which is designed to entertain and instruct a modern public which tends to fly over the Atlantic rather than steaming through its waters.

only a static museum display. As a ship operating at sea, she expressed the high levels of British maritime construction and luxury hotel service which were the standard during the interwar years. The patrons of the vessel represented money and class, and their presence turned a trip aboard the *Queen Mary* into an exciting living event. As is true for so many preserved shells of buildings, factories or transport vehicles, it was in their use and within their contemporary context of society that they intrigue us today. For the contemporary holidaymaker who is interested in seeing history, action must accompany atmosphere so that the old feature will continue living and profits will be made from its operation. However, the basic need is to arrest destruction of features from the past, which once achieved, permits the steps leading to restoration and recycled use to follow. Our legacies from the past must compete for space with other contemporary human activities. In this connection one well appreciates the current British concern over the disappearance of ancient field relics when they are ploughed up or when hedgerows are destroyed to produce larger, more efficient fields. At all times the competition is severe for funds and labour suitable for the preservation task and the development of historic museums or parks, but convincing advocacy is necessary to compensate for the weaker competitive position of the past.

A fundamental position for the preservationist would demand that an historic preservation appendix or element be prepared as a part of every standard regional plan or urban development or renewal proposal. This requirement would ensure that the past received a fair and equal presentation when community resources of time and money were being apportioned. The inventory of historic sites, which is an essential part of any such element, can function as a warning light to alert a planning officer whenever urban renewal or road building threaten relics from the past (Fig. 5). With sufficient prior warning, the relic could be evaluated in comparison with the plan's anticipated improvements and a reasoned decision made.

British reservations concerning overly precipitous alteration of rural or urban landscapes inherited from the past are well expressed by Nan Fairbrother in *New Lives, New Landscapes*.[4] If these old landscapes must change in order that the present may flourish, then the changes should be programmed with foresight. On the European level, concern for the urban past has been expressed during the European Architectural Heritage Year in 1975 by the Council of Europe when it provided a forum for the expression of opinions

Fig. 5   Urban renewal in Glendale, California as the recent urban past gives way to unused open land, parking lots and attractive plans for high rise business complexes. With semi-antique bricks being sold here for 15 pence each and the timbers being equally valuable, it clearly pays to demolish the past with care. Will a better alternative use develop on this site which had to offer only relatively undistinguished commercial buildings of the 1920s and 1930s? (Photo by the author.)

arguing for the husbandry of the built fabric of ancient European cities now under rapid attack from forces producing profound physical changes.[5] The responses from sixteen nations in Western Europe and the Mediterranean were as varied as one would have expected. Projects in the United Kingdom for the cities of Chester, Edinburgh and Poole contrasted with one for a rural setting in the County of Fife and an exhibition in Århus, Denmark illustrating resources of handsome buildings in town and suburb.[6] Programmes such as these are designed to cultivate interest in the architectural history visible in European towns and cities so that future urban planning will contain an awareness of the benefits of such scenic and useful resources (Fig. 30). The consequent hope is that this greater awareness will promote earlier and more complete preservation of the urban patrimony.

The groundwork which such efforts may build in the future is suggested by the state of development which preservational planning has reached in three contrasting nations. Denmark seems to have advanced the farthest in this field with its national planning studies. The present survey of the entire 43,000 sq. km (16,000 sq.

miles) of the realm in terms of the intrinsic value of its open lands is one such planning milestone. At the national level a co-ordinated effort is under way, according to a standard procedure, to evaluate and plan the use and development of relic historic features which are part of the scientific, educational and recreational resources of the nation. Britain is a leader by reason of its energetic efforts directed at an inventory of prehistoric and historic features which together represent the national resources of tangible history. She has built on a long history of concern with field antiquities among archaeologists and has enlisted the effective labour available in local societies. The laudable attempt to organize and finance a network of district archaeologists charged with the inventory task, among other duties, is remarkable in a nation which, of late, has not been in the best of economic health. Lastly, since 1966 the United States has been investing its pragmatic energies and financial resources in a programme of historic preservation for its dwindling stocks of field monuments and old buildings. The result of the comprehensive data collection, committee meetings and civic ordinances has been to ensure that many kinds of historic items have been spared from destruction and have been given conscious consideration when land use and urban plans were being drawn up and adopted. The American approach has been designed to reward the alert, the persuasive and the persistent, for, although the 1966 Preservation Act spells out what is generally desirable, it is quite up to local bodies to see preservation plans through to real accomplishment.

The scope of the Historical Geographer's Concern

The British geographer imbibes a familiarity with the historic landscapes of the nation as a standard feature of his school and university curricula, but not all individuals become intoxicated with the past. Hence, the application of geographical skills to the preservation or use of the past is not everyone's favourite beverage. Nevertheless, foreign geographers, including those in the United States and Denmark, much admire British contributions to the study of historic landscapes and applaud their successes in interpreting the complex geographical challenges posed by the impact of several millennia of physical and human changes on a so varied physical landscape (Fig. 6). The variety of methods used and the research case studies which deal with the visible history of town and country in Britain have together produced a number of outstanding

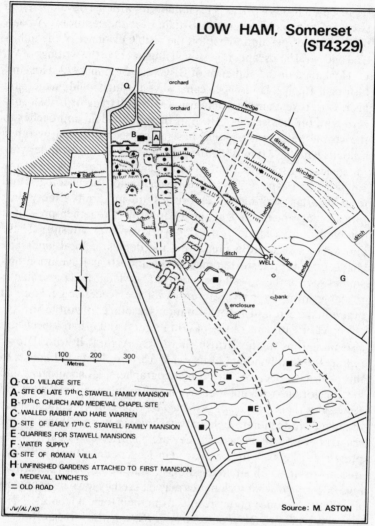

Fig. 6   Sketch map of Low Ham, Somerset, by M. Aston.

publications, and it is from among these riches that the author has made the following selection.

The impact of H. C. Darby has been great upon the school of landscape reconstruction in historical geography, as is evidenced by his Domesday studies and his summary of the evolution of England's geography.[7] The refinement of methods for handling historic documents and for the interpretation of field evidence are fully

represented by his work as is his familiarity with the developmental
sweep of geographic events in Britain over the centuries. A complementary disposition to exploit the visible evidence of the industrial and rural landscapes is very well illustrated in the writings of W.
G. Hoskins. For the audience of BBC television in 1972, Hoskins'
historical English landscapes came alive through vivid images and
his text to reveal another dimension in the shaping of British concern with old landscapes.[8] Both of these individual approaches to
the visible past on a regional basis have been adopted by other
scholars who have described the features and processes underlying
the genesis of specific counties in England. In the 'Making of the
English Landscape' series, Christopher Taylor (archaeologist and
local historian) writing on Cambridgeshire and Frank Emery (historical geographer) in treating Oxfordshire, together present a
complementary sample of the fine work which may result.[9] These
two authors succeed in presenting the details of local landscape
changes from prehistoric times to the Industrial Revolution and
studies such as these, well grounded in knowledge and presented in
readable form, are basic references for the academic guidance of
others in the care and use of the nation's resources of visible history.

Topical treatments of the past in its rural and urban aspects are
also numerous in the British literature. A rural historical topic
requires special handling of its evidence, and illustrated guides to
this skill have been produced by geographers, archaeologists and
local historians working together in a fruitful manner. Aston and
Rowley in their *Landscape Archaeology* have offered much more
than an introduction to fieldwork techniques in post-Roman landscapes because their case studies are themselves valuable interpretative insights.[10] In a similar vein Rogers and Rowley, an historian working with an archaeologist, indicate in their *Landscapes
and Documents* what techniques may be used by local investigators
in order to produce better results from their topical labours.[11] The
absorbing story of *Rural Settlement in Britain* which Brian Roberts
has told and the surrounding *Fields in the English Landscape* which
Christopher Taylor has described depend upon the same documentary, cartographic and field-work materials.[12] The grand developmental themes of the urban revolution within the historic towns and
cities of Britain are discussed in Darby's *A New Historical Geography of England,* and the appropriate geographical methods of study
available to all are presented in *The Landscape of Towns* by Aston
and Bond.[13] The wealth of accumulated physical evidence for urban
revolution, contained beneath the foundations and cellars of con-

temporary urban Britain and illustrated in the Council for British Archaeology publication on medieval towns, is a recommended data source useful in continuing preservational efforts.[14]

If one views the landscapes of Britain as comprising an outdoor museum which illustrates the achievements of the past in a way which can awaken our admiration today, Darby's Domesday studies suggest the intelligence of our forefathers and Hoskins' vivid rural settings serve to augment our appreciation and understanding of the scenery about us. The social historian's sense of the past, which also may contain traces of nostalgic cultural history, finds expression, for example, in a study of the rural roots of post-industrial city dwellers as in Peter Laslett's *The World We Have Lost*, or in Raymond Williams' *The Country and the City* which lets contemporaries of the exodus from village to town express their reservations about this dynamic adventure in Britain's historical geography.[15]

The Geographer's Specific Contribution to the Preservation Process

The geographer's approach to the past is set forth in a lucid manner by Alan Baker when he states that historical geography consists of the study of the geographies of past times, that is, the things, events and processes typical of some place during some interval in its cultural history.[16] Working in an historical manner, the geographer seeks to produce the best possible synthesis of the changing character of a region as it was shaped through time by man. Our demonstrated need to know about the past provides both a market and a motivation for such a geographical undertaking, and our hope is, in Baker's happy phrase, that our studies may improve the quality of life. Specifically, historical geography may contribute to the solution of present-day problems by illuminating landscape legacies which still affect our contemporary world for better or worse. This pragmatic use of the results of academic research may help to clarify a problem or suggest a solution to our contemporaries involved in resource planning, historic preservation or urban renewal, all activities which are directly influenced by the legacy of the past. Historical geographers – like all others who study aspects of the past systematically – can help to show others where we as a people or a nation have been, in terms of time and constructions, and to sketch the outlines of where we are going in terms of our collective efforts to make a home for ourselves. Lastly, if truly foresighted, students of the past can suggest how to arrive at a future which will be humane and resource-wise. It is quite possible, therefore, for the pure research of academic historical geography to make a contribution to the work of the planner or the futurist. Our heritage of antique lands, in the expression of Hugh Prince, must be discovered and evaluated if this peculiar resource is not to be squandered but, rather, is to be exploited to produce a utilitarian appreciation of the historical depth and harmony residing in our surroundings.

The geographer, as a practitioner of his art and repository of information concerning history which is visible on the landscape, is well qualified to contribute to and participate in the historic preservation process. What this process consists of in terms of its theory and practices is well represented in the colour film, *A Place in Time*, which opens with a scene of a London Transport double-decker bus crossing London Bridge to the sounds of Big Ben striking the hour.[17] The camera's viewpoint thereupon recedes to reveal that this classic scene of British urban history has been resurrected as a tourist attraction at Lake Havasu City, Arizona! The film then goes on to examine historic urban preservation as being a variety of expressed civic pride, an example of ethnic rediscovery of the group past, and a good business investment. The geographer, it is felt, should be able to make a contribution to any of these undertakings, and if he is an historical geographer, his input will reflect an additional acute appreciation of the time element and its importance in shaping contemporary rural and urban landscapes. It is hoped that these landscapes, with their cargoes of relict features, will be in greater harmony within themselves than is London Bridge in Arizona.

The self-confessed professional contribution by the historical geographer to historic preservation is to some extent summarized by the three following selected authors. L. R. Ford makes the most general statement and provides sound theoretical underpinnings when he describes the 'new preservation' in the United States as being able to profit from the contributions of the geographer who draws on his ability to reconstruct and interpret the geographic past so as to provide a better understanding of the present for the benefit of both planners and preservationists.[18] In specific terms, the geographer's sense of place is heightened by his sensitivity to the processes of landscape growth and his appreciation of the human scale factor typical of older environments. His reminders of historic urban functions, which may be enduring legacies or reintroduced, are frequently welcomed by both planners and residents in a rehabilitated old quarter of a city. Secondly, Hugh Prince provides a catalogue of the varieties of historic objects which are of preservational interest and which are also familiar to the historical geographer.[19] Anachronisms, ruins and ghost features of either vernacular or official origin abound, and the facts of their state of repair, whether they are unspoiled or decayed, can be expertly evaluated and recorded by the geographer. Lastly, the potential contribution by the geographer within the specific context of Danish preservational planning has been outlined by the present author with particular attention being paid to the uneven areal distribution of artifacts and the suitability of the outdoor museum for their display.[20]

Among the realities of the California state preservation planning programme, a geographer interested in the relics of the past, as well as in the planning process and modern recreational land use, can find abundant challenges and opportunities. The Federal passage of the Historic Preservation Act of 1966 set into motion the bureaucratic machinery which produces the guidelines, planning studies and reports necessary for carrying out the intent and purposes of the new law. The populous and wealthy state of California has responded to this mandate with a series of indigenous publications which illustrate the implementation of this national legislative programme at the local level. *The California Land; Planning for People,* published in 1975 by the California Land-Use Task Force, includes recommendations to the State Department of Parks and Recreation which administers many of the prehistoric and historic resources of the state, and the study also addresses the peculiar problems characteristic of the Public Lands upon which many of these features are located.[21] An official document directly relating to historic preservation was published by the California State Office of Planning and Research in 1976.[22] This publication, the very well regarded *Historic Preservation Element Guidelines,* was a practical guide to making an inventory of historic features, to the drafting of preservation ordinances and to the generation of public support for preservation programmes. The completion of a comprehensive state census of places and things, the first and essential step in the preservation process, was signalled by the publication in 1976 of the excellent *California Inventory of Historic Resources* which included 3,000 historic and 22,000 archaeological sites.[23] The interpretation of the intent and the precise language of the Historic Preservation Act is vital since these national guidelines must be applied to local problems in a context of congruent state and local laws, and the

1975 publication of *Historic Preservation in California. A Legal Handbook* sought to clarify the legal situation, at least for that particular state.[24]

What historic preservation programmes, which involve old buildings and districts, can mean to the municipalities or public bodies which pay for and use the results has also been elaborated. Within the US national context, Alderson and Low produced a report in 1976 which takes up the many questions surrounding the interpretation of individual historic sites.[25] One must distinguish, for example, between sites designed for passive viewing and those to be used for active audience participation, and the possibilities for site development in terms of local history and local needs are seemingly without limit. To return to California for an actual example of site interpretation, the Sonoma County Planning Department in the northern part of the State published a general plan in 1976 which was notable because it included the more homely artifacts of the farming countryside, the field patterns, settlements and tree-lined rural lanes.[26] This succession of related publications which ranges from state-wide studies down to local specifics concerning scenic vistas and farm buildings within just one of the fifty-eight counties of California, illustrates both the complexity of establishing an integrated approach to historic preservation and the wealth of local sites and structures which may find a place in any comprehensive master plan. The geographer's contribution may be made equally well in state planning and inventory work or in studies of local landscape history. The tasks involved are interdisciplinary in nature; the challenges to find meaning in and uses for the past are both local and universal.

Recreational Use of the Past

The concern for the visible past expressed by historical geographers and preservation planners can be understood, but what do the pleasure-seeking public and those who provide their entertainments think about visible landscape history? The answer is that the relics of the past are conspicuously popular with the public and are, consequently, of great interest to the recreational industry. As an example, *theme parks* with historic exhibits and concessions flourish in the United States, and their numbers continue to increase as new approaches and attractions are explored to attract the patronage of an affluent and mobile public. Theme parks are organized around a unifying idea, a characteristic setting them apart from conventional

Fig. 7   A mini Bodiam Castle crowns the artificial motte at Golfland, San Fernando Valley, California. Young and old come to this entertainment facility in order to play miniature golf through and around the castle walls, a Chinese pagoda, a Dutch windmill and other historic embellishments. Carefully located so as to be accessible and immaculately maintained, Golfland represents more than two dozen such places where thousands can find inexpensive family entertainment amid diverting scenery. (Photo by the author).

amusement parks (see Fig. 7). In addition, theme parks are so expensive to build and operate that they depend upon the financial resources of corporations for their construction and campaigns of mass advertising for their success. An historic theme based upon the national past, a regional peculiarity or a particular ethnic group is usually popular and draws the crowds.[27] The layout of the facility and its operation on a day-to-day basis call for expert financial management, a fine touch with labour-management relations and great insights into the use of the media to merchandise a product. In short, theme-park history is a commodity which is popular but one which is expensive to produce and sell.

Immense numbers of the public visit theme parks in the United States, with Disney World in central Florida presently attracting fourteen million visitors a year to enjoy, in part, its themes of make-believe, managed history. Its older brother, Disneyland in Southern California, draws eleven million people who come to enjoy its revival of mainstreet USA circa 1900, among other notable historical attractions. Knott's Berry Farm, just around the corner from California's Disneyland, is the place where 'the West Goes Wild', and opportunities for audience participation in the creation of the Old West attract over 3·5 million customers annually. These three theme parks alone account for nearly one-third of the total estimated American patronage of the 200 examples of this type of historically aware, commercial recreational park. Not all, to be sure, feature historical attractions, but the drawing power is so evident for the Wild West, American Revolutionary times, the Colonial South and bygone village life that at least a portion of park areas can safely be given over to the past. An optimistic student of the past might well hope that the flourishing theme-park industry will cultivate an audience which will also be drawn to visit some of the more academic 2,000 house museums or 125 museum villages which today also populate the recreational landscapes of the United States.

If the theme park with historical pretensions is still a commercial stranger to Britain, living museums, to use Roy Christian's term, which combine relics dating from the Industrial Revolution, the Middle Ages or pre-industrial rural folklife exist in numbers and present a tourist attraction.[28] The idea that the British landscape is a repository for history and hence must be treated with care emerges in Patmore's chapter on 'Conserving the Heritage: Paradox and Conflict' in his book *Land and Leisure*.[29] At the most general level of recreational preferences, the universal popularity with foreign tourists of England's historic attractions such as the Tower of London, Stratford-on-Avon and Hastings, is well recognized and provides the basis for a very successful national industry.

The interest which the public on both sides of the Atlantic demonstrates for historical places and events requires sensitive and intelligent handling in either a museum village or theme park. Whether the commercial exploitation of the past is carried out by public bodies or by private firms is not as important a factor as is the degree of historical veracity which is insisted on in the undertaking. What should always be remembered is that relatively few of the visiting public will be well acquainted with the facts of the historic episode being presented, and, with children in tow and a tour schedule to keep, their resources of patience available for expenditure upon pedantry, poor presentation or shoddy preservation are indeed limited. The management of a theme park can afford to retain the best in technical and academic consultants, but their advice cannot be expected to dominate the mix of economic and administrative considerations which direct the park as a business venture. On the other hand, house museums and museum villages may excel in the degree of managerial guidance provided by their professionals who are well versed in the techniques of museum administration, but often the financial resources available are inadequate for carrying out the full display, and the educational and recreational tasks at hand. Something less than the complete reconstruction of an ancient hamlet or of an urban Victorian railway station will be all that can be done, and yet we must be grateful for what is achieved and see that it is fully utilized.

The arresting and instructive relics of the past crowd in on us from every side (Fig. 39). There exists a strong if latent interest in the past for many people who today have both the leisure time and financial resources to indulge their interest. The conserving talents of students of history can be mated with the planning skills of technical experts so that the past may be preserved and made accessible to the public. In addition reasonable expectations for making a profit from the visible past encourage investment by the private sector as well as by accountable public agencies. Along a broad front recreational use of the past is an active and growing enterprise in the contemporary world, and historical geographers, among others, can contribute their knowledge and energy to the end that the least possible damage is caused to the visible past while at the same time informing and entertaining the public to the utmost.

The Preservation-Recreation Outlook

The combination of preservation with recreation to promote the husbanding of the visible past whilst making it accessible and intelligible to the public is common enough in current practice if not always obvious. Britain is full of excellent examples, and one has but to think of the Tower, Westminster Abbey and the Horse Guards to realize that preserved historic structures, traditions and practices exist in an abundance and are very much appreciated by visitors to London. The past, in this case, serves to adorn the urban present and to entertain visitors in a pleasant and potentially informative manner in return for earnings in sterling which accrue to the national economy. The geographer interested in this interdisciplinary subject finds it necessary to master the complexities of preservational planning as well as the field of recreational studies. Since there is money available to support research and project reports, both subject areas are currently undergoing accelerated growth, and the investigator who studies them must work quickly just to keep abreast of developments.

Overshadowing both preservational planning and the recreational use of the past are the general threats of damage or destruction which, either through ignorance of their significance or through the competition of space or financing, can obliterate the fragile remains of the past on the landscape. Meyer's *The Plundered Past* vividly reminds us of the ruthless exploitation of portable antiquities in order to satisfy the narrow self-interests of museums and private collectors.[30] British rescue archaeology has led the way in issuing an arresting call for last-ditch or foxhole excavations before the bulldozer's blade carves up the past to make way for a new motorway, a real estate development or an industrial park.[31]

National experiences with this loss of patrimony and the varied approaches to assure its preservation and sound managed use are varied, as one would expect. Britain's philosophy of preservation is related by Wayland Kennet, the field experience of the subject by landscape historians in Rowley and Breakell's *Planning and the Historic Environment*, and the pioneer effort to introduce the preservation park concept to modern recreational practices by Patmore.[32] In the New World, Travis and Jakle focussed the viewpoint of the historical geographer on the recreational use of the past as a variety of environmental management, and Ann Falkner summed up the many-sided Canadian approach to the central problem of preserving that nation's architectural heritage while yet assuring continued use of the structures and their availability for enjoyment by an informed public.[33] Lastly, European nations, both individually and through the Council of Europe, have expressed their awareness of the problems incidental to the arrest of building and landscape destruction while at the same time seeking techniques and programmes which will be effective in promoting preservation and which come within national budgets. In Denmark, for example, Koester and his associates, while providing a guidebook to the legal jungle of building preservation legislation, have produced one of the most complete descriptions of the impact which national laws designed to promote architectural preservation can have on national perceptions of the larger dimensions of historic landscape preservation.[34]

The chapters which follow comprise a two-part exploration of the three themes which become intertwined in any effort to plan the past. The present-day uses of the past must be examined as well as the laws which concern the preservation of our past so that it may last sufficiently long to be enjoyed. These two themes make up the four chapters included within Part One which cover recreation, planning and the law in relation to historical landscape features. The second part of the book is devoted to an examination of the specific landscape relics which attract the historical geographer and the preservationist and which bear a potential for instructive recreation. The chapters in Part Two will consider the categories of historical landscape features in a planned recreational context. Conclusions will be in the form of prescriptions for a more effective approach to landscape analysis which, from the point of view of the preservationist, is the integrating step between site and object inventory, on the one hand, and the recreational land-use plan on the other. It is the actual landscape relics we can see and use which comprise the third and most enduring theme to be discussed here.

Part I

Recreation, Planning and the Law in Relation to Historical Landscape Features

The four chapters in Part I describe recreational usage of the past and the preservation planning process. Chapter 2 looks at current recreational usage of the past in museums, outdoor parks and theme parks with historical attractions. An inventory of our resources of historical landscape features is a basic requirement for both planning and usage, and this undertaking is described in Chapter 3. The stocks of Prehistoric barrows, medieval field system remnants and early industrial buildings, among other legacies of the past, must be examined, classified and evaluated before we can advance with plans and proposals. The many and varied legal instruments which support the study, inventory and preservation of the landscape patrimony are reviewed in Chapter 4. Because the law assumes nationalistic characteristics and reflects varied economic priorities, our case studies are drawn from three different nations whose structures of preservation law complement one another. Chapter 5 examines the development of recreational usage of the past as this may be expected to evolve, given the preferences and economics of the leisure-time industry and the legal machinery which exists.

2

Present Recreational Usage of the Past

Introduction

The thirty-five members of our one-day, bus tour group had reco-vered from the delicious luncheon taken at the trout fishermen's inn by the time we reached the private, open-air museum of Hjerl Hede in north Central Jutland. This popular museum of ancient and historic rural Denmark was started in 1930 by H. P. Hjerl-Hansen on a site which has expanded to include 2,000 hectares (3,000 acres) of rolling heathlands, pine forests and lakes. Currently, some 150,000 people visit the park in the summer season, with a low entry fee posing no real financial barrier to their entry.

Starting with a fine half-timbered farm from 1530, the museum has grown to its present size of over forty buildings, and although the emphasis is upon the reconstruction of a pre-enclosure Danish village, the time-span covered by the exhibits stretches from the New Stone Age (c. 2500 B.C.) to about 1900 A.D. so as to include the impact of the Industrial Revolution on rural industries such as forestry, dairying and peat lifting. Laid out within a generous space of 500 metres (1,500 feet) each side, the immediate impression one receives at the museum is of a dispersed village built upon a gentle slope, with the post mill and the stone church dominating from above the half-timbered and straw thatched barns and farmsteads.

As we wandered through the village, the liveliness imparted by the creaking ox-drawn cart full of visiting children, the songs of the costumed children at the village school of 1823 and the salty com-ments of 'Jens Vejmand' the road mender at work, did much to give the buildings a sense of belonging to a genuine rural community of a hundred years ago. The smith was fashioning miniature horseshoes, the miller was prepared to grind corn, the potter worked her wet

41

clay, and the staff of the steam-powered sawmill were busy ripping planks. Just beyond the sawmill with its magnificent and shiny British steam engine lay the new exhibit which combined a narrow gauge logging railway with a horse-powered turf brickette manufacturing complex. The stir and activity here contrasted strongly with the silent, sunny interior of the raw stone village church and the grassy undulations of the ridge-and-furrow fields below (see Fig. 8).

One was struck by the interest shown by the visitors, old and young, and it was evident that for many an uncle or grandmother Hjerl Hede provided an excellent opportunity to demonstrate their knowledge of old village crafts and techniques. Experimental archaeology was used here to instruct and entertain in the form of a reconstructed Iron Age house, complete with clay forge and loom; a Bronze Age house under construction; and the ever-popular Stone Age settlement inhabited by archaeology students, where the men were fashioning a dugout canoe and the women, in foxskin bikinis, were making pots or cooking fish, while their children rolled and tumbled about the threshold (Fig. 9).

In terms of its scale and layout, its variety of exhibits and its human interest I believe Hjerl Hede to be one of Scandinavia's best outdoor museums, a model against which other lands can measure their own efforts to bring visible history to the public. At Hjerl Hede one finds encapsulated the five basic requirements for a successful public outdoor museum.[1] These factors include *publicity*, to make the attraction known to the public and to keep them informed about new additions and special showings, and *parking space*, a vital requirement for patrons from motorized societies. Freedom and enjoyment for children and family groups should be enhanced by *protection* against vandalism, unobtrusive crowd-control, park *maintenance* and efficient litter control. Lastly, the *profit margin* should be sufficient to keep the park attractive and in good repair, and reinvestment funds should be used to add new exhibits and attractions to the existing complex.

These requirements are obvious, and their practice is presumed by visitors to those attractions which are recognizably going concerns. What is somewhat less self-evident, perhaps, is that recreational usage of the past must employ these principles as faithfully as does the proprietor of any amusement park or facility. Merchandising the past in a park which stresses history is much the same sort of business as organizing and operating a park which stresses amusement rides or wild animal exhibits.

The useful American term, *theme park*, is applied to entertain-

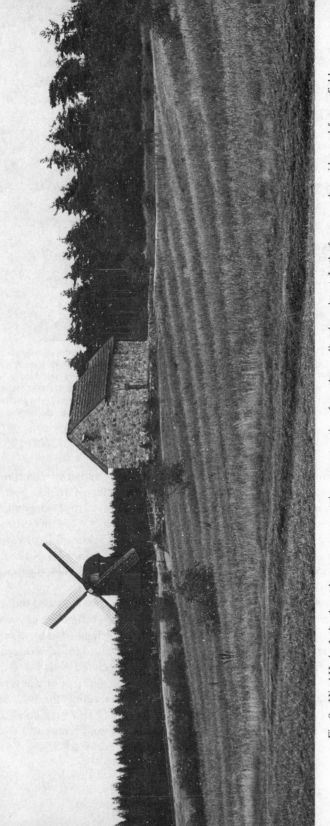

Fig. 8 Hjerl Hede, Jutland, outdoor museum contains reconstructions from the medieval rural past. In the foreground are ridge-and-furrow fields reconstructed with great care and under scholarly guidance. The stone replica of a twelfth century Christian church, complete with interior furnishings of a font and altar, shares the skyline with a rebuilt but antique postmill which can still grind corn. The museum visitor is free to wander around these exhibits with guidance from available literature and from appropriately costumed museum personnel.

Fig. 9 The reconstruction of a Stone Age Village at the private, outdoor museum at Hjerl Hede, Jutland in Denmark. Archaeology students live and work here during the summer high season, building houses, making pots, cooking and fishing by dugout canoe under the gaze of an interested public. This traditional type of Scandinavian reconstruction of the past provides popular entertainment and education to the public at large as well as to school groups and bus tours. (Photo by the author.)

ment complexes which focus on certain types of activities or certain groupings of attractions.[2] The classic examples of theme parks which have succeeded to a fabulous degree are Disneyland, California (now over twenty years old) and Disney World in Central Florida near Orlando, which has been most successful since its opening in 1971.[3] Both parks incorporate the principles outlined above with such dedication that a total of twenty-five million people visited the two facilities together during 1977.

Among the multitude of delights available to young and old at these two parks, American history is included in the form of New Orleans Square, a type of Main Street USA which glorifies town life as it was at the romantic dawn of the automobile age. In addition, the entire range of symbols and objects associated with the Old West is employed to furnish Frontierland. Regardless of whether one admires the Disneyland approach to marketing the past or views it critically, it is an approach which sells and its successful shadow will be cast upon the following discussion of museums and theme parks devoted to historical events or places.

Enjoying the Past at the Museum

On entering the prehistoric section of the National Museum in Copenhagen, one is immediately confronted by the paradox of the museum world. Here, neatly displayed in glass cases, are thousands of polished stone and flint implements, all originating from Danish fields and forests. In this example the museum is a storehouse but one with a potential for silent self-improvement; it is an educative social service supported by public funds. The museum serves two functions somewhat in conflict with one another. First, it must protect, preserve and study antiquities which have been removed from the perils of the open field or of the damp cellar. Secondly, it must instruct, if possible in an entertaining manner, members of the public, particularly school children. Since study is seldom entertainment in the sense of providing amusement or diversion, a conflict arises between studious intent and public expectations. How to make the past interesting, how to make it *fun*, is the challenge; otherwise the museum will remain a storehouse visited only by curators and night watchmen.[4]

These observations are well recognized among museum staff[5], and resources of time, money and intellect continue to be expended to find ways for the museum at national or local levels to meet the demand for enlightening entertainment while continuing their research function (Fig. 10). The care and presentation of exhibits are practical goals, but the organization of museums and their financing are frequently matters of national policy. The 270 museums open to the population of Denmark have come under close scrutiny within the last five years as efforts to achieve a balanced programme of subsidies have progressed parallel with efforts designed to democratize their administration.[5] While the professional future for the trained museum worker is being evaluated, there is also a debate on the social functions of his institution.

Enjoying the past within museum walls may, therefore, present nothing more than vistas of glass cases filled with glorious strings of amber beads or examples of delicate, prehistoric flint work. Alternatively, the museum displays may be made less burdensome visually and be equipped with greater amounts of textual material, including brochures for self-guidance or radio headsets which will pick up a broadcast commentary delivered *en route* through the exhibits of flint tools, art objects and rune-stones. A third possibility is that the museum will develop and maintain an outdoor, working-display exhibit which, for example, involves the

A. The Traditional Museum

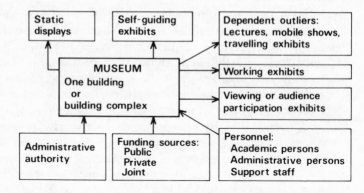

B. The Outdoor Museum

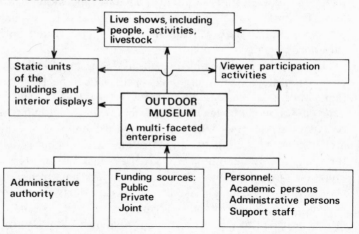

Fig. 10   The traditional museum contrasted with the open-air museum.

construction of a Viking house using reconstructed tools of that era. The summer visitor may even find scout troops and school classes involved in the reconstruction work itself. In the summer of 1976, for instance, 13,000 members of the Danish Boys' and Girls' Brigades encamped near Skanderborg, and part of their activities included the construction and habitation of ten different 'towns', six of which had historic period themes extending from the Stone Age to village life in 1876.[6] The novel element added here to the equation of the working museum is audience participation. For many, participating in or watching such constructive activities serves most dramatically and in a valuable manner to make the past work for the gainful entertainment of the present.

The Outdoor Museum

In moving out from the four walls of the traditional museum building into the courtyard or the surrounding fields, we can consider a distinctive transitional type of historical museum, housed within an historic building itself. The old mill, the country cottage, the old town hall are well-known examples, and the building may contain a heterogeneous assemblage of items which range from local flint implements to a sea captain's collection of scrimshaws (ornaments made from shells or whale teeth). On the other hand, the old watermill building may become a museum devoted to the visible and working relics of the miller's art. The single-building museum housed in an historic structure is the half-way step between the traditional museum and the collection of old buildings which form what is called in Scandinavia an open-air museum but elsewhere an outdoor museum.[7]

Two aspects set this type of *display centre* apart from the traditional museum. First, the museum and its exhibits and activities are located within terrain which itself enhances the museum's functions. The visitor invests a good deal of energy in traversing the museum preserve, and in a kinaesthetic manner involves himself in the sights, sounds, textures and scents of the museum, its activities and its environs. For the family with young children this requirement of active participation is frequently a positive factor, for the energies of the restless young are hereby usefully diverted. The vagaries of the weather will add a stimulating dimension to the museum experience.

Secondly, the piece of territory encompassing the museum structures and activity centres can add an enlivening dimension to the museum experience. The possibilities offered by a village environment, the presence of vegetation, connected pathways or meeting points such as the pond or mill are visual and functioning features which can shape and broaden the museum experience for the visitor. Space, the weather and one's own muscles are all enlisted by the open-air museum so that it may better do its job.

The outdoor museum, as indicated by Fig. 10 (B), involves more audience participation in its live-shows or demonstrations than does the traditional museum. Passive viewing is, of course, still very much a part of the museum experience in both cases, but the sense of liveliness is emphasized more by the outdoor than by the traditional museum.

Hence, when experiencing open-air museums such as the one at Lyngby north of Copenhagen or the Skansen Museum of Swedish county architecture in the centre of Stockholm, the visitor has the impression of an old village which, by some freak of time, has been preserved untouched from an era a century or more ago. At the Copenhagen open-air museum the presence of sheep and goats on the green and the rumble of the horse-drawn waggon which takes visitors about help greatly to make a lively scene and to simulate a village atmosphere out of buildings which date from the seventeenth to eighteenth centuries.[8] At Skansen, the pioneer among this type of museum, the handicrafts practised by potters and weavers enliven the interiors of the farmhouses and outbuildings. At both of these outdoor museums the tree-lined paths with their curving configurations provide the pedestrian with many views of gables, portals and wooden walls. The absence of the background noise of automobiles means that natural sounds can enhance the bucolic mood.

As representatives of the historic urban environment, the Old Town at Århus, Denmark, and the Old Bergen district of Bergen, Norway each make a contribution to the preservation and enjoyment of examples of pre-industrial urban architecture. In Århus, private initiative was responsible for the opening of the museum in 1914 with a prime example of a two storey, half-timbered merchant's house from 1597. This particular building had occupied a parcel of land close to the centre of town until it was carefully moved and used at the Århus International Exhibition of 1909. Peter Holm took the opportunity of this building becoming available at the close of the show to obtain it as the centrepiece for the new museum, and during the ensuing thirty-four years under his direction the museum developed a high rating among the open-air museums of urban buildings to be found in Scandinavia.[9]

The Århus Old Town today charms and instructs the visitor through its harmonious collection of over fifty examples of pre-1900 urban buildings. Since its early start, the Old Town Museum has continued to receive examples of old urban buildings while at the same time adding to its collections of technical and artistic artifacts. The visitor today can stroll on the flagstones of a reconstructed marketplace which looks much like that of a Danish merchant town in the late eighteenth century. Within the surrounding buildings are housed a functioning collection of bakery equipment, a print shop, a glazier's workshop and a merchant's shop and home. The fact that museums such as those in Århus or Bergen are open all the year means that their attractive environs are always accessible. The fifty-odd buildings of the Århus Old Town aptly fulfil the function of a repository museum of urban arts and crafts, serve as a research museum, and act as a public museum and year-round urban amenity. In the best sense of the word, this is living preservation and restoration of relics from the urban past.

The Historic Theme Park

The restrained, enlightened outlook of Scandinavian open-air museums contrasts sharply with the amusement park atmosphere and the colourful liveliness of the American historic theme park. As an example, twenty km (twelve miles), from the modern, high-rise heart of Tucson, Arizona one can roll time back a century and walk the streets of the Old West in order to see some of its more spectacular sights. Old Tucson was built originally as an outdoor stage setting for the filming, in 1939, of the motion picture *Arizona*. From this compact nucleus of false-fronted stores and buildings facing a dusty street has grown the modern tourist attraction which today greets half a million visitors per year. Within a compass of 130 hectares (320 acres) one will find everything from an adobe mission to a replica of a one-room school of 1870, from a blacksmith's shop to the ever-present if incongruous Chinese laundry. The buildings, as excellent examples of the stage-set builder's skills, are well researched and well constructed. The furnishings of many of the interiors are authentic and well displayed. The ice cream parlour housed within the saloon building and the curio shop in the merchant's trading post may jar upon some sensitivities, but together they provide necessary compromise with contemporary demands.

The fact that nearly thirty films and television shows have been made here is responsible for higgledy-piggledy layout of the park which centres on two independent foci, the dusty main street and the mission compound. These two elements would not be so clearly identifiable nor so spatially separated from each other in any real western settlement, but their construction and subsequent preservation at Old Tucson means that the visitor can sample both the Spanish and Anglo architectural contributions to the West. One additional indication of the park's origins in the entertainment industry is the daily 'live gunfights' which vie with stagecoach and train rides for the visitor's attention.

If one demands the 'pure', silent, museum-based historical entertainment for the masses, the positive aspects of an enterprise such as
Old Tucson with its population of western folk – real Arizonians of
local residence – and its dust and horses will probably not be
admired for its educational value. The 'Old West Lives Again' is on
lively display here amid the expansive scenic wonders of the
Arizona desert. This popular chapter from an idealized past reconstructed within the context of the commercial, open-air entertainment business holds its own well against the celluloid West of the
television screen, and the economic success of this and other similar
examples is easy to understand.

The Museum as National Symbol

A special example of the museum as a repository of popular history
occurs when it is founded and used to display national symbols.
Selected episodes or versions of national history may be impressively and conveniently displayed within such an institution.
Colonial Williamsburg and Williamsburg Historic District, a joint
municipal and private outdoor museum in Virginia, conveys the
atmosphere of Colonial America. The Tower of London in its daily
role as a national museum displays the might of the state throughout
British history. Such museums or groups of preserved buildings may
be state-supported or private outpourings of patriotism. Additionally, historic museums may even express nationalistic sentiments
and patriotic feelings in spite of themselves.

The individual entrepreneur offering a tour of the childhood
home of a national figure at fifty pence a head represents a vastly
different operation from the battlefield monument maintained at
state expense with all the powers of the bureaucracy used to adver-
tise it. Common to both approaches, however, is the conscious
decision to stress an individual or a chapter from national history in
order to capitalize on the interest of a broad public in particular
historic relics, buildings or outdoor sites.

Some buildings or places convey such strong and well-known
messages of national significance that no promotional efforts are
necessary. Dybbøl Mill in southeastern Jutland in Denmark is such
a place, containing associations which represent an entire chapter in
Danish national history, for a decisive battle in the war with Prussia
took place here in 1864. The fact that Hastings as a place is so
clearly associated with its role in British history means that it needs
no private or state efforts to enhance its significance.

A point worth making about these sites of nationalistic symbolism is that some of them are endowed with painfully ambivalent characteristics. The combined public and private expanse of Gettysburg National Military Park, a battlefield site in Pennsylvania, is as full of significance for those who view the American Civil War as a victory over slavery as it is for those who consider it a conflict which revealed what was best in the cause of the southern Confederacy. Culloden Moor in Inverness-shire, which is today owned by the public and is a site little changed since the day of the great battle, must bear a similar bi-polar significance for people dwelling north or south of the Border who possess strong nationalistic sentiments regarding the outcome of the events of 1746.

Since the Second World War, when so many previously colonial lands have received their independence, attempts have been made to enlist the house museum and the open-air museum in the service of the state to help engender patriotic sentiments about the new land and a personal identification with its future. Such a pragmatic exploitation of history with its relics need not be devoid of positive results. For the Republic of Indonesia, Indonesia in Miniature – an outdoor museum – was one answer. Within a park of 120 hectares (300 acres) the vastness of the Republic and the many cultures which it enfolds are represented. Of particular interest here is the attention devoted to the varieties of architecture and crafts found in abundance among the more than two-score provinces which today make up Indonesia. Historic house types and methods of construction, for example, are hereby preserved for appreciation by the Indonesian and foreign tourists who visit *Taman Mini Indonesia Indah*.

History is a powerful shaper of opinions which can be used to direct national goals and rationalize national policies. The museum, whether a traditional or outdoor type, can be enlisted to further such aims. The result for the museums can be abrasively chauvinistic, simplemindedly adulatory or instructively entertaining. At the least, selected elements from the national past are preserved, while at the best, an inspirational lesson from the past may be received.

Fitting the Past into a Museum

Since there are 25,000 museums in the world today,[10] why even consider the establishment of any more? This question arises because new museums and theme parks with historic dimensions continue to be established, seemingly regardless of any need other than as a contribution to the entertainment industry. 'Tucktonia', a theme park to be built near Bournemouth, is billed as potentially the largest model landscape in Europe. The park will include historic buildings and sites befitting the complex cultural landscape of Britain it is setting out to depict. With museums devoted to historic bottle collections, to wines and wine production, to barbed wire and to the barbarities of taxation, why not a museum to commemorate the role of the potato in Irish history or a 'Museum of Emigration' to represent the quarter-million Danes who sought fame and fortune in the New World?

If we consider the varied personal approaches to the past on which the world of museums is based, we may be able to suggest additional types of historic museums which will fulfil needs of the public at the same time as preserving things of value from the past. Table 1 lists six personal approaches to the past which may be

Table 1   DIFFERING APPROACHES TO THE PAST VIA THE MUSEUM

1   Diversion and entertainment derived from the past as preserved within the museum.
2   Scholarly research conducted within the museum.
3   Use of the museum as a teaching device for school children of all ages.
4   Searching for moralistic confirmations of the present by the past through the museum's contents.
5   Searching for a confirmation of one's vision of the present by the physical relics housed within the museum.
6   A flight from the present in search of the nostalgic past, whose simpler and purer standards may be revealed or imagined through the museum's exhibits.

catered for within the museum. For the adults who pay the suppor ing taxes, diversion and entertainment are probably the chief gai experienced from a museum visit. It is assumed in all cases that tl. institution will both serve the research worker and will certainly make a positive educational contribution. Instruction may also be derived from a point of view which sees the material preserved in the museum as contributing a type of moral guidance for the present.

Instruction and entertainment of a different sort are represented by two final personal approaches which together can be regarded as a search for alternative visions to the present as hidden within or revealed by the past on display. A confirmation of one's image of the present, for example, may be sought in the past as revealed by the museum. By contrast, the flight from the present in search of the nostalgic past may also be a motive. Here it is expected that relics from the past may themselves be superior objects and speak of purer motives and greater harmony within the lives of their makers and users, or may be manipulated by a romantic person in order to imagine a perfectible past as a means of escape from the troubles of the present.

Using these six varied approaches to the past accessible via the museum, is it possible to suggest an omnibus type of museum which will satisfy most or all of them? It would seem that a variation of the outdoor museum which depicts rural village life may be one satisfactory answer. A multi-faceted environment such as a collection of farmstead buildings, all carefully restored when rebuilt upon the museum site and filled with antique furnishings of parlour, kitchen and barn will suffice. In such a place the scholar, the teacher with the school group and the romantic or nostalgic dreamers can all find a degree of fulfilment. Diversion and entertainment can be provided by varieties of working exhibits and by 'tools and techniques' demonstrations offered by craftsmen. As an example, the carding, spinning and weaving of wool derived from the museum's own sheep, as demonstrated at Lyngby open-air museum north of Copenhagen, can fascinate even the most blasé of audiences, especially when the day is mild and a neat farmyard seems the natural place for such a demonstration to take place. Whether or not the audience itself can be allowed to participate to any degree in such a programme of skills and chores depends on the size of the anticipated audiences and the budgetary resources available for funding instructors and programme directors. The museum which involves itself in such an undertaking directed at the public is assuming a difficult and expensive addition to its normal programmes.

Moving out of doors, the possibilities are great if we recall the populated Stone Age village at Hjerl Hede or the roadmender and ropemakers. An indication of the possibilities is suggested by the replicas of pre-Enclosure ridge-and-furrow fields at Hjerl Hede (Fig. 8). These were carefully fashioned under the supervision of Prof. Axel Steensberg, one of Denmark's foremost authorities on ancient fields. Such a concern for accuracy and appropriateness requires both time and money. Once built, the second phase of the project would be to cultivate these field strips by means of a wheeled plough and several brace of oxen. If such a colourful undertaking were feasible, one could foresee lively discussions regarding the relationships between plough type, direction of ploughing and length of ox goad and the resulting field system dimensions. At Hjerl Hede in about 1970 an attempt was made to cultivate a piece of heathland using an ard and a brace of domestic oxen in connection with the Iron Age house exhibit. The skill and stamina of the participants, both men and beasts, were apparently not up to the demands of the experiment, for the oxen made some cursory attempts at the tough heath and then simply lay down on the job. It is consequently difficult to envisage any success with a demonstration of medieval ploughing using soils, equipment and draught power in keeping with that period. In addition, to consider that such a programme would have to run for years before one could ascertain the role of plough type and ploughing direction in the formation of ridges and furrows, and given labour costs and audience resources of patience, the feasibility of such a complicated undertaking may be remote.

The success of arts-and-crafts activities at a museum such as Hjerl Hede depends on the recruitment of country craftsmen from the surrounding area and their retention at a satisfactory rate of pay. Rope makers, coopers and basket weavers are craftsmen in short supply in most parts of Europe and North America, if not so scarce in other parts of the world. Their involvement as living participants in museum activity exhibits is highly diverting and entertaining but expensive for season after season. If such craftsmen are not to be found, then their skills need to be taught to others who can perform within the museum context. Success in this regard can be reported at a time when traditional, hand-work skills are becoming attractive to young artisans, whilst the wares produced by the museum craftsmen may be sold profitably as souvenirs. Houses and outbuildings can present more of a long-term problem. However faithfully they are constructed according to Iron Age or Viking patterns and tools, they would seem to have little use other than as passive exhibits on the museum's grounds. The Viking house at Mosegård archaeological museum south of Århus, Denmark is perhaps an exception, for there the seasons are noted in the building of boats, the baking of bread and the brewing of strong mead, all according to Viking plans or recipes. The fact that upwards of 125 of these outdoor museums are today functioning in the United States[11] illustrates the attractiveness of this particular answer to the needs expressed in Table 1.

If we turn from the chilly, windswept streets of the rural open-air museum during the winter season when no one delights in visiting such places, what are the potentialities in the museum of urban history or the living, old village or small town itself? This type of museum is greater in size than a single building and may be located on a plot of land within the city centre or a preserve somewhere on the periphery. In these latter examples, reconstructions of original buildings on a new site provide the centrepieces of the physical display. The buildings themselves may be laid out to reproduce a more or less fanciful urban unit, so that the buildings may be clustered about a pond and a mill, as is the case with the Old Town open-air museum of urban buildings at Århus. The resulting feeling of structural unity does much to offset the fact that not all of the buildings so collected are from the same time period nor are they representative of a single town but rather the collected legacy of many different towns.

The usage of the buildings making up such a museum can be varied, and the structures may house various collections or provide space for research work on the history of printing or baking in the pre-industrial town. For the public, the museum may provide entertainment and activities which will require that some of the buildings will be open and supervised. In addition, functions such as restaurant facilities, gift shops and information kiosks which greatly differ from the buildings' original purpose can also be housed within the museum structures. The result is a museum which has a life and a usefulness which surpasses that of the enclosed, display cabinets of a traditional house museum.

When such an urban museum precinct becomes directly involved in the daily life of the surrounding city, as is the case when the museum park is frequented on a daily basis by visitors and by pedestrians *en route* to work or residence, the extent of the museum's contribution to the urban milieu can be realized. The attractive Århus Old Town Museum functions as a most lively and appreciated park and transit route. This normal urban role is augmented for one week each year when, during the Århus Festival Week, an old town market is recreated, complete with antique roundabouts, a Punch and Judy show, a wine cellar, an old-fashioned outdoor restaurant and serenades from a genuine Black Forest calliope (steam organ). If a museum of urban architecture is located peripherally to the town centre, then its vitality will be promoted by the arrival of school excursions and by summer vacation days.

The urban historic district or precinct is quite another story, for in this case the aim is to further the use of old buildings by contemporary urban activities or to recycle old structures into modern roles. In addition to the district, one also should consider the individual building of historic interest located within contemporary urban areas. Further discussion of these possibilities, which relate more to historic preservation than to museums of urban houses, will be taken up in Chapter 7.

In neither the museums of rural buildings with their exhibited trades and practices or in the urban equivalents, can we expect to recreate and maintain a living, functioning settlement unit which works as it did in the past. The best that the outdoor museum can hope to accomplish is to breach the barrier put up by the traditional four walls of the house museum and to get the visitors out of doors where they can walk and observe as well as perhaps participate in activities which simulate the historic farm village or market town. The historic theme museum should be designed to illuminate the past, not to recreate it as a viable alternative to the present day.

The 25,000 or so museums in the world serve, first and foremost, to store valuable and interesting, unique and fragile relics from the past. They provide places to which school children and the public may come in expectation of constructive and vivid instruction. If there is a professional staff in residence, study, conservation, and modern display may all be achieved. The outdoor museum may be quite similar in appearance and have identical functions, but in addition its experience will be enhanced by a liveliness of activity – including audience participation – and a spatial element which combines an ensemble of structures with the outdoor climate.

The museum can function to preserve shrines of the past which have outlived their original functions but continue to be well regarded as a relic of the national patrimony. In many new and self-consciously patriotic nations, the museum may be enlisted in the service of the state to function as a mirror which will reflect recent achievements or serve as a rallying point for the stimulation of public awareness. Museums may also be erected at sites where there is a need to preserve new archaeological discoveries.

An historical museum may serve as a peripatetic institution which takes the past to the public if the public is slow to find its way to the museum. Brown-bag seminars about the history of the city have been attempted in Los Angeles among the city centre workers who share their lunch with forty minutes of history alfresco.[12] Travelling displays which reach out with a theme or artifacts from the past provide opportunities of enrichment for remote, isolated communities beyond the pale of big city museum facilities (for example, the travelling exhibitions arranged by London's Victoria and Albert Museum). History projected via television is a popular proposal, but peak time programming usually exceeds its financial resources and its audience attraction ratings tend to fall below the threshold of commercial success. Whatever their programmes, museums demand and consume money and labour in their maintenance and collecting activities. Public funds administered through granting agencies serve the needs of those institutions which are not privately endowed. Labour is hired or, in some cases, may be volunteered. An arresting example of museum employment is the practice in Danish museums of using conscientious objectors from national service, a practice which may produce lasting and positive gains for both parties in the agreement. The unemployed might be useful to museums if in-training and motivational programmes were implemented. Lastly, when thinking of free or inexpensive labour sources for the understaffed museum world, contributions might be elicited from members of the academic leisured class who have sought – or have been forced into – early retirement.

One major recreational use of the past occurs in the museum of either conventional or outdoor type. The house museum full of display cabinets crammed with all manner of antiquities or natural wonders is only a warehouse of the past, and this is a necessary but not particularly stimulating function for it to perform. The commercial theme park with historic areas or attractions catches public patronage if efficiently operated, but the academic messages of the past are all too easily lost or diluted when competing with a larger-than-life Mickey Mouse or with five exciting, adventure rides for a two pound entry fee. The outdoor museum of rural or urban history can serve in a balanced way as a warehouse, a place of study and a stimulating arena for attractive and productive recreation if funds, labour and imagination are made available.

3

The Inventory and Resource Assessment

Introduction

In the course of a Spring afternoon in 1973 our group of Danish students of historical geography had visited the site of the Roman town at Alchester in Oxfordshire. One student chanced upon an object which looked like a lead loom weight. The next morning we visited the City and County of Oxford Museum located in the beautifully preserved Fletcher's House in Woodstock, north of the city of Oxford. In the course of our visit, our small trophy was entered in the Sites and Monuments Record, maintained by the Museum, which recorded our loom weight at the appropriate find-spot shown on the 6-inch Ordnance Survey map and at the same time an index card was completed. An immediate, accurate and retrievable record had been made, and one additional, tiny contribution had been added to the known inventory of historical relics in Oxfordshire.

Our example of the inventory process in action illustrates three basic aspects of this operation.[1] First, the inventory process was executed by a responsible body according to an established, standard format. Secondly, the significance of the reported find was assumed according to the vacuum-cleaner principle which says that *all* field observations should be noted. Left unresolved – and not a relevant matter in the case of our loom weight – is the question of assessing the relative importance, and hence, value, of the observation or find. The third aspect revealed by our example is that the registering body is related to other bodies and offices in a complex network existing within the county of Oxfordshire and which reaches further afield to connect with national bodies. These entities all subscribe to policies which prescribe the registration of items of interest towards maintaining a national register which can support the preservation of historic sites in the larger world of planned landscape changes. We shall be looking at these three points and discussing the magnitude of any inventory undertaking as well as making some suggestions for its improvement.

The basic field inventory of historic landscape items has two purposes. First of all, the inventory, whether an all-inclusive or a special topic one, seeks to find out what actually exists in the field, and in what quantities these items are to be found. It asks, for instance, are there many Stonehenges or only a single example? The second purpose reflects a pragmatic effort to influence preservational and planning decisions about the allocation of fiscal resources. To have any influence, one must be able to argue cogently with support from hard data. If, for example, through comprehensive inventory work, we establish that there exists but a single Stonehenge, we can concentrate the available planning resources on the needs of this lone relict item. On the other hand, if we find that twenty Stonehenges exist, we can set priorities and take measured decisions about which should receive protection. If we establish that the twenty Stonehenges exhibit different levels of preservation, we are in a position to evaluate them in terms of one another so as to establish priorities of preservation before any plans are drawn up. If our inventory survey establishes that no Stonehenge remains in the form of a visible field monument, we might consider the reconstruction of a replica for educational and scientific purposes. In each of these hypothetical examples the contribution of the field inventory is central.

Sources of Inventory Information

Field inventory consists of active, energetic work outdoors and of archive and office work. It usually starts with a survey of existing lists of field monuments variously compiled by individuals or organizations. J. B. Harley, in his *Ordnance Survey Maps: A Descriptive Manual*, recounts the significance to contemporary inventory takers of the fact that General William Roy in his role as one of the founders of the Survey was also a competent archaeologist.[2] Following the Napoleonic Wars, when the disruption of valuable field monuments was not yet a problem, it became the conscious policy of the Survey to record antiquities in the field and to mark them on the printed maps. Consequently, there exists in Britain manuscript and printed sources with which to begin the inventory enumeration of items of archaeological interest. The recording of relics from urban history and from the industrial revolution was a much later development.

The Danish experience was similar to the British since cartographic recording of antiquities began early in the nineteenth century and was continued, although not at the comprehensive level of activity characteristic of the Ordnance Survey. The large-scale working maps (1:20,000) used by the Danish Royal Society *Kongelige Videnskabernes Selskab* as the basis for its map of the kingdom, published between 1771 and 1825 at a scale of 1:120,000, abound with Megalithic stone monuments and earthen barrows. This tradition of mapping at least some varieties of antiquities was passed on to the Topographic Department of the General Staff when it took up the responsibility for producing large-scale maps in 1842 and it has been continued since 1928 when the present-day Geodetic Institute was organized.

The early involvement of the Inspector for the Conservation of Antiquarian Monuments, J. J. A. Worsaae, coupled with the strengthening of nationalistic sentiments after the Danish defeat by Prussia in 1864, meant that by 1873 an official programme for the inspection and protection of Danish prehistoric monuments already existed. Hand in hand with this policy went what Ole Klindt-Jensen has termed the first systematic survey of prehistoric monuments attempted by a nation.[3] At the end of the nineteenth century, thanks to royal support from a prominent archaeologist, King Frederik VII, the state cartographers and the youthful National Museum, Denmark could boast of nearly eight thousand recorded and scheduled prehistoric field monuments.

The beginnings of historic site inventories in the United States grew from late nineteenth-century concern over the loss of natural and historical monuments through settlement expansion and national growth. The Antiquities Act of 1906 established protection for features located on federal land and empowered the President to set up national monuments within the public domain. In 1916 the Organic Act created the National Park Service, and it was from these two national legislative actions that support was engendered for inventory-taking by public agencies, such as the National Park Service, and by concerned individuals (Fig. 11).

Subsequent legislative enactments and expressions of national policy have led to three quite different but complementary approaches to the inventory problem within Denmark, the United States and Britain. Since the medium is preservation law (discussed

Fig. 11 An inventory of threatened historic buildings in Los Angeles, California revealed the Rochester House. This noble if dilapidated Victorian mansion was moved bodily to a vacant corner of a railroad yard in 1970, pending a decision regarding relocation and restoration costs. These technicalities and costs continue to increase with inflation as a decision is awaited. (Photo by the author.)

below in Chapter 4), it will suffice here to sketch the respective national policies. Danish legislation from the Great War onwards reflected statements of concern about field monuments, but it was with the passage of a nature preservation law in 1969 that the current impetus to inventory work began. As part of the preparation of county or *amt* land-use plans, a complete inventory of pre-historic and historic landscape relics must be executed. The Danish approach reflects inventory-taking on a national level according to the requirements of conservation and land use planning. 1966 proved the turning point for inventory studies in the

United States with the passing of the National Historic Preservation Act. Previous legislation had helped, but this latter act laid upon local agencies a requirement to report on historical and archaeological resources, and the legislative mandate was accompanied by federal funds so that effective inventory work could go forward. Within the first decade of this energetic programme, the National Register of Historic Places has grown to 7,000 entries against the anticipated, eventual total of 50,000 items.[4] It is very probable that a good half-million entries will eventually exist in all of the local, state and federal listings and catalogues.

The British experience has followed a course of development mid-way between that of Denmark and the United States. She has the most vigorous and best-manned inventory programme which has grown up out of local and state initiatives but is relative to no discernible, over-all planning legislation. Keen and effective local amateurs in the tradition of John Aubrey and William Stukeley and trained in the archaeological legacies of Sir Richard Colt Hoare and Augustus Henry Lane-Fox engage in field-walks and compile painstaking parish lists of antiquities. The bulging inventory files of the Ordnance Survey, containing upwards of a quarter of a million entries, and the conservation efforts of the National Trust add to the data-bank of old places and things.[5] The rise of rescue archaeology within the last twenty-five years has contributed to inventory work in Britain. In the face of rising excavation expenses, it is important to know in advance whether a site is the best or even the only representative of its class, and here too inventory data is most helpful.[6] Under the 1973 proposals which would organize British archaeology upon a regional basis with county field archaeologists at work, a timely and co-ordinated approach to the needs for a definitive national survey seems possible.

National Inventories: Numbers and Types of Items

Given the background of inventory programmes in three representative nations, it is time to look at their inventory listings and to see what is being counted.

Denmark

This nation of five million inhabitants occupying 44,000 sq. km (16,000 square miles) can boast of a nearly complete inventory of its prehistoric landscape relics, as outlined in Table 2. The most numerous antiquities are the fifty to sixty thousand barrows

Table 2   INVENTORY OF DANISH ITEMS OF VISIBLE HISTORY

Prehistoric features	
Earthen barrows of all periods	50,000–60,000 recorded
	20,000 scheduled
Megalithic features, including tombs	2,000 scheduled
Assorted Prehistoric items, including standing stones,	
old field systems, Viking camps	1,800 scheduled
Medieval and later features	
Parish churches of Romanesque age	1,800 (all scheduled)
Manor houses, Medieval or younger	700–800
Medieval moated habitation sites	1,000
Abandoned Medieval farmsteads	2,500
Abandoned villages, Medieval or younger	100
Old field systems	12 scheduled
Iron Age systems	several hundred in Jutland alone
Historic buildings, post-Viking to *c.* 1850	2,500 scheduled
Other features, inventory totals unknown	
Medieval field systems, post-Viking to Enclosure	
Relics of the classic Enclosure field patterns, *c.* 1800	
Historic parish and estate boundary alignments	
Roads, fords and old bridges	
Vernacular buildings of note and value, rural and urban examples	
Features relating to the Industrial Revolution, *c.* post-1850	

Sources: R. M. Newcomb, *Annals, Association of American Geographers*, 57 (1967); R. M. Newcomb, *Geoforum*, 9 (1972).

recorded in the files of the National Museum. They range in age from the Neolithic to the Viking period and nearly one-third have been scheduled within the past century as historic monuments. Whilst it is shocking to learn that nearly two-thirds of Denmark's barrows have disappeared into the maw of the gravelpit or have been relegated to barely discernable swellings in the barley fields, with twenty-thousand examples remaining, a basis exists for reasoned decision-making when faced with motorway construction or factory expansion.

The omnibus category of items from the Megalithic period includes the prominent and scheduled passage graves and cairns which are fascinating adjuncts to the rural countryside of Denmark. In all, about 30 per cent of the known items are scheduled, but this is a misleading figure, for it assumes that inventory knowledge is as complete concerning other pre-historic features as it is about barrows. In the case of ancient field systems, for instance, Gudmund Hatt recorded 116 occurrences in Denmark but recent researches by P. Harder Sørensen have suggested over twice that number in the northern half of Jutland alone.[7] Consequently, earthen barrows are in a better state regarding inventory and scheduling than are cairns or Iron Age fields. In addition, if one were to include all the archaeological find sites in Denmark, the total inventory would probably exceed 200,000 known occurrencies.

Looking further at Table 2, the supply of medieval and later antiquities seems large, but the completeness of the inventory for the individual groups of feature varies and in some cases is nothing more than an educated guess. Hence, though the 1,800 parish churches which date from the Romanesque time are secure in their protected status under the Church Ministry and National Museum, not all of them are of equal historic or architectural value, and each year renovation work reveals hidden wonders in the shape of wall paintings and constructional details. The total of 2,500 scheduled buildings of more than a century old is obviously on the low side when the data of Table 5 is considered. Those scheduled buildings included on the list of the Special Building Survey (*Saerlige Bygningssyn*) would include a high proportion of the 700 to 800 manor or country houses which particularly characterize certain regions of the country. An estimated total of moated habitation sites has been suggested, which is surprisingly large compared with the equivalent British figure in Table 3. Abandoned medieval farmsteads numbering 2,500 reflect the settlement losses experienced as a result of plague, enclosure and drifting sand. With time and continuing research, several of these totals are likely to increase.

One hundred examples of abandoned villages for a country the size of Denmark and with a history so full of rural tribulations would seem to be too small a total. This figure is indeed an estimate by Viggo Hansen, and the continuing efforts by the Danish Division of the Scandinavian Abandoned Settlement Project are certain to turn up additional examples. Regarding the category of fossil field systems, the work of Gudmund Hatt, P. Harder Sørensen and Viggo Nielsen has suggested that examples of this intriguing agricultural relic far exceed the total of scheduled sites. The present-day landscape of Denmark bears traces of agriculture from the late medieval era fossilized within modern fields. Their number of occurrences as well as the incidences of ridge-and-furrow are even more debateable topics, for no study has yet mapped these old field forms for all Denmark, and a definitive inventory of old fields remains is yet to be completed.

Given the antiquity of settlement in Denmark, something of the network of old land routes might well be worth preservation if we knew the full extent of such remaining routeways. The same would apply to old bridges and fords. The topic of vernacular buildings is equally lacking in definitive totals, and this will be discussed later on in this chapter. The assumption of 1850 as the termination date for studies of vernacular architecture removes from consideration the entire chapter of the Industrial Revolution in Denmark. Industrial archaeology and relics from this eventful era are only partially covered, although Kenneth Hudson can name 20 sites of significance.[8] It is to be hoped that the current effort to study buildings and habitations associated with industrialization, as sponsored by the Research Committee for the Humanities (*Industrialismens bygninger og boliger, humanistiske forskningsråd*), will lead to a census of structures dating from this active period so that strides can be taken toward necessary preservation and appreciation.

United Kingdom

An indication of the wealth of visible history to be found in the United Kingdom is contained in Table 3. Within a nation of 244,000 sq. km (94,000 square miles) with a dense population (fifty-six million), an entire range of prehistoric archaeological field monuments occurs. Judging from the Danish experience, the full total of barrows should be greater than that listed, and apparently a lower percentage enjoy scheduled status. The category of megalithic tombs, for instance, might well increase in numbers if additional field work can establish the nature of the collections of stones in the country which may either be of natural origin or represent a ruined burial chamber. The recent upsurge of interest in the interpretation of megalithic standing stones and stone circles for their astronomical significance will serve to increase the recorded incidences of henge-type monuments. Stone alignments and ruined henges are very difficult to authenticate by field observation alone without resorting to excavation to establish the existence of certain of these features, and inventory listing may have to follow excavation and identification of the remains.

The British quota of Iron Age hill forts is known with a good degree of certainty, but totals for habitation sites and burial places would be more numerous if sufficient field archaeology had been possible. However, the paucity of recognized habitation sites for pre-Iron Age Britain is now being redressed as intensive studies of stream valley gravel terraces, initially identified through aerial photography, succeed in adding new locations to the files and maps.

Agrarian features of Roman Britain and rural relics of the post-Roman and medieval periods have been tallied up and appear to

Table 3 INVENTORY OF UNITED KINGDOM ITEMS OF VISIBLE HISTORY

Prehistoric features

Flint quarrying sites	Grimes Graves, the best-known example
Neolithic long barrows	200
Cursus monuments	20
Megalithic tombs	600
Henge-type monuments	40–50
Stone alignments	70
Small stone circles and standing stones	numerous
Bronze Age round barrows, all types	10,000–20,000
Iron Age settlement sites, England and Wales	469
Iron Age burial sites, England and Wales	154
Iron Age hill forts, England and Wales	1,382
Iron Age brochs, Scotland	500

Roman Britain

Roman villa sites	500–600
Extent of Roman roads in Britain	8,000 km (5,000 miles)
Roman mining and industrial sites	numerous

Dark Age Britain

Linear defensive earthworks	10–12 examples

Medieval Britain

Vanished or shrunken village sites in England	1,000–2,000
Examples of surviving open field patterns	4 well known
Examples of ridge-and-furrow	many acres
Examples of lynchets and lynchet terraces	numerous
Ancient and old hedgerows	250,000 running km (160,000 miles)
Medieval mining and industrial sites	numerous

Other features, other periods

Listed buildings in England	183,000
Historic country houses	2,000
Moated habitation sites	2,000
Civil war and other battlefields	numerous
Remains of the Industrial Revolution	numerous
Total archaeological find sites on record with the Ordnance Survey:	250,000

Source: R. M. Newcomb, *Annals, Association of American Geographers,* 57 (1967), as revised.

exist in numbers sufficient to gladden the hearts of archaeologists, historians and preservationists. However, more extensive rural remains such as field patterns are less well identified for any clearing-house procedures to be applied. The Deserted Medieval Village Research Group has added greatly to our total of deserted or shrunken villages, but no equivalent group has concentrated upon the distribution of ridge-and-furrow and of agricultural lynchet terraces. The more narrow topic of Roman and medieval mining and quarrying sites is complicated by subsequent exploitation of these raw material sources whilst the unspectacular tip heaps and temporary smelting works of the older enterprises have disappeared beneath the attacks of picks, shovels and bulldozers.

The last category of Table 3 is a miscellaneous one for buildings, battlefields and industrial plants. If one adds to the scores of existing castles nearly 2,000 notable country houses, then the monumental architecture of settlement is well represented. The over-abundance of valuable country houses in England, more of them than either individuals or the state can take care of, is a complicated and sensitive issue in terms of preservation and public enjoyment. The estimated 2,000 moated habitation sites are of greater interest to academics than to the general public. John Cornforth's total of 183,000 listed buildings in England serves greatly to expand our ideas about inventory totals when we are confronted by the hundreds of classic examples of medieval half-timbered buildings after having been conditioned by the unique examples of Stonehenge or Avebury.[9]

Turning to the unenumerated relics of Britain's Industrial Revolution, it is easy to be convinced that hundreds of sites of early coal or iron working exist, that many Cornish wheelhouses endure in reduced circumstances, and that miles of original railway routes remain from the pioneer days of steam. By contrast, there is only one Coalbrookdale complex, a prime site heavily laden with significance.[10] Much clearly remains to be done before an inventory of remains dating from the two centuries of the Industrial Revolution in Britain can be completed, but a take-off point can be the 160 sites listed by R. A. Buchanan in his book, *Industrial Archaeology in Britain*.[11]

United States

The United States inventory of historical features is large and varied as is to be expected for a nation of 9·4 million sq. km (3·6 million square miles) and 220 million inhabitants. The division of time into a pre-Columbian, aboriginal period and one dating from 1492, if artificial, is nevertheless understandable. The American National Register of Historic Places has worked to bring these two groupings of places and objects closer together by assessing the individual sites and structures in terms of what they reveal about the nation's diversified archaeological, historical, architectural, and cultural personality.

The items include properties and landmarks registered with the National Register of Historic Places, the National Historic Landmarks Survey, the National Park Service and the Historic American Building Survey, and by June 1973 some 7,000 items had been proposed and accepted for the register. It reads like an episodic history of the nation with references to Sandia Cave, New Mexico, an archaeological site representing the Folsom bison hunters who were active between 9,000 and 8,000 B.C.; the Pony Express Stables in St. Joseph, Missouri which date from 1860; the San Francisco cable car system, an English technological contribution to the city in 1873 and the only mobile national monument on the inventory; and the meadow in Massachusetts where Robert H. Goddard launched the world's first liquid propellant rocket in 1928.

If we consider the state of California as an inventory example, Table 4 provides a fair sample of the breadth of topics and periods represented by the American inventories.[12] Among the fifty-eight counties which comprise the 480,000 sq. km (158,000 sq. miles) of the state, the California items include 3·6 per cent which are devoted to Indian remains which impinge on either the Spanish or Anglo periods of the state's history in the form of mission-related activities or military confrontations. The 30·5 per cent devoted to economic and industrial features, including the many mining and railroad relics in the state, and the 23·7 per cent covering the wide

Table 4   INVENTORY OF CALIFORNIAN ITEMS OF VISIBLE HISTORY

A total of 3,000 items or sites are listed for California, including those currently to be on the National Register, and they are grouped according to nine organizing themes.

Themes	Site totals
Aboriginal: primarily associated with Indian activities	107
Architecture: buildings and structures of note	477
Art/Leisure: homes of writers and artists	129
Economic/Industrial: a large grouping of mining towns, fishing facilities and ports	901
Exploration/Settlement: a large grouping of trails, passes, early settlements, *ranchos*, etc	698
Government: historic buildings, treaty sites	110
Military: forts, battlegrounds	101
Religion: notable church edifices	170
Social/Education: original school buildings, libraries	257
Total sites	2,950
	Plus:
Recognized but unpublicized archaeological sites, registered but not accessible to the public in order to protect them from 'pot hunters'	22,600

Source: California Dept. of Parks and Recreation, *California Inventory* (1976).

range of exploration, mission construction, land grant *ranchos* and pioneer communities constitute the bulk of the items catalogued and represent the main historical-geographic imprints on the landscape of California. These sites include the Kit Carson Trail through the Sierra Nevada mountains of Alpine county and the Baseline Road of San Bernardino county which was surveyed in 1853 and became the basis for the establishment of land titles within the courts of the new state. Within Los Angeles county the San Gabriel Archangel Mission, founded in 1771 and still in church use, represents a feature of exploration and settlement, whilst in Alameda county the Alameda Terminal of the first Transcontinental Railroad, dating from 1869, represents the economic and industrial category.

The true wealth of California in its resources of historic and prehistoric items is indicated by the totals of archaeological sites which are recorded but not described in order to preserve them from eventual harm at the hands of amateur archaeologists. To the total number of sites in California accessible to the public must, therefore, be added a further 22,600.

This large total for a single state suggests the impressive number of sites of historical and prehistorical significance which may exist for the nation as a whole. If California represents 10 per cent of the USA in this category, then a site total of a quarter of a million items might be anticipated. This total when compared to the estimated 250,000 registered sites in the files of the Ordnance Survey for Great Britain, seems reasonable given the historical depth of the latter country versus the territorial expanse of the former.

An Inventory Estimate of Valuable Buildings

Approximately fifty to sixty buildings are submitted to the American National Register each month as candidates for registration (Fig. 12). Even if all of these were accepted each year, how significant a contribution to the potential US total would the resulting 700 buildings make? On the basis of experience with historic building registration carried out in Denmark, Table 5 has been constructed to illustrate the size and costs of similar structure inventories if carried out for all of Denmark as well as for the UK, USA and Canada.[13] My estimates derive from data which showed that in a municipality of 250,000 inhabitants, 12,000 buildings served to shelter and meet in part the work needs of 30,000 people. Statistically this gives a ratio of 2·5 inhabitants per building. In addition,

Fig. 12 The Doctors' House, Glendale, California is a well maintained example of 1880s Queen Anne Eastlake-style architecture. Privately owned, the house is an item of prime importance in the city's historic preservation plan and one of the gems discovered in the inventory phase of the investigation work. This home is a living relic of early Anglo settlement in Glendale, and for this reason as well as for its excellent state of repair it will receive preservational consideration. (Photo by the author.)

500 valuable buildings were identified within the total of 12,000 structures, which produces a valuable-building ratio of 1 to 24 buildings. Using these two simple ratios Table 5 shows total buildings and total historically valuable buildings per nation by assuming that the Danish ratios are applicable elsewhere. The total of buildings to be surveyed ranges from two to eighty-eight million. The potential totals for historically valuable buildings range from 100,000 in Denmark to a staggering 4 million in the US.

Passing on to a consideration of the fiscal resources which would be required for such inventory surveys, the Danish experience is again relevant. The modest survey in 1974 of 12,000 buildings required approximately one man-hour per valuable building for the collection of complete inventory information. At the then going rate of 25 Danish kroner (approximately £2·00 or $4·00) per hour for workers (university students), and not counting the costs incidental to the production of resulting reports, it is possible to estimate the labour costs of a comprehensive inventory. Two million pounds for a survey of the million valuable buildings in Britain might be a difficult proposition to sell either to the public or Parlia-

Table 5   REQUIREMENTS FOR AN INVENTORY STUDY OF OLD BUILDINGS IN
DENMARK, UNITED KINGDOM, USA AND CANADA

	Denmark	UK	USA	Canada
Total population	5 m.	55 m.	220 m.	22 m.
Theoretical total of buildings*	2 m.	22 m.	88 m.	8·8 m.
Theoretical total of historically** valuable buildings	80–100,000	900,000–1 m.	3·5–4 m.	300–400,000
Estimate of labour requirements for study of valuable buildings (expressed in man–hours)	80–100,000	900,000–1 m.	3·5–4 m.	300–400,000
Estimate of labour costs of survey of valuable buildings (1974–5 costs as basis for estimate)	2–2·5 m. kr.	£1·8–2·0 m.	$14–16 m.	$1·2–1·6 m.
Estimate of total labour costs for basic inventory survey plus valuable building survey (1974–5 costs as basis for estimate)	5 m. kr.	£4·4 m.	$33 m.	$3·3 m.

Sources: Estimates derived from the Århus, Denmark Village Project and from
Kaj Gottlob, architectural historian, Copenhagen, Denmark.
*Estimate of total number of buildings based upon 2·5 persons per building.
**Based upon one valuable building to every 24 buildings.

ment; the fourteen to sixteen million dollars which would be
required of US taxpayers would probably be regarded as a quite
outlandish sum.

It must be noted, however, that these would be the costs only
after buildings of potential historic value had been located and
identified – another undertaking entirely – from within the much
larger building mass of the respective nations. The many-sided
Danish study was carried out on 12,000 buildings, comprising 105
separate villages and hamlets, at a cost to the 250,000 municipal
rate payers of a mere kroner per head, equivalent to 8 pence or 15
cents. Using this information the estimates for total costs have been
generated and appear in the bottom section of Table 5. Hence, the

total project sum for Britain might be on the order of £4·4 million
and for the US $33 million. These are indeed substantial simply for
basic inventory research.

The Role of Field Inventory in the Planning Process

The arguments in support of basic inventory assessment may be
strengthened if we look at the advantages to be gained from a
full-scale inventory of valuable buildings. Without knowledge of the
numbers and varieties of historic relics present as regional or
national resources, no progress beyond speculation can be
expected, for time-consuming and expensive tasks of enumeration
and classification provide the foundations for our grander efforts at
planning the past. Figure 13 illustrates in a schematic manner the
nature of this dynamic interaction.

At the inventory level one will find the greatest number of people
involved; it is the one place within the planning hierarchy where the
efforts of the unpaid amateur are welcomed. Grass-roots inventories of every hedgerow, half-timbered out-building or antique
municipal pumphouse depend on the efforts of knowledgable and
devoted laymen who can provide data which might otherwise never
be recorded and whose informed opinions regarding preservational
priorities should be communicated to the central planners. At the
same time, diplomatic relations with local investigators are essential
to ensure that inputs of raw data continue, though these must be
checked for accuracy and relevance.

The desideratum, as nearly as possible, is for exhaustive inventories, but such completeness is frequently simply not feasible. In
fact, we may have to use rescue-style field work or standardized
mass surveys to collect a minimum amount of data. On the other
hand, local areas, particularly in the United Kingdom, may be able
to use some of the wealth of inventory data which already exists for
parishes or particular categories of antiquities. As an example,
Vivien Russell's *West Penwith Survey* contains minute data about
thousands of field antiquities in the fourteen ecclesiastical parishes
of West Penwith in Cornwall, and would serve as a marvellous
source for a solid base-line inventory.[14] Here, the accumulated
observations of one person's dedicated field work can serve the
rapidly moving deliberations of contemporary preservation planners.

Once the inventory has been completed, it is fed into the plan
under the section dealing with resources of historical interest. Then,

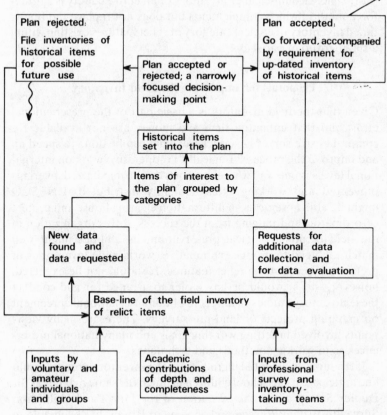

Fig. 13 A schematic representation of the role of the field inventory in the historic preservation plan.

if the plan is accepted, there will be need for expansion of the inventory to embrace other categories reflecting new topics or new interests in the plan itself. If, however, the plan is rejected, the inventory work need not be lost, for if properly filed and indexed, it can survive to assist academic or local workers when a new opportunity arrives for planning.

Good inventory work cannot be rushed, especially if supporting documentation is attempted. To assign twenty workers for a short inventory may not produce as good results as are possible when a single person works over a longer period of time. However, given the exigencies of the situation, the application of mass efforts may be dictated. Frequently, decisions must be made as to which items should receive inventory priority, especially if time and funds run short. The vacuum-cleaner inventory of an entire county is a brute-force method which complements but does not replace the finely-tuned inventory of a select category of relict features existing within a small group of parishes.

Proposals for Improving the Field Inventory

Given that the field inventory is a basic part of the preservational effort and that unlimited time and money are not available for comprehensive surveys everywhere, what can be done to speed up and improve the process? Logically, co-operative work on international levels is one way whereby efforts can be maximized, overlaps prevented and working skills equitably distributed. UNESCO might be able to serve as an information clearing house and project co-ordinator, and judging from the success of this organization in the field of archaeological preservation, its abilities might well match the need to produce cumulative, world-wide inventories of prehistoric and historic relict features. It should not be expected, however, that it would be any easier to arrange for and conduct these inventory studies than it is to obtain international agreement on mapping projects or land-use surveys. There are many viewpoints involved in setting working goals and many national preferences as to working methods and techniques.

If labour is an essential ingredient in the inventory process, could one anticipate using school children in much the same manner as Sir Dudley Stamp did in the execution of the First Land Utilization Survey in Britain. Rescue archaeology in Britain has been able to use this type of labour, but British success does not necessarily imply that child labour would prove an equally good resource on a world-wide basis. Unemployed persons could provide another labour pool, but here too, sufficiently strong motivation and a degree of competence in rough field archaeology are necessary. However, some nations are plagued by academic overproduction of qualified architects, engineers and geographers, who might well be excellent inventory labour if the financing of such a programme was feasible.

Is it possible in any way to speed up the inventory process, to use data sources other than or complementary to the human field worker? Remote sensing imagery, whether taken from aircraft or satellites, whether vertical or oblique, in black and white or some more exotic film type, comes readily to mind as being a possibility. The fascinating field of air archaeology can supply the necessary techniques and a wealth of interpretative experience. Major George Allen's pioneer efforts during the early 1930's in Wessex come to mind as does the exciting work of John Bradford in the Mediterranean Basin and the fine examples presented by Beresford and St Joseph from England.[15] The work of these authors depended on the availability of good, comprehensive photographic coverage, an interpretative background and basic documentary source materials. Neither of these conditions can be met for large portions of the earth today if we restrict ourselves to thinking about imagery from aircraft.

If, however, we consider satellite photography, new and exciting prospects open up for the historic inventory.[16] The high quality and ready accessibility of the LANDSAT imagery from the United States has particular potential offering good coverage of 90 per cent of the Earth's surface in black and white according to several different spectral bands, each of which commends itself for the depiction of vegetation, cultural features or land-water contrasts.[17] Colour is also available, and the next generation of spacecraft in this programme will expand the available coverage from the infrared portions of the spectrum. The results are readily available at a modest price and through this medium virtually unknown parts of the globe become available to the inventory-taker. The limitations of LANDSAT photography reside in its resolution threshold of 80 metres (240 feet) which precludes many items of historic interest. However, enhancement of the photography, enlargements and use of the colour transparencies allows extraction of the maximum amount of information available.[18] The use of manned satellite photography, such as that available from the three SKYLAB operations in the mid-1970's, especially in oblique format, allows for the study of large, areal views for synoptic purposes, whilst the interpretation from colour images often reveals the presence of features of significant interest to inventory studies. With the press of destruction of landscape relics and with the restrictions as to labour and money which are endemic to historic planning work, we should be ready to adopt any technique which promises to assist us in the inventory effort. Photography from space, when used according to the techniques of air archaeology, can reveal information about relict forms which have either an areal extent or a linear one, and any such information from little-known portions of the globe will be welcome as a basis for new county lists and topical inventories.[19]

The field inventory of landscape relics allows us to evaluate our stock of such items and to keep track of any changes in their numbers. The scope of the census may be a world-wide archaeological atlas or a narrow study in depth of a single province.[20] Inventories may be based upon descriptive notes taken by an amateur antiquarian or upon questionnaires and index systems used by professional inventory workers. The inventory may be used in the scientific interpretation of the spatial distributions of cultural artifacts and as a guide to excavation and restoration or it may serve as the backbone of a preservation plan or provide information essential to a preservation and recreation land-use programme. In the two chapters which follow and which deal with preservation law and new trends in recreational uses of the past, the basic item-inventory will have an important, if largely unsung, role to play.

4

The Law and the Visible Past

Introduction

During two very hot days in May 1976 nearly two hundred people gathered within the cool walls of the historic Riverside Inn in Southern California to attend a symposium on preservational planning in the United States. The Inn, which encapsulates many of the challenges and problems characteristic of preservation planning, is a huge, rambling, idiosyncratic creation built in the Mission revival style by a hotel keeper between 1902 and 1932. Dedicated to the premise that service comes first – service meaning many legs and hands to run and to fetch – the Inn's enduring charm is today matched by its hopelessness as an efficient, modern hostelry. Here lies the crux of the preservation problem which concerns buildings of noble value which can no longer be maintained or used for their original purposes.

This symposium was designed to inform and to stimulate us into action on behalf of preservational planning as it has grown up in the United States over the past decade. The need for enlightened law-making, a careful dispersal of preservation funds and the shaping of mutual confidence between planners and politicians were the goals stressed. The subsequent placement of the Inn upon the National Register and efforts to co-ordinate its revival as a hotel with a new attempt at developing a viable commercial downtown mall in Riverside, suggest the tangible preservation actions which may be taken.

Conflicts over Definitions, Goals, and Methods

Part of the Riverside Inn problem is that various groups are not using the same glossary of terms or pursuing related goals. In the beginning almost everyone agrees that an *Inventory* is both desirable and necessary. Thereafter, opinions diverge when *Preservation, Conservation* and *Restoration* are mentioned as being desirable for a specific building or a group of structures, because the meanings of these three words are not clear to the interested parties nor are they even accepted by all of them. There exists, consequently, a need to seek clarity of definition and agreement about methods in order that misunderstanding, suspicion and ignorance can be reduced. The completion of an inventory, a sufficiently modest undertaking, requires that private property be subject to inspection, an action seen by some as an infringement upon their inalienable right to hold property and to dispose of it as they wish. The California legislature debated during 1976 a proposed law which would make such inventory studies unlawful by reason of their being an unwarranted intrusion upon the privacy of property owners. Had a law of this sort been enacted in a leading legal community such as the state of California, then the whole future of the National Registry in the United States would have been jeopardized.

Moving up the scale, the opportunities for misunderstanding are without limit within the active phases of preservation of a given building (Fig. 11). Immediately there arises the problem of the controls to be placed upon continuing present or proposed future usage of a scheduled building or site. Secondly, even if preservation and scheduling are accepted by all parties, the type and amount of financial aid to assure its maintenance can become a source of dispute. If the scheduled-property owner is allowed a payment or tax-relief, he may feel that the amount is insufficient, given the stringent controls and standards which restrict him. On the other hand, the rate payer, if he becomes aware of the existence of this variety of tax-supported largess, may feel upset when his undistinguished home or shop is deemed as being not worthy of such support payments. Should the question of restoration arise, then a veritable Pandora's box of contentious forces may be released. Restoration, although sometimes useful in job creation schemes, is usually a very costly and time-consuming business whether one is talking about repairing or rebuilding an ancient farmstead, country house, parish church or covered bridge. Someone must meet the bills for this attentive craftsmanship, and the ins and outs of the cost accounting means that it tends to be either the very well-to-do with estate tax problems or liberal organisations who can lobby effectively in parliament who are attracted to support such work.

Fig. 14 The preservational and restorative effects of the law are represented here by a view up Low Petergate towards York Minster in one of England's most scenic and venerable cities. Something of the dimensions of preservation law and its complexities can be appreciated when considering all the facets of modern urban life and land use which coincide in this single street scene, all of which have a bearing on the maintenance and use of the urban history resources which occur here.

Making the past useful requires planned expenditure of large sums of money, whether the goal is business, pleasure or profit. Whether the result is preservation for scientific and pedagogic use or for public and recreational enjoyments, the attractive idea is abroad that the visible history of our landscapes can be integrated into contemporary life through the processes of scheduling, conversion or recycling of useage (Fig. 14). The problems arise when we start to decide whose plan for the recycling of an historic urban district we are to adopt. The area becomes for one person a park, for another an Elizabethan-style shopping precinct while a third envisions a half-timbered discotheque and restaurant complex. Vivid horror stories abound wherein the forces of good seek to preserve old canal locks from bridgebuilders or abandoned village sites from real estate developers. Often these tales reveal conflicts over the meaning of words between those who revere the past and those who look first for honest profit.

Preservation Law in Action

Increasingly, groups which seek to use the visible past for a variety of purposes come into contact with a third great force: the weight of preservational law. We must become familiar with this body of law in order that planned preservation for recreation or study can advance, since it is able to guide or constrain, encourage or frustrate.

Preservation can, however, take place without support or hindrance from the law (Fig. 15). An enlightened landowner may expend his own time and money to keep an old barn or area of garden landscaping from decay. An urban homeowner may lovingly restore the faded Victorian glories of his residence, using weekends and the energies of his family for the task. Such restoration or last-ditch repairs could profit from the structured support of an organization and the shared interest and enthusiasm which an organized group can generate. The gains to be realized from a consistency of practice and from the strength of group advocacy will outweigh the dampening effects which organized effort frequently produces upon motivated and effective individual effort. In addition, organized efforts to broadcast the preservation message can offset the forces of ignorance or indifference which, through acts of commission or of omission, can easily damage relics of landscape history.

An enlightened and liberal outlook would seem to be a necessary prerequisite for the setting-up of preservational mechanisms, for not everyone feels that old field systems, copses of woodland or semi-derelict farmsteads are valuable in terms of their contribution to history, cultural development or pedagogic potentialities. Initial efforts at preservation were being made more than a century ago by liberal landowners and academics able to exploit the antiquarian proclivities displayed by the royal house in Denmark and by landlords trained in the liberal arts who supported the National Trust in Britain.

Acting to stop destruction, the initial task, is still a complicated undertaking. Information about proposed or current destruction of objects or sites must reach the preservation office in time for action to be taken to stave off irreversible loss. This is the early-warning stage. Secondly, some administrative mechanisms should exist to take up a threat of destruction and conduct hearings which can lead to a disposition of the case. The third device needed is a set of promulgated regulations governing relics and sites so that their

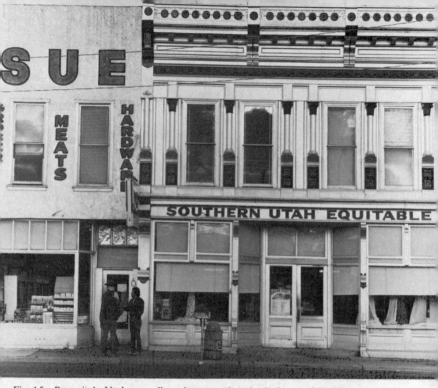

Fig. 15 Panguitch, Utah, a small market town deep in the heart of the Mormons' Dixie, survives in arresting architectural form more as a result of its remoteness in the scenic southwest of the state than by any intended laws relating to preservation. The Great Basin Classicism, illustrated here as an accomplishment of local designs and workmanship, deserves consideration as a useful monument to the small rural communities of America.

discoverers or developers may find guidelines for their legitimate actions in order to prevent plunder or blunder.

The Danish example is helpful since it illustrates a complete cycle of regulations backed by responsible jurisdictions.[1] On the discovery of a field antiquity such as a gold torque or buried grave, the Danish law states that the Antiquary of the Realm shall be notified in order that he may visit the scene and make an assessment of the nature and importance of the find. If the site of the find is deemed sufficiently valuable, then a preservation order is worked out, and under it the landowner is guided by very detailed regulations as to how much farm work, for instance, can take place on the site. In return, he may receive a state stipend for his efforts in the interest of official preservation. Later on, if a proposal is made to sub-divide the farmland for a suburban housing estate, part of the planning deliberations will examine whether the future of the scheduled site can be assured or whether its value is outweighed by the proposed construction to the extent that the alteration or even destruction of the site will be permitted. Such an apparently clear-cut procedure would be worth adopting in any land which consciously seeks to preserve its physical patrimony.

Closer inspection of the Danish situation in practice will reveal, however, where the preservational chain of decisions and responsibilities is weak and may break down. One cannot be certain, for example, that only the scrupulous discover golden torques, undamaged grave sites or foundations of abandoned, medieval farms. The Danish laws relative to treasure trove (*Danefælov*), which derive from medieval ordinances, are reasonably clear, but even the present Queen cannot pass legislation concerning the conduct or conscience of her subjects to the same degree as was possible five hundred years ago. Suppression of evidence revealed by a mechanical ditch-digger on the excavation for the line of a sewer may be turned to the construction project's advantage if a delay to allow a rescue archaeology dig can thereby be avoided. The eyes and ears of the Antiquary of the Realm, planning office employees or archaeological co-ordinators cannot possibly see or hear enough to ensure that such temptations do not overrule the citizen's patriotic good sense.

Additionally, the Danish regulations can be abridged in the enforcement of preservation regulations which specify, for instance, that within one hundred metres of a scheduled burial mound no activities shall take place which might result in the basic alteration of this monument and its site. The traveller through rural Denmark will repeatedly see cultivation coming so close to burial mounds that their bases are being cut away. In other examples, access by livestock to sites and the presence there of pasture has meant that trampling has precipitated erosion. If a fundamental alteration such as forestation is permitted, antiquities such as burial mounds may be lost within the darkness of young coniferous plantations, and the relationship of the mounds to their surroundings becomes fundamentally altered and much of the scenic significance of the site is thereby lost.

The third area where the Danish regulations have proved vulnerable is evident whenever widening of a highway or motorway results in damage, through topographical encroachments, to megalithic or Bronze Age graves. The highway engineer is, of course, not to be viewed as a monster who would destroy all that is historic and scenic. His task is to build the roadway in such a manner and according to such a routing that the end product is the best available for the budgeted money. If it is a Bronze Age barrow which is endangered, what can one say when it is one of nearly 20,000 which are already scheduled in Denmark? Should this sacrifice of one to the common transportational good be allowed? Can a rescue dig be fitted into the tight construction work schedule, and is it at all certain that this particular barrow is unique and needs to be preserved above all else, or is it merely an average example of its particular group and age? Danish preservationists and engineers have been unable to find a true and balanced route through these obstacles toward the ideal of responsible and realistic preservation.

In contrast to the step-by-step, accretional approach to preservation law practiced in Denmark, the United States has, since 1966, attempted a comprehensive if complicated approach to this particular branch of applied law.[2] In building on the Historic Sites Act of 1935, whereby the Department of the Interior was directly involved in historic preservation work, the enactment of the National Historic Preservation Act of 1966 broadened the scope of legislation both in terms of who and what was to become involved in this national effort directed toward the 'protection and enhancement of the cultural environment.' This latter phrase comes from the Executive Order number 11593 of May 1971 which served further to strengthen and broaden the preservation effort and its planning instrumentalities in the United States.

Figure 16 illustrates the national historic preservation programme of the United States as depicted by *Preservation News* in May 1976.[3] The basic goals of the programme appear to be several. The first desire is to involve both governmental and private organizations and individuals at local, state and federal levels. No one, theoretically, would be left out of the preservation deliberations. From the diagram there would appear to exist a clear liaison channel from the individual owners of historic properties through the offices of a preservation society to the Advisory Council. The Department of the Interior, custodian of historic parks, sites and monuments, answers to both the executive and legislative branches of United States government, with a line of administrative control to the former and appropriation ties with the latter. Once again, the diagram suggests that all lines of authority are clearly marked and that no individual or office should fail to receive information or be omitted from relevant consultation because of a lack of contact.

The second goal concerns the pressing need for a national register of historic places to be completed before any further blind or malicious inroads are made upon the historic and cultural resources of the Nation.[4] Not until each of the fifty states, the District of Columbia and the four overseas territories which together make up

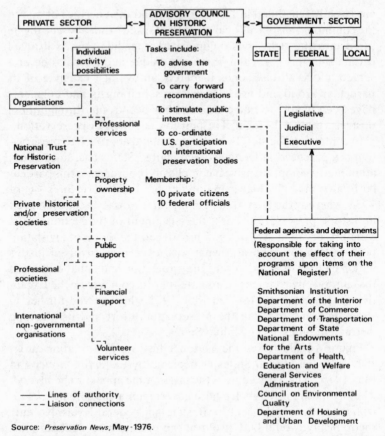

Source: *Preservation News*, May-1976.

Fig. 16 Organization of the National Historic Preservation Programme in the United States (1976).

the United States are covered by full and accurate inventories of their historic riches, can really comprehensive decisions be made and national programmes effected. While pursuing the goal of a full and perfect inventory, it is intended that all those involved will avail themselves of the opportunities for preservational action.

The third goal in this historic preservation plan concerns the desirable aim of bringing together the many separate but related national preservation and grants programmes in order to increase overall efficiency and reduce debilitating and costly overlaps and disputes about jurisdictional responsibilities[5] (Fig. 17). Figure 16 hints at this potential for good as well as the certainty of strife when illustrating the ten federal agencies and departments constrained to

Fig. 17 The historic Plaza of the City of Los Angeles, California is today a state historical preserve administered by the municipality. Two hundred years of existence as an urban core under, successively, Spanish, Mexican and Anglo influences has provided a rich ethnic and architectural background upon which the modern park developments may draw. This side of the plaza, which features the city's first firehouse and an early multistorey office building, is much less lively than the Olvera Street portion with its many Hispanic shops and great amount of local colour. The administration of an urban preserve with such a varied ethnic background is a demanding diplomatic task. (Photo by the author.)

take into account the effects on registered cultural property of all duly licensed undertakings.

Planning Law and Preservation Policy

What the existence of a reasonably complete National Register of historic places can mean in the context of preservation law will be considered next in our discussion of the ties between planning law and preservation policy.

At present, it is possible to view planning law as being a sub-unit within a larger concern about environmental policy in general. By the 1970s, politicians and bureaucrats had become acutely aware of the potent influence exercised by organized environmentalists on behalf of clean air, pure water and pristine landscapes. It is generally recognized that some natural resources are exhaustable and others are available only at increasing costs. Air, water and land-scape are reckoned to be finite resources and their careful exploitation ties in naturally with concerns about environmental quality. In order to ensure that the quality of the human habitat is recognized legislation needs to be enacted. Since the environment contains both physical and cultural features and the latter encompasses the historic patrimony represented by monuments, fields and buildings, then environmental quality and historic preservation policies will have much in common. There thus exists a somewhat circuitous connection between national consciousness about environmental quality, the legislative phases of environmental policy regulations and the final enactment of some form of national historic preservation law.[6] A direct connection is theoretically supposed to run from the highest councils of the national policy-making bodies down to the local group which seeks to assure a future for the old churchyard or railway station. A channel of communication in the reverse direction should also exist, and Fig. 16 depicts, for the United States, the circuitry of this ideal two-way traffic.

The national responses to recognized needs for environmental planning legislation and historic preservation have been varied, as one would expect. What has emerged as national policy reflects the history of the preservation movement and the basic national philosophies regarding the regulation of individual rights in the interests of group needs. For example, the United States' experience is both ambitious and youthful and depends upon people at grass-roots levels being alert enough to seize opportunities which the state is presenting. Secondly, a contrasting programme has arisen in Denmark where, in this matter at least, the state is viewed as both instigator and administrator of land-use planning and historic preservation. The British experience, our third example, represents a plan which has evolved gradually over time and is one which, although increasingly bureaucratized, nonetheless still calls on the enlightened self-interest of the citizenry for implementation of designed programmes.

United States Preservation Legislation

Relative to Britain and Denmark, the movement in the United States towards preservation of the national patrimony is a recent thing, but its roots lie in the nineteenth century when the wonders of the West were first brought to the attention of the nation. Table 6 indicates this orientation in the West with the passage of the Antiquities Act of 1906. Nearly thirty years were to elapse before legislation regarding historic buildings and associated sites was brought into force. The Historic Sites Act of 1935 which, by authorizing the Secretary of the Interior to make a survey of historic

Table 6   NATIONAL LEGISLATION INFLUENCING HISTORIC PRESERVATION IN THE
UNITED STATES

Date	The legislation
1906	Antiquities Act
1933	Historic American Building Survey established
1935	Historic Sites Act
1949	Act establishing the National Trust for Historic Preservation
1966	National Historic Preservation Act
1969	National Environmental Policy Act (NEPA) which sets forth the Environmental Impact Study (EIS) requirement
1970	Executive Order 11514 Protection and Enhancement of Environmental Quality
1971	Executive Order 11593 Protection and Enhancement of the Cultural Environment
1972	Act to Facilitate the Preservation of Historic Monuments, amending the Federal Property and Administrative Services Act of 1949
1974	Preservation of Archaeological and Historical Data Act amending the Reservoir Salvage Act of 1960 Housing and Community Development Act

Source: National Trust for Historic Preservation, 1976

sites and buildings, set in motion the process whereby national historic landmarks could be established. The historic inventory was hereby given a great boost, and it advanced beyond the excellent start given by the Historic American Building Survey which was set up in 1933 to provide employment in the depression era.

For preservationists the establishment of the National Trust for Historic Preservation in 1949 was a most important legislative act because it brought into existence a legalized information office or lobby which could work actively to advance the cause of a national programme for the protection of the past. There was, however, much more to come from the legislative hoppers of Washington, DC, and the current decade has seen historic preservation strengthened directly by legislation as well as indirectly by measures which include preservation policies under the more comprehensive umbrella of environmental protection.

For direct preservation planning law, with its positive impact upon the historic features of the United States, 1966 was a banner year because of the enactment of a key piece of legislation: The National Historic Preservation Act of 1966. This created a programme which could provide matching grants-in-aid, up to 50 per cent, from the Federal government to agencies within the fifty states, the District of Columbia, the Commonwealth of Puerto Rico, Guam, American Samoa, the Trust Territory of the Pacific Islands, the Virgin Islands, and the National Trust for Historic

Fig. 18 Heritage Square outdoor museum under construction in Los Angeles, California. For nearly a decade the Cultural Heritage Board has been promoting the relocation here and subsequent restoration of buildings which illustrate the city's architectural traditions and phases of its late nineteenth and early twentieth century growth. Legal and financial programmes have been established to assist this undertaking. As an attractive and educational leisure attraction the museum holds promises of success, but its location in a transitional neighbourhood continues to be a limiting factor to its full development. (Photo by the author.)

Preservation. The purpose of these grant funds was to support agencies interested in carrying out surveys and in developing plans for historic preservation. Additional funding was available for the acquisition and development of properties listed in the National Register if their future would be more secure when placed in public ownership (Fig. 18). Where previously, good intentions and valuable volunteer work had been the chief preservational tools, after 1966 when Federal funds became available, a set of new and powerful instruments were accessible for the advancement of planning with history as its main interest. The Mission Inn Symposium of 1976, mentioned already, was in part motivated by and financed from the provisions of this Act – ten years on and in the midst of the national celebration of the Bicentennial.

The National Environmental Policy Act of 1969 and the Executive Orders of 1970 and 1971 established plans concerning the environment as a whole, but they included provisions tied to historic sites via the requirement for environmental impact statements, using new co-ordinating bodies, channels for consultation and specialized site inventories. The 1972 Act to Facilitate the Preservation of Historic Monuments involved the General Services Administration in the conversion of historically significant surplus properties, either for use at local levels or for sale with the revenues going into preservation efforts. In 1974 the Preservation of Archaeological and Historical Data Act provided guidelines to the Department of the Army concerning features of historical interest which might be threatened as a result of programmes carried out by the Corps of Engineers to develop water resources. Once again, a department of the Federal government was specifically enjoined to pay close attention in the course of its normal duties to the historic patrimony of the nation. The last legislative enactment in Table 6 is the Housing and Community Development Act of 1974, designed to provide loans to help preserve residential properties listed in the National Register. In this case, Federal housing policy in its piecemeal evolutionary history had been enlisted to give buildings of the past a useful present as residences or places of business.

The seventy years of preservation legislation in the United States have bridged the gap from pioneer inventories to sophisticated programmes designed to promote urban renewal. The increasing size of government and its costs have been reflected in the number of preservation bills and in their internal complexities. The existence of such laws does not necessarily mean an unclouded future for old houses and decayed urban historic districts. Communications are slow and the co-ordination of efforts is hard to achieve, but apparently genuine concern with the national past, evident in the corridors of Washington, is a heartening sign.

Danish preservation legislation

Danish developments, outlined in Table 7, began with inventory efforts in the middle of the nineteenth century and with an earlier modification of the ancient laws governing treasure-trove. The past sixty years of legislative development parallels, in part, the United States pattern. In 1917 and 1918 laws were passed which specified the place of antiquities as an adjunct to the landscape, and also addressed the technical matters of saving old buildings. The law of 1937 strongly echoes, in part, that passed in America in 1935 with its emphasis upon inventory, but the Danes added effective provisions designed to ensure preservation.

In both nations it has been the post-World War II period which has seen the most sustained development of comprehensive legislation regarding the planned preservation and use of historic

Table 7 DANISH HISTORIC PRESERVATION LEGISLATION

Year	Effecting legislation and its nature
1737	Law of 22 March
1752	Law codifying the ancient Danish Law of treasure trove and its provenience
1917	Nature Preservation Law. A statement of basic principles, including preservation of antiquities as part and parcel of general environmental preservation legislation
1918	Law on preservation of historic buildings
1937	Law covering the inventory of historic features and a policy of fines and assistance for landowners with features upon their property
1947	Law on maintenance of churches and churchyards
1949	Circular of 26 January from the Church Ministry giving guidance for a voluntary programme for preservation of parish churches
1961	Various needed adjustments to the law of 1937 enacted Commission on Nature Preservation established
1963	Legislation Law passed to protect shipwrecks located within Danish coastal waters
1966	Law on the preservation of historic buildings
1967	Instruction of 13 October from the Commission on Historic Buildings
1969	Law of 18 June which is a nature preservation law covering the planned, multiple usage of Denmark's open lands and which includes provisions for preservation planning and the execution of local level inventories and landscape disposition plans. Includes the concept of the multi-faceted nature park and planned development of these in Denmark
1969	Law of 19 December amending the law on preservation of historic buildings
1970	Law on City Planning which includes provisions for the preservation of historic city portions
1973	Law on milieu protection. A multi-faceted law which with two appended laws, also of 1973, set standards for waste disposal, air cleanliness, noise pollution, etc on a nation-wide basis, and charges municipal governments after the effective date of 1 October 1974 with administration and enforcement
1975	Law concerning municipal planning which comes into effect 1 February 1977 and which, among other things, directs local planning authorities to carry out data collection involving historically significant urban and village milieus in connection with comprehensive studies of the potentials and needs of local administrative units

Sources: Danmark, Miljøstyrelsen, *Miljøreformen og Borgerne* (København, 1974); R. M. Newcomb, 'Has the past a future in Denmark? The preservation of landscape history within the nature park', *Geoforum*, 9 (1972); Viggo Nielsen, 'Status for den Antikvariske Lovgivning', *Fortid og Nutid*, Bind XXIV, Haefle 5 (1971).

landscapes. Table 7 shows five legislative enactments between 1947 and 1969 relating to historic churches and buildings. These highly visible and venerated relics attracted much attention during this interval. With the development of underwater archaeology, the preservation of submerged wrecks, particularly remains of Viking ships, received special treatment in legislation passed in 1963.

The most interesting Danish development in preservation planning began in 1961 with the establishment of the Commission on Nature Preservation. This group was assigned the preparation of documentation necessary for legislation aimed at the fully integrated development of the Danish countryside for recreation, scientific study and school use. The law which emerged from the Commission's white papers is a forward looking, comprehensive blueprint for the planned study and development of the resources of Denmark's countryside. Included within the law are provisions for systematic, nation-wide surveys of both prehistoric and historic items, as well as requirements for the production of feasibility studies of multiple-use nature parks in the particularly favoured parts of the nation. Denmark possesses in this law a potent device for the planned exploitation of great stretches of its historically rich open lands (Fig. 40). The multiple-use concept, whereby pedagogic and leisure-time activities are to be encouraged, is an admirably advanced idea.[7]

Since this legislative landmark, the Danish parliament passed (in 1969) an amendment to the regulations governing historic buildings, and in 1970 passed a measure designed to assist the preservation of historic portions of city centres. The environmental quality legislation passed in June of 1973 includes such measures as the better control of waste disposal which will promote the retention of landscape qualities augmenting the attractiveness of fossilized history, and will help to assure better preservation of old buildings and old village environments.[8] The municipal planning law of 1975, which came into operation early in 1977, requires local authorities to include the built historic patrimony in their deliberations and proposals regarding urban growth, development and renewal. Equipped as they are with sound legislative enactments and a strong underlying commitment to the preservation of their visible history, only a lack of fiscal resources will prevent Denmark from carrying through its admirable programme.

British preservation legislation

Table 8 provides a summary of the century-long history of legislative acts aimed at the inventory and preservation of antiquities, buildings and monuments in Britain.[9] Since the early nineteenth century the Ordnance Survey has accumulated data on the antiquities of Britain until today a quarter million entries are included in the Departments records. This legacy is one of which many nations would be envious. The Ancient Monuments Protection Act of 1882 was the legislative cornerstone upon which much that followed was

Table 8   BRITISH HISTORIC PRESERVATION LEGISLATION

Year	Legislation
1791	Ordnance Survey begins systematic collection of archaeological data
1882	The Ancient Monuments Protection Act. Originally 68 monuments were scheduled
1895	National Trust for Places of Historic Interest or Natural Beauty founded. Incorporated by act of Parliament in 1907
1908–1910	Three Royal Commissions on historical and/or ancient monuments established to conduct inventory surveys in England, Scotland, Wales and Monmouthshire. Ancient Monuments Boards for these three areas were also set up at this time
1913	A succession of amendments to the Ancient Monuments Act following on in 1931, 1937 and 1943
1947	Town and Country Planning Act, a far-reaching and fundamental piece of British planning legislation. As subsequently revised in 1968, it introduces preservation of historic buildings into the work of local planning authorities
1953	Historic Buildings and Ancient Monuments Act
1957	Civic Trust founded with the goal of elevating standards in planning and of encouraging historic conservation
1966	Report of the Committee of Inquiry into the Arrangements for the Protection of Field Monuments 1966–8 (Cmnd 3904)
1967	Civic Amenities Act. Designed for environmental preservation and enhancement, including historic preservation. This Act was incorporated into the 1971 Town and Country Planning Act. Includes criteria for Conservation Areas
1968	Town and Country Planning Act. Oriented towards planning policy. Incorporated into 1971 Planning Act
1969	Housing Act. Setting up General Improvement Areas designed to improve urban housing and environments and to encourage the rehabilitation and recycling of old housing stocks
1970	Establishment of the Department of the Environment with strong organizational representation for archaeology, the preservation of ancient monuments and historic buildings. The positions of Director of Ancient Monuments and Historic Buildings and Under-Secretary for Archaeology are established
1972	Expansion of the National Buildings Record into the National Monuments Record
1974	Department of the Environment plus the Secretary of State for Wales undertake formation and staffing of regional advisory committees to deal with rescue archaeology, including augmented inventory studies
1974	Town and Country Planning Amenities Act. Concerns the functions and administration of the 3,000 conservation areas which have grown out of the provisions of the 1967 Civic Amenities Act. Includes improved support for historic preservation activities

Sources: R. Taylor, M. Cox and I. Dickins (eds), *Britains Planning Heritage* (London, 1975); and Rescue and CBA, *Archaeology and Government, A Plan for Archaeology in Britain* (Worcester and London, 1974).

built. This pioneering effort antedates the American Antiquities Act of 1906 and the initial Danish law of 1917.

The accretional aspect of British preservation legislation is revealed in the succession of Acts directed to ancient monuments, which started with the initial law of 1882. Related Acts were passed in 1913, 1931, 1937, 1943 and 1953. In one sense such a string of laws indicates a failure to do the job correctly the first time, but a more generous interpretation is that British lawmakers learned through experience and were willing to adapt as conditions changed.

With the adoption of the epoch-making Town and Country Planning Act of 1947, Britain expanded planning to cover development of all lands and began compiling a list of buildings which were considered to have historic interest. This Act reflects the national resolve to improve both urban and rural environments using a co-ordinated, planned redevelopment thrust and by exploiting the opportunities provided by the wreckage of World War II. With the advent in 1970 of a state portfolio – Secretary of State for Environment – dedicated to the preservation and betterment of the nation's environment as a whole, a second shift in emphasis can be observed. Subsequently, work with ancient monuments became closely identified with the preservation of environmental amenities and, as a result, professional lobbying was able to give a sharper focus to the role that archaeology could play in the protection of the nation's visible past.[10] An Under-Secretary for Archaeology was appointed in the Department of the Environment in 1973 and policy regarding ancient monuments was co-ordinated in this new ministry. With the release of additional funds through the Department of the Environment in 1974, thirteen Archaeological Advisory Committees were founded to oversee rescue work as well as inventory and preservational programmes in England. Archaeological work today encompasses urban and industrial history, and inter-disciplinary contributions from geographers and local historians are encouraged. The attractions of a grand plan for historical preservation in Britain are greater today, partly as a result of concern about the increasingly faster paced maelstrom of landscape changes, and partly as a recognition of the usefulness of the legal tools which Parliament has provided.[11]

Planning Incentives and Controls

The police power of preservation law functions through its punitive clauses which set fines for the destruction of registered antiquities or historical monuments. Control may be quite strict over the types of land use permitted in areas which include historical features or within areas immediately surrounding such features. In Denmark, for instance, a 'protective shield' zone one hundred metres in depth is specified around scheduled antiquities such as barrows or megaliths. By law an historic house may be defined in such a way as to preserve both its external facade and its internal geometry against unauthorized alterations. Current practice in the United States employs listing on the National Register as a type of early-warning device to alert local authorities and building contractors about the existence of an historically important structure before bulldozers start their attack.

In recognition of the fact that often the legislative carrot is more effective than the stick, an entire arsenal of positive incentives has been developed in order to further historic preservation.[12] One well known technique is the exercise of 'eminent domain' or 'compulsory purchase' to force a transfer of property ownership in the public interest. Here a combination of the stick and carrot are used since property is taken from an individual by a public agency but due compensation is paid. The technique of eminent domain may be used to write an ordinance which establishes an historic district within either an urban or rural area. The zoning regulatory powers of such districts provide for a special evaluation of a piece of land and restricts its use in order to promote preservation of structures or of an urban neighbourhood located there. This device is, clearly, a complex instrument, for criteria to define historic significance must be established and the mechanisms for funding and control have to be set up. Zoning regulation by means of this technique is a matter for the city architects, the local planning authority, or the urban land-use council to employ.

Another technique available to planners at local or municipal levels is the manipulation of easements so as to preserve building and street facades or open spaces adjacent to historic structures. Architectural style controls provide an excellent technique for the preservation of building facings or even of entire street frontages. When used in combination, these two planning instruments may give formidable protection to an urban vista of half-timbered houses or restore the Victorian nobility of a row of downtown office buildings.

The use of taxation relief and grants provide very effective incentives to property owners and developers with some relic of the architectural past under their control. Tax incentives in the form of allowable charitable deductions for expenditures made for the rehabilitation of an historic structure, as proposed in 1972 by the Environmental Protection Tax Act in the United States, is one such proposal. Another and more controversial idea would channel government funds into the rescue and upkeep of historical items located on private property under the concept that privately held land is in part a community asset to which a government may allocate funds for upkeep in the interests of the general welfare. John J. Costonis has advocated this device which he calls development rights transfer.[13]

Finally, two more techniques may be suggested for the tool kit of the planner with an historical conscience: these are aesthetic zoning and the more comprehensive category of urban renewal regulations. The use of aesthetic criteria as major factors in the promotion of a preservational plan has been tested in the United States courts and upheld. Such a technique is commonly used as a screening mechanism to remove junkyards from public view, but the acceptance of age-based criteria in a zone plan for an old village core or for an historic industrial complex is an encouraging legal precedent. Operating at a more rarefied level in the planning hierarchy, the introduction of historically-based aesthetic criteria into a technocratic plan to rejuvenate a decayed urban core can mean that an historic urban quarter becomes worth preserving.

Clearly, none of these technical incentives exists in a vacuum, for all are derived from existing canons of rural and urban planning theory and practice. If, however, they are applied with an historical bias guiding their usage, they can serve to reward the owners of historical monuments rather than merely threatening them with the negative consequences of the law. Positive incentives, which reward as they control or direct the course of historic preservation, may help to ease friction between citizen and bureaucracy and thereby encourage a more appreciative acceptance of historic scenery and the need to save portions of it while we yet can.

In Chapter 3, Fig. 13 emphasized the inventory phase in historical planning projects. The subject matter of Chapter 4 is represented by the sections of the figure occupying the uppermost portion and labelled 'the Plan'. Here an unspecified but significant process was taking place within a suitable 'black box' into which was fed the results of the inventory study. The plan was depicted as being either accepted or rejected with appropriate inventory-related actions to follow. A full-blown national programme for preservation is depicted in Fig. 16 where all of the working and consultative bodies existing in the USA are illustrated. The administrative structure for planning shown in the upper portion of Fig. 13 is depicted by an entire constellation of 'black boxes', each with responsibilities and lines of authority or liaison. Although this is the American example, it is used here to represent a fully realized national programme.

In order to fill out the framework shown in Fig. 13, the legal instruments used by three different countries are listed in Tables 6, 7 and 8. It is informative to have some appreciation of the legal instruments which have been designed and perfected for the preservation task as perceived within three varied national contexts, for, although they have common backgrounds of liberal concerns for their visible historical relics, their individualistic administrations have evolved quite different legislative answers to the problems of preserving and usage. Historical preservation has been converted from an individual hobby activity to a recognized and essential component of plans for environmental conservation, for public access to open lands, and for heightened public recreational use of the out-of-doors.[14]

People involved in historical preservation planning need more than a casual familiarity with the law as this affects these pursuits. Specialists in applied history, historical geography or recreation geography may need post-graduate instruction in resources, recreation and preservation law. These specialists may also need to cultivate more than a passing knowledge of city finances, zoning applications and land-use controls. The proposals for new types of recreational uses of the past (discussed in Chapter 5) and the use of the special techniques of landscape analysis (covered in Chapter 10) are related products of the requirements and opportunities presented by preservation law as it continues its rapid evolution.

5

New Trends in Recreational Uses of the Past

Introduction

Our group met beside the sparkling waters of Ringkøbing Fjord on the west coast of Jutland in a stately building from the early nineteenth century, as guests of a group which was drawing up a regional plan for the full use of the open land resources of the county. The Law for the Preservation of Nature, passed in 1969, had charged each Danish county with the task of producing such a plan, augmented with detailed studies of local areas which were considered to be suitable for development as Nature Parks. Skovbjerg Bakkeø (Woodhill Glaciated Remnant), lying east and north of Ringkøbing town, had been selected by the local planners as a likely candidate to serve as a playground and classroom for the 30 per cent of the county population which resided in four nearby towns. For a whole day our group of geologists, botanists, archaeologists, naturalists and geographers traversed the back roads, busily recording our impressions of this varied landscape. Our grassroots inspection and the ensuing discussion of our observations were part of an exercise in practical land-use and recreational planning. The range of scientific opinion would be used by the technicians in planning how to extract the greatest use from the historical and natural resources of this small piece of Denmark.

The Geography of Recreation

A day's professional consultation in the Ringkøbing area illustrates the contemporary business approach to outdoor recreation as being a variety of land-use expression which can profit from professional planning. The items which we saw and discussed represent the

97

resources which the public would exploit. In the interval since World War II outdoor public recreation has grown into a big business, and the pressures placed on the natural and historic resources used by the industry which caters to a vigorous, mobile population have produced problems of a size to match the industry itself.

A great change has taken place in the study of recreation since the days when a traditional course in economic geography mentioned the recreation industry briefly, if at all. Today the situation is one where major programmes exist to service the geography of recreation and where curricula in architecture, engineering and business management have been developed to deal with resort design, construction and operation. In short, public demand has risen to the level where the resources of leisure time and money are sufficient to fuel an industry which caters to mass recreation. This is an undertaking that needs and certainly can profit from a measure of planning in its development.[1]

The evolution of the pursuit of leisure, from an undertaking available only to the well-to-do during Victorian times to the contemporary world where mass audiences exist for every possible outdoor entertainment and pursuit, forms one of the main themes studied in the history of the geography of recreation.[2] The Grand Canyon of the Colorado River in Arizona encapsulates, in its growth into a major outdoor park attraction, this history. Originally it was accessible only to the intrepid few until the opening of the railroad to the South Rim in 1900 and the construction there of the Bright Angel Lodge opened the way to modern tourism. Today, by contrast, millions of visitors come to the South Rim in private vehicles or buses, and those seeking passive views of the scenic and geologic wonders compete with the hikers and campers for a vantage point. The traffic on foot, mules and horses going from the rim down the steep trails to the river at the bottom or to the Havasupai Indian settlements threaten to erode both the sides of the canyon and the fragile culture of the Indians. Grand Canyon National Park is a major natural attraction of North America, and in addition to its geologic wonders it contains a wealth of plants, animals and relics representative of over eight centuries of human settlement. The demands upon its facilities require careful conservation as well as thoughtful planning for the Canyon's future when, it is to be hoped, individual visits need not be rationed just so that public demand for access can be brought into balance with the carrying capacity of the monument itself.

The many facets of recreation studies include the behavioural

Fig. 19 The old village smithy in Tilst, Jutland, Denmark has taken a new lease of life since being converted into a snug public house five years ago. The village guild of the smith contracted with a schoolteacher in the village in support of a project to convert this derelict structure into a local amenity, while at the same time preserving some of the physical relics of this important trade for the modern generation to view. Within a stone's throw of the village church, the generous forge inside the smithy counteracts the dampness of the Danish summer weather, while the horseshoeing shed on the right houses the visitor's bicycle.

aspects of the public, the economic impacts of the industry and the presentation of recreational facilities to the public. The way that people view the outdoors as an environment for recreation is a type of study of spatial distributions and activity preferences which lies close to the core of the field of geography. Attempts to isolate varieties of behaviour and to quantify their manifestations challenge the best that we as professionals can offer in the way of academic or applied research.[3]

If recreational pursuits consume the resources of an area, their practice can also mean economic gain to the local inhabitants and to the local business structure (Fig. 19). For instance, the money-making potential of the 'Shakespeare Industry' in the Stratford-upon-Avon community is obvious, and the impact of this income upon the town itself can be appreciated even if local facilities built from the taxes which it has generated are not so easily seen. Within the realm of the tourist information kiosk and the travel handbook we come into contact with the dissemination of information – the ways by which one conveys to the public the existence of attractions, their history and their arresting peculiarities. The environmental impact of recreation upon a landscape and the planning problems related to the exploitation of historic landscape features are topics which are sufficiently important so that separate attention will be accorded to them.

Planning of Recreational Facilities

In order better to appreciate the integration of historic landscape relics into a recreational facility, Fig. 20, and a few appended comments are offered on the subject of the actual planning process involved. The *Inventory Data Collection* phase involves a survey of the available natural and cultural features which can be used for recreational purposes. In addition, the environmental conditions which must serve to support the facility have to be studied as do the competing land-use practices in the vicinity (Fig. 17). With such a mass of data in hand, the *Tourism Development Plan* would naturally come next. At this point decisions must be made as to the kind of facility envisioned, whether it is to be a commercial theme park or a state historic monument. The plan itself, in order to be consistent with the physical, economic and legal characteristics of the chosen locale, must take into account as many of these variables as possible. Restrictions upon economic developments within the chosen area and building codes or zoning regulations are examples of critical limiting factors. Most crucial to the whole enterprise is the search for the *Financial Resources* which will allow the project to be built and set into operation. The exact mix of the many potential sources of funding depends on whether the project is a private undertaking or a state sponsored project. Actual *Site Selection*, an outgrowth of the first three phases but made possible by the available finances, is a key point within this entire chain of events. Assuming that all has gone smoothly so far, then the *Building Phase* proceeds so that on-site and support facilities for the park will be produced. After completion and the opening of the facility has taken place, *Project Operation* on a daily basis, including routine maintenance, begins. If subsequent expansion of the project area or of its theme features is anticipated, then a parallel recapitulation of the foregoing series of steps must take place, with the hope that the experience gained in the initial planning work will be used to guide the subsequent improvements.

Environmental Impact of Recreation

Table 9 provides a summary of the various physical and social

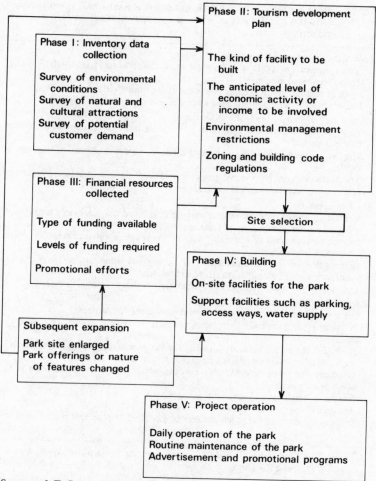

Phase II: Tourism development
plan

The kind of facility to be
built

The anticipated level of
economic activity or
income to be involved

Environmental management
restrictions

Zoning and building code
regulations

Phase I: Inventory data
collection

Survey of environmental
conditions
Survey of natural and
cultural attractions
Survey of potential
customer demand

Phase III: Financial resources
collected

Type of funding available

Levels of funding required

Promotional efforts

Site selection

Phase IV: Building

On-site facilities for the park

Support facilities such as parking,
access ways, water supply

Subsequent expansion
Park site enlarged
Park offerings or nature
of features changed

Phase V: Project operation

Daily operation of the park
Routine maintenance of the park
Advertisement and promotional programs

Sources: J. T. Coppock and B. S. Duffield *Recreation in the Countryside. A Spatial Analysis* (London, 1975); and the author.

Fig. 20   Planning steps appropriate in the construction of recreational activities.

impacts which a recreational facility may impose on its surroundings.[4] Once built and set into operation, the theme park or historical monument becomes submerged in its surroundings in much the same manner that any other private or public enterprise does. Depending upon the type of leisure or recreational facility in question, the resulting impacts may be categorized according to whether they are behavioural, economic, or environmental. There is a difference in the nature and magnitude of these impacts according to

Table 9   ENVIRONMENTAL IMPACTS OF RECREATION: BEHAVIOURAL, ECONOMIC AND
ENVIRONMENTAL ASPECTS WITHIN SCENIC AREAS, RURAL LANDSCAPES AND
THE CITY

Behavioural response – the visitors
   Active tourism or sports with personal involvement versus passive viewing and
   closely controlled itineraries.
   Mode of response to the scenery or site can range from awed delight to disinterest.
   Frequency of visit ranging from the annual pilgrimage to once in a lifetime.

Behavioural response – the local inhabitants
   Views on day-trippers and long-term guests vary from condescension to definite
   financial interest.
   The 'we' of the locals giving a sense of solidarity versus the 'them' of the visiting
   tourists.
   The fluctuations in the seasonal economic impact of the tourist industry promotes
   economic opportunism as well as fiscal conservation.

Economic impacts
   Recreation-tourist industry income may be distributed quite unevenly throughout
   the local economy, especially in scenic park areas.
   Income derived from this industry may be the result of catering activities which
   serve the visitors directly.
   Income derived from this industry may be enjoyed within the strata of the in-
   frastructure which supports recreation and tourism.
   Direct income from the industry may be subject to sharp seasonal fluctuations.

Environmental impacts
   Is the pursuit of recreational tourism damaging to the environment?
   What is the degree of visual intrusion characteristic of a particular recreation in-
   dustry?
   How does the level of activity intensity for the recreation industry compare with
   the levels of other activities going on in the same area?
   What are the types of observable changes which recreation and tourism bring
   about in a given area?
   Are there short-term and long-term changes?
   Are such changes reversible or irreversible?
   What is the degree of care which must be exercised in placing a recreational ac-
   tivity in a given area?

Sources: Nan Fairbrother, *New Lives, New Landscapes* (Harmondsworth, Middx.,
   1972); and the author.

whether the recreational facility is located in the city, the countryside or in an isolated scenic outdoor setting. The types of recreational activities involved will also affect the type and degree of
environmental impact, for the passive enjoyment of natural scenery
is very different from active sports such as skiing or boating in this
regard.

   All three environmental arenas may be used in active or passive
recreational pursuits, each suited to the arena. The *Behavioural
Responses* which can be anticipated range from those of skiers and
mountain hikers, who take pleasure in both viewing and being
active in a particular scenic arena, to tourists closely tied to the

scheduled route of a tour and views of the scenery passing by the bus window. The manner in which the visitor views the scenery or the displays presented for his entertainment is also of interest to us. It may range from a delighted sense of awe before a particularly commanding landscape prospect to a lack of historical curiosity only alleviated when the bus stops at a kiosk or restaurant. The degree of individual preparation to extract the maximum from a museum visit or a tour through the historic heart of a European city will vary to a corresponding degree. The behavioural characteristics of the visitors are also shaped by the frequency of visits, whether it is a once-in-a-lifetime fling to see Rome or it is the annual ski or spa pilgrimage which is being undertaken.

As important as the behaviour of the visitors is the outlook and conduct of the local inhabitant, the person working in the tourist industry or subject to advantages or disadvantages which this business brings to his home village or town. Whilst day-trippers may be regarded with a degree of condescension, the long-term guest may be more warmly received since the expectations of financial reward may be greater. An attitude of the locals versus the visitors may have an important bearing on how comfortable the tourist feels and how successful the business becomes. Lastly, the seasonal aspect of tourism is a dimension of the industry which more strongly and adversely affects the local population, many of whom must plan carefully if the golden harvest of the tourist months is to tide them over the slack season.

The *Economic Impacts* as they are sketched here consist, first of all, of the uneven distribution of derived income throughout the local economy. The fact that hotel keepers may prosper while school teachers are not affected illustrates this disparity. There are two types of income derived from the recreation industry: firstly income realized from direct catering services for the guests, and secondly from the general support services essential to the whole tourist community. The income which the industry provides to the infrastructure of the local economy, through the provision of jobs and salaries to local civil servants, road menders and farmers, may be also of considerable importance. Last of all, and having a great impact, is the seasonally uneven flow of income from the industry which produces a feast or famine situation.

The third category of effects characteristic of the recreation industry falls within the group labelled *Environmental Impacts* in Table 9. One asks initially whether recreation is damaging to the environment, a question as difficult to answer as it is to define. We assume, for example, that the delicate and easily disrupted natural environment of the high mountains is more easily damaged than the city called on to absorb yet another theme park. An assessment of potential damage is usually formulated in terms of the recreational pursuit itself, but should also take into account the facilities provided to support that activity. Visual intrusion by the recreation industry takes different forms, from forest clearance on mountain slopes for skiers to uncontrolled advertising of restaurants and curio shops adjacent to a national shrine. As in the case with environmental damage assessment, a completely objective determination of the degree of visual intrusion is not easily achieved. For instance, the activity level of recreation may dominate in an undesirable way the general business and commercial profile of a given area. It may, on the other hand, provide an attractive distraction from undistinguished surroundings, or furnish an appreciated focus to a diffuse activity environment. The commercial landscape of Southern California is, for example, definitely improved in places by the presence of colourful and diverting theme parks. By contrast, a group of prehistoric monuments standing unobtrusively on the Irish landscape augment the general scene in a harmonious way since their distinctive details are an essential part of the whole vista.

Two concluding points regarding environmental impacts are worth stressing. The types of observable changes which recreation and tourism bring about within a given environment may be short-term or long-term in their effects and either reversible or irreversible. The use of a man-made reservoir for pleasure boating and fishing will leave few changes affecting either the appearance of the lake or its primary use once recreation has ceased. By contrast, desert or alpine environments are marked almost irretrievably once tourism or recreation have been introduced. The degree of planning care required when recreational activities are introduced into any area underscores the potential magnitude of their impact and the need for clear thought before action lest, for example, an enshrined battlefield be surrounded by parking lots and snack-bars.

Examples of Historical Features Classified According to Landscape Type and Popularity

Having looked at the recreation industry, the way in which its construction is planned and some of the environmental impacts which it may produce, the next stage in the argument is to consider the features from the past which may be used as centrepieces in history parks or as subordinate attractions in recreation complexes. Once this survey has been completed, three case-studies will be examined in detail.

Table 10 has been compiled partly from Patmore's book and partly from personal knowledge.[5] Part A of this table illustrates the type of places and things which would be suitable for illustrating the past as it occurs in large scenic outdoor areas, in rural areas and in bustling urban areas. Estimates of the popularity of the same set of historic features for a leisure audience are contained in Part B of this table, in terms of spheres of impact. The selection of sites is a personal one, and others might well draw upon another listing of the 'historic Top Twenty'. The estimates of potential audience attraction are also personal and are presented more as illustrations to be discussed than as examples for which quantative data exists.

Looking first at the examples which illustrate the *Landscape Types*, the largest in terms of size and the most complex in contents are the *Scenic Outdoor Areas*. The entire 1,750 km (1,100 miles) of the Californian coastline constitute a recreational resource with many and varied scenic attractions. Included are historic features representing settlement history during the Mexican and Spanish periods as well as prehistoric sites in abundance dating from the Native American era. The more recent landscape imprints by the Anglo Americans are clearly evident, and even the early Russian penetration from the north shows in the form of the preserved wooden buildings at Fort Ross. Other large features in this category include Bodmin Moor in Cornwall, the Mols Mountains of east central Jutland in Denmark and the Appleton Ranch research area which covers 3,200 ha (8,000 acres) in Arizona south-east from Tucson. Within the 25 sq. km (10 sq. miles) of the Mols Mountains one may find features which span the long interval from the last Ice Age to enclosure of the farmlands in 1800. The Appleton Ranch is currently being used to study the return of natural flora and fauna now that cattle grazing has been stopped and the landscape is reverting to its appearance *c.* 1500 when grazing was first introduced.

The smaller features in *Rural Areas* illustrate more tamed landscapes dominated by agriculture and populated by farms and villages. The six examples included here range in time from the New Stone Age (Mosegaard), to the Industrial Revolution (Beamish). At Mosegaard Historical Park the prehistoric walk leads one among the restored prehistoric tombs, whereas the Bobcaygeon lumbermill site in Ontario reflects the nineteenth-century settlement of the

Table 10 EXAMPLES OF HISTORICAL RELIC FEATURES CLASSIFIED ACCORDING TO LANDSCAPE TYPE AND POPULARITY

(A) *Landscape type:*			(B) *Degree of popularity:* Sphere of audience impact		
Scenic outdoor area	Rural area	Urban area	National impact	Regional impact	Local impact
Appleton Research Ranch, Tucson, Arizona	Bobcaygeon, Ontario, Canada	Angel's Flight, Los Angeles, California	Bodmin Moor, Cornwall	Appleton Research Ranch, Tucson, Arizona	Angel's Flight, Los Angeles, California
Bodmin Moor, Cornwall	Mosegaard Historical Park, Denmark	Brighton Old Town Centre, England	California Coastline	Bobcaygeon, Ontario, Canada	Brighton Old Town Centre, England
California Coastline	North of England Open Air Museum, Beamish, Co. Durham	Los Angeles Old Plaza, California	Mols Mountains, Denmark	Los Angeles Old Plaza, California	Mosegaard Historical Park, Denmark
Mols Mountains, Denmark	Old Harlev, Denmark	Museum of the City of London	Museum of the City of London	North of England Open Air Museum, Beamish, Co. Durham	Royal Burgh of Culross, Scotland
	Royal Burgh of Culross, Scotland	Norwich City, Historic Centre	Traelleborg Viking Site, Denmark	Norwich City, Historic Centre	St. Katharine-by-the-Tower, London
	Traelleborg Viking Site, Denmark	St. Katharine-by-the-Tower, London		Old Harlev, Denmark	

Source: J. A. Patmore, *Land and Leisure* (Newton Abbot, 1970 and Harmondsworth, Middx., 1972); and the author.

Canadian Shield and the development of its timber resources. At the Trælleborg Viking site on the island of Zealand in Denmark one finds the reconstruction of a precise military camp of nine centuries ago, and the Royal Burgh of Culross remains as a scenic legacy of mercantile prosperity during the seventeenth century. Beamish Open Air Museum displays reconstructions illustrating the mining industry in North East England at the height of its industrial awakening, but Old Harlev village in rural Jutland depicts the scenic attractions of the Danish countryside of a century ago when an agricultural revolution was in progress. Among these examples, Beamish, Culross, Mosegaard and Trælleborg exist in the form of preserved or reconstructed sites which are open to the public with an interest in the visible past. Bobcaygeon mill site is at present a carpark, with its potential for representing a stirring chapter in the history of Canadian resource development being realized only in the imaginations of informed visitors. The prospects for Old Harlev are covered in greater detail later on in this chapter.

The last landscape type is composed of *Urban Areas*, illustrated by six examples in Table 10. These represent a range of sizes and of temporal periods, from a town centre reflecting the glories of medieval urban England in the case of Norwich, to the intimacy of the Spanish and Mexican plaza which was the centre of the old *pueblo* of Los Angeles. The growth of the urban landscape under the impact of industrialization is fossilized in the docks and warehouses built in London by Thomas Telford during the early decades of the nineteenth century on the Thames at St Katharine-by-the-Tower. The impressive vistas of urban history are conveyed to the visitor by the new Museum of the City of London with its variety of displays or by a stroll through the rehabilitated pedestrian precinct in Brighton's old town centre. The status of these sites varies, with the Museum of the City of London representing a going concern, the St Katharine's project only partially completed and the tracks and trolleycars of Angel's Flight still in storage. This will be discussed in further detail.

The second portion of Table 10, Section (B), classifies the same sixteen site-examples according to their levels of popularity and in terms of their spheres of impact as recreational attractions. A classification in terms of whether an historic feature exerts a national, regional or local pull upon potential visitors is altogether subjective because comparable statistical measures are not available. Hence, the five sites of *National Impact* include the scenic and cultural wonders displayed along the California coast, amid the granite tors of Bodmin Moor and within the hills and dales of Mols. London, the great attraction, can depend upon the Museum of the City of London to demonstrate its unrivalled resources dating from the past, and the Trælleborg Viking camp is worth making a detour to see.

Six places have a *Regional Impact* sufficient to draw visitors from East Anglia and North-East England to Norwich's historic heart or to the impressive machinery in the Beamish outdoor museum. The Old Spanish days recreated at the Los Angeles Plaza draws people from all over the Basin, and residents of Arizona might easily manage a stop at the Appleton Research Ranch in the course of an extended day tour. Residents of Ontario on vacation can easily combine a trip to the Canadian Shield vacation lands with a stop at the empty site of the Bobcaygeon sawmill but would be more likely to do so if a museum were to be built there.

The last section in Table 10, *Local Impact*, lists five features which certainly would attract visitors from within the locality. Walking through the picturesque stone streets and lanes of Old Culross or beside the watery expanses of Telford's handsome docks and buildings at St Katharine-by-the-Tower would be very attractive to urban history enthusiasts if maps and guidebooks were available. The restored attractions of Old Brighton or the Mosegaard History walk beckon families for an outing on a sunny day, as would a renovated Angel's Flight clanging up and down Bunker Hill in Los Angeles. These examples of attractive and interesting existing or restored historic landscape relics, and many others which come to mind, illustrate the possibilities which exist for constructive enjoyable recreation among the remnants of our past, if care is taken in their planned development.

Three Proposed Historic Sites Illustrating the Tenets of Recreational Planning

In order to illustrate in more detail how an historic feature can be developed as a recreational attraction, three case-studies are described here.[6] They are diverse in terms of the national traditions and landscape history which they represent, and they are also varied in terms of their size and the potential tourist hinterlands which they command. In addition, these illustrations have been chosen so as to illustrate urban, village and rural environments.

The urban scene, local interest and Angel's Flight

We are concerned here with a homeless relic from the glorious past of Bunker Hill in downtown Los Angeles, California. Built around the turn of the century, Angel's Flight was a member of that family of small and efficient urban transporters which includes the elevators of Lisbon, Portugal, the famous cable-cars of San Francisco, California and the cable railways of Innsbruck, Austria. Angel's Flight was a funicular railway installed to negotiate the steep 100 metre (325 ft) east face of Bunker Hill between Hill and Olive Streets along Third Street. For almost seventy years, until their removal in 1969, two cars named the Olivet and the Sinai, provided for the price of five cents a round trip which ascended via a narrow slot in this densely built quarter. Once atop Bunker Hill, the City of the Angels could be glimpsed stretching into the distance beyond the silhouettes of the renowned Victorian houses which crowned the hill.

As part of the urban redevelopment of the Bunker Hill area, Angel's Flight was dismantled and put into storage in 1969. Protests against this action and proposals to restore the trolley line have swirled back and forth through the corridors of urban-renewal power in Los Angeles ever since. Inflation has pushed up the costs of rebuilding the railway and of restoring the rolling stock, while the cars themselves continue to repose in semi-derelict storage. Bunker Hill is dominated today by severe shapes in steel, aluminium and bronze glass which provide an environmental context quite different from that of the solid hotel apartments and gloriously elaborated Victorian houses which used to dominate the area. Now that massive redevelopment is well advanced on Bunker Hill, it is reasonable to examine whether the Olivet and the Sinai could ever again be at home amid the contemporary towering blocks and slabs.

While the name of Angel's Flight is perpetuated only by a roof-top revolving bar amid the splendid cylindrical stacks of the Bonaventure Hotel, alternative uses for the original installation are being discussed. One proposal, put forward by Warren Christensen, epitomizes this chapter's theme of planned recreational use of existing historical relics within the urban milieu.[7] Some 6·5 km (4 miles) to the northwest of the Los Angeles Civic Centre and Bunker Hill, on the eastern margin of Hollywood, is Barnsdall Park, a pleasant urban minipark. Within this 4·4 ha (11 acres) which occupies a dominating site on the southern fringes of the Santa Monica Mountains is located Hollyhock House, Frank Lloyd Wright's first commissioned project in Southern California. A private home which was built in 1918 for Aline Barnsdall but later fell into ruin, it became a property of the city in 1927 and has been recently restored under the guidance of Lloyd Wright, the architect's son. Today, above the traffic noise and confusion of nearby boulevards, with a vista over a vast parking lot and busy shopping centre, Barnsdall Park, crowned by its exotic Wright house and the newer art gallery, is a focus for art shows, workshops and conferences. The green spaces and shady slopes of the minipark provide picnic and meditation space for many local residents. Christensen's idea is that Angel's Flight should be resurrected at the margin of Barnsdall Park. If this little funicular railway were to be installed against the sheer, east-facing slope of the park grounds, it would provide a stunning route to the park buildings and portions of the parking area could be used for visitors' cars. Such an installation would provide easier access to the park and serve as an arresting symbol from the past for a neighbourhood currently dominated by that which is most unsightly from the present.

In terms of planning, clearly the original equipment and cars of Angel's Flight would have to be inspected to determine whether restoration is still feasible. If this were not so, then should replicas of the originals be built or would it be better to use some more modern design based, perhaps, upon the original horse-car lines? The financial resources required for such a scheme would be considerable, and during a time of fiscal austerity private funds might have to be called upon. In terms of its environmental impact, such a scheme would mean a greater use of Barnsdall Park with associated wear and tear on the buildings and facilities. The prospect of combining a Victorian trolley system with a useable monument to American architectural genius in a park setting is appealing. Even though tied to an urban milieu and operating at a local level of interest it should still be possible to capitalize upon the existence of these two legacies from the past for the benefit of contemporary local residents.

The scenic village, regional interest and Old Harlev

Old Harlev is a suburban village which could well offer a view of the preserved past to the residents of Århus, a city with a quarter of a million inhabitants, located on the coast of Central Jutland 13 km (8 miles) to the east. The village of Old Harlev at present contains about sixty-five people who inhabit or utilize twenty-nine buildings, including twelve which have been described as being of outstanding historic value. Situated upon an ancient terrace remnant adjacent to the Århus River, Old Harlev sits by itself within the Århus glacial spillway valley and is separated from its nearest neighbours by 1·5 km of fields and meadows. In the course of the Village Project

Survey carried on for the Municipality of Århus by the Geographical Institute at the University of Aarhus, Old Harlev came out near the top of the ratings in terms of its aggregate building quality, its total village physical milieu and its combined social and physical milieu value.[8] It is a very attractive place and a residential environment which is well regarded by its inhabitants.

The historic fabric of the village includes a distinguished example of a Danish Romanesque church representing 800 years of history. The adjacent vicarage farm is a high class example of Danish half-timbered, thatched roof, rural elegance, and within sight of the church is a handsome building dating from 1721 which served as a pioneer centre for state-supported elementary education during the eighteenth century. Nearly 60 per cent of the buildings in Old Harlev date from the early periods of vernacular architecture, which means that they were built prior to 1850. Whether these structures serve today as modernized residences, barns or outbuildings, when coupled with the attractive gardens, stands of trees and the curving street pattern, the village as a whole is a treat for the eyes and an instructive open-air collection of Danish rural architecture at its best.

To use such a complicated and delicate relic from the past for recreational purposes would require descriptive materials to be made available on site, and vehicular access to the place would have to be controlled in order not to overtax the existing roadnet and the limited facilities for off-street parking to the detriment of the interests of the inhabitants. A potential solution lies with the near-by old foundations of the Århus-Hammel Railway, which united the city with the town via some 40 km (24 miles) of curving track threading its way through green fields and small villages from about 1904 until its demise as a route fifty years later. Though the tracks are long gone, the right-of-way exists for the majority of its extent, and informal use of this routeway is well established by contemporary pedestrians and bicyclists. If it were possible to develop the 15.5 km (9 miles) of roadbed from Århus city to the cross-roads town of Framlev-Harlev as a bicycle path, then the result would be a means of access to Old Harlev which was much less demanding of road and parking space. Beyond that, only 1·5 km (1 mile) of access path need be built either along a scenic stream from the east or across the valley from the north in order that bicyclists and hikers could reach Old Harlev with ease from the scenic old railway route.

With respect to environmental impact considerations, the atmosphere of Old Harlev could easily be disrupted by a mass of day-trippers, even if they came by foot or by cycle, and at present the village is not able to accommodate visitors in any numbers. The provision of information, refreshments and toilet facilities would require tact and unobtrusive siting in order that the very scenes which one is trying to preserve for the visitor are not at the same time disrupted by attempts to make the place accessible.

Given the dense and overlapping network of Danish planning legislation and zoning ordinances, merely bringing such a recreational development into being might be much more difficult than finding the finances for such a project. After nearly twenty-five years of existence as a disused right-of-way, the Århus-Hammel line has yet to be declared a bicycle path and to be so developed. The planned imposition of energetic tourism upon such a village with its fragile social and physical structure is so delicate an undertaking that one needs to proceed with deliberate caution and be certain that the potential risks of failure are outweighed by the gains in entertaining instruction which such an historic site can offer to modern urbanites.

Rural expanses, national interest and Bodmin Moor

Bodmin Moor is an example of a potential nature park with great historical resources and national appeal, and a brief description of it completes our trilogy of proposed recreational features for the future. In an ascending order according to size and popularity with visitors, Bodmin Moor ranks as the largest and the most magnetic. When looking at sheet number 200 of the Ordnance Survey 1:50,000 Series or leafing through the historical section of *The South West Peninsula* by Millward and Robinson or Balchin's *Cornwall*, one is struck by the dense accumulation at Bodmin of prehistoric and historic relics of many types.[9] Within its 200 sq. km (80 sq. miles) of Cornish granite, embossed with elongated ridges, capped by tors and smoothed by boggy hollows, one finds a landscape dominated by grazing land beneath open heavens (Fig. 21). Right up to its peak elevation of 400 m (1,375 feet) at Brown Willy, Bodmin Moor demonstrates why it so richly deserves its designation as an area of outstanding natural beauty. Four millennia of human occupation are memorialized here in features as disparate in appearance and function as Trethevy Quoit and the Hurlers from the Stone Age, and Stowe's Hill Iron Age fort, contrasting with the numerous remains of Bronze Age habitations and remnants of Iron Age field systems not far distant from indications of early medieval moorland colonization.[10] The alignment of the Roman road across

Fig. 21 The scene is on Bodmin Moor, Cornwall, England with a view from Bronze Age hut circles near Rough Tor across to glistening white piles of waste from a nearby china clay pit. The vast temporal span typical of the Moor and the impact of the present upon the past are illustrated. The Cornwall Archaeological Society is conducting an exhaustive survey of field antiquities in the area, and information of that type is vital if a proposal is to be developed for making the Moor into a nature park with strong elements of landscape history. (Photo by the author.)

the Moor, perpetuated by the modern road, contrasts with portions of late eighteenth century turnpike roads which are still visible. The extraction of stone and minerals from Bodmin Moor has occupied the energies of men from the beginning, and evidences occur of tin streaming in the valley of the River Fowey as a complement to the remains of granite quarrying on the heights and the old china clay workings hard by the Moor itself. Within the towns and villages which surround the Moor on all sides, one finds a wealth of medieval crosses, churches and holy wells which attest to the waves of human faith which have washed its margins. The indefatigable energies of the Cornwall Archaeological Society have been invested in an attempt to raise the level of inventory information for Bodmin, and a recent Society exercise in field archaeology in the vicinity of Rough Tor, during the Spring of 1975, revealed over 150 features which had not been previously recorded. Once the Parish check-lists for Bodmin Moor have been completed, the true wealth in landscape history which this area possesses will be clearly revealed.

Meanwhile, the recent summary by the Cornwall Archaeological Society of activities currently threatening the Moor provides good reason for proposing that the area be made a National Park.[11] Though the windy, rocky heights of Bodmin Moor are unattractive for most contemporary human activities, the more sheltered fringe areas and the linear portions along public access ways have felt the impact of developmental processes. A proposed reservoir of nearly 320 ha (800 acres) in the centre of the Moor near Colliford Downs would produce an over-dominating visual intrusion into the landscape. A car park to be built at Draynes Bridge on the southern edge will spawn extraordinary foot traffic along the trail to Golitha Falls on the River Fowey and threaten forested portions which are reputed to date back to Domesday times. Lastly, as an example, the pollution by aircraft noise of the south-western moorland is a questionable by-product of the Treswithick airfield.

Although Bodmin Moor has served man for thousands of years, the contemporary exploitation of its water resources, mineral deposits and recreational attractions actively attack this area where it is most vulnerable and where the results of such inroads are most clearly vislble. The challenge is to promote a balanced use of Bodmin Moor and its attractive margins by resource developers, tourist interests and environmentally conscious societies. This granite protuberance, extending 20 by 20 km (12 miles square), is filled with an abundance of arresting and interesting natural features as well as with a rich cross-section of the visible works of human history and deserves to be considered as being a national respository. In that role Bodmin Moor further suggests itself as a fit candidate, because of its riches and its relative degree of sparse useage today, to become a national park wherein the scientific, pedagogic and recreational interests of the nation as a whole and the South West as a region may be cultivated. Intrusive uses, whether to further public utilities, access or entertainment should be assigned roles there within a sensitive scheme for planned development. Near Rough Tor on the western side of the Moor, one can in a single glance savour the sweep of developmental time from the remote past to the present with a view across a collection of Bronze Age hut circles to the distant glistening heaps of china-clay waste. In suggesting the best possibilities for the three granite moorlands of the South West, perhaps one can generalize and say that if Exmoor is most appreciated as a locale for comfortable modern retirement and tourism along its northern side, and if Dartmoor excels as the home of vast natural panoramas, then Bodmin Moor serves best as a retreat in which we may contemplate our collective past as it is etched upon a living landscape.

The geography of recreation and leisure as a topic offers in its ramifications so many technical byways that it has been possible here to give but a short synopsis in order to place comments on the uses of the past for leisure-time enjoyment within an appropriate context. The planning of recreational activities is also a discipline by itself, so here it has only been possible simply to note the places where it impinges in a regulative manner upon our enjoyment of items from the past. The main concern within this chapter has been to show by means of examples how recreational planning can include items of historic interest.

In Fig. 20 we show the succession of steps involved in the development of a plan for a recreational project, and Table 9 sums up for us the impacts which recreation activities may produce. Thereafter, Table 10 illustrates a number of specific historic features according to landscape types and then in terms of their potential recreational attractiveness. Three examples were then selected for discussion in greater detail with respect to these resource attributes and the planning constraints peculiar to them individually. Within these three case-studies the potentials for development are stressed in order that we may advance our discussion in Part I of the book from the inventories of historic items to present-day recreational use of areas which do include some of these features. Part of the focus has also been upon the law as an instrument which can promote planned preservation of our past and part upon recreational planning as a feasible guide for the enjoyment of the past now and in the future. To paraphrase the words of Glyn Daniel, we have discussed here in Part I the careful recreational use of the understood past by an interested and informed present.[12]

Part II

Categories of Historical Landscape Features in a Planned Recreational Context

Once the historical geographer has looked at present-day uses of the past for recreational purposes and briefed himself on the law as it relates to preservation, his interest naturally moves on to the inventory of landscape items with which this whole enterprise is involved. Having a grasp of possible uses of items from the past, the geographer wishes to know more about the specific periods of human activity which are so represented and the distribution over the earth's surface of the relic forms themselves. The four chapters which follow will consider the physical legacies of landscape history typical of the rural scene and the modern urban milieu. The emphasis is placed on field patterns and settlement forms in the former case, and on old buildings, historic neighbourhoods and urban redevelopment within the latter chapter. In addition, the imprints derived from the complex history of Industrial Revolution in the Western World will receive our attention. Finally, the many attempts by the state to affect the landscape will be examined. A plan for recreational entertainment or for building rehabilitation may exist of itself, but what interests the historian and the geographer is the type of past relics which are to be manipulated and the historical truth of men's efforts to shape the world which they can yet convey.

PART II

Categories of Historical Lapse: the Lecture as a Planned Radio-sound Programme

6

Landscape History Relics
of the Rural Scene

Introduction

On a summer's day in 1972 our excursion group from the International Geographical Congress left the tour bus at a gravel road which ran through an undulating and swampy landscape; we were about to absorb through the soles of our shoes some impressions of Irish agricultural colonization in Peterborough County, Southern Ontario, Canada. We toiled up steep and stony slopes, passing swampy areas in the hollow, to end our trek atop the rise where the soils were thin but the terrain more level. Here was some of the land allotted to members of the Peter Robinson emigration of 1825 when they arrived after an exhausting trip from County Cork in southern Ireland. This geological and geomorphological interface between the Laurentian Shield to the north and the more gentle Palaeozoic rocks to the south was and still is a harsh and fickle environment, and the consternation of those assigned a swampy area could well be imagined as we walked through this silent wasteland. The guide, A. G. Brunger, drew our attention to the contrast between the permanence of cadastral surveys as conveyed by the topographic maps we carried and the transient nature of such adventures in rural settlement.[1] The swampy bottom lots were still untilled and the poor, rocky slopes athwart our route seemed never to have bloomed under the ploughman's hand. Unmarked by modern development, this stony and swampy land slept with its memories of the anguished comments uttered by Irishmen 150 years ago.

Our field example helps make the points that rural landscape history appears in many guises, and the full significance of its relic features is often difficult to unravel without the help of expert

119

knowledge. In addition, one finds that modern settlements and artifacts will often overlay the remnants of the past producing a confusing but richer landscape. A last point concerns the well-known propensity of geographers to invest their energies in attempts to unravel the mysteries of the rural way of life which has shaped our lands since the remote days of the discovery of agriculture. This is so despite the fact that our residential preference is for the city and much of our concern focuses upon the housing and work-spaces which impart the most to people today. This means that whilst the major balance of our preservational energies are invested in the urban environment, our clear preference for the countryside as a recreational arena dictates that fields, farmsteads and villages do figure in recreational planning and that the discreet, historically significant items of the countryside have been itemized and restored for our edification and amusement.

Where History Appears Upon the Rural Landscape

In Hugh Clout's *Rural Geography* there is a figure which illustrates the major components and the activities which together make up the landscape of the dynamic rural scene.[2] Within this constellation of physical, institutional and economic objects are a number which characteristically may bear forms and features derived from the past. Figure 22 is a schematic expression of these specific features which, although embedded in the larger complex, command the primary attention of the students of rural landscape history.

The demands placed upon the rural landscape appear on the right of the diagram, and the rural responses are shown on the left where they focus on the *Farmland* and the *Settlement* boxes. As an example, the urban demand for foodstuffs would ultimately be reflected in the production of corn and livestock from the farmland as an expression, in turn, of the physical characteristics of the land, the components of utilization and the exact utilization pattern itself. The land, divided into fields, is cultivated so as to produce products which will satisfy the urban demands. Within the settlement portion of the diagram, it is farm labour employed in various activities within farmsteads and villages which gets the actual work done.

There is nothing of profound novelty in this description, but what we may sometimes forget is that economic, agricultural and settlement history all may be produced and endure for later discovery as a result of this chain of functionally interdependent actions and pursuits. Fossilized field patterns from medieval times would be a land

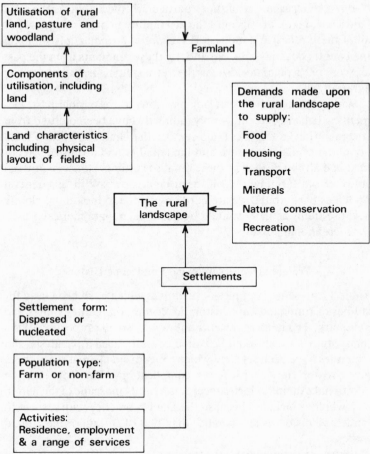

Source: Hugh Clout, *Rural Geography. An Introductory Survey* (Oxford, 1972).
Fig. 22   The rural landscape in its historical dimension.

characteristic, and their role within the old pattern of farming would constitute a visual relic of medieval agriculture as an economic enterprise and as a particular pattern of land-use. Within the settlement portion of the diagram, a demonstrable shift from dispersed to nucleated settlements would qualify as an historic relic as would surviving houses which represent the residences of farmers and labourers, or the work-places of smiths and millers. The urban market stretching out its demanding lines to the countryside would also produce relics in the form of tithe barns for the collection of produce, drover roads for its transport and country estates for the residence of those who controlled and administered the system.

Nature Conservation, while not a particularly old activity in the rural landscape, takes into account the desirability of preserving some or all of these relics, and modern *Recreational Demands* placed upon the countryside may seek out and use these remnants from the past as scenery, a place to visit or the setting for learning about the agrarian past.

Within the framework of our bias toward the visible past, elements which are detectable only indirectly have been omitted from consideration in Fig. 22. Land tenure, the characteristics of rural populations' age-sex ratios, and land quality and farm size are not included although each of these details is of importance in any full study of old farming and old farm landscapes. With this general sketch as background we are better equipped to look more closely at those items actually studied by historical geographers and used for recreational pursuits.

Preferred Topics in Rural Landscape History

Table 11 presents examples of the topics which have been used for studies of rural landscape history in Britain, the United States and Denmark. The table represents only a very small proportion of the many studies which could be called upon for such an analysis, and examples have been selected which concern small areas, in order to give greater clarity with fewer complications. For Denmark, an additional example which concerns the rural landscape of the nation as a whole is included because the Danish practice with respect to landscape history is less familiar than that of Britain or the United States.

Emery's treatment of *Oxfordshire* reflects in its selection of topics the admirable British approach to rural landscape history.[3] By concentrating upon the visible evidence in the landscape to describe and illustrate the dynamic processes which have shaped it from prehistoric times to the end of the Victorian era, the author is able to pack a great amount of detail about a wide variety of topics into a manageable format. Historical cross-sections in time are the basis of his narrative structure, and descriptions of case-studies add vividness to the text. The elements of the rural landscape stressed include field patterns, built structures, transportation lines and landscape parks. The three-dimensional volumes represented by individual buildings and settlements add much to Emery's story since they represent habitations and work sites as well as visibly manifesting human architectural skills and aesthetics.

It is equally worth noting the topics of landscape history which a study in the tradition represented by Emery's volume does *not* cover. The much-discussed dynamic processes which shape landscapes are presented only in narrative form and not as models, equations or behavioural curves. A student of landscape history working within the tradition represented by this Oxfordshire volume cannot become much involved with the underlying strata of decision-making among politicians, Parliamentary enactments or the social currents which help determine the making of landscape at a given time. The socio-economic forces at work upon the land comprise an alternative historic approach which does not lend itself to a focus upon the human use and production of landscapes nor upon the heritage of visible relics which endure through time.

The local history written by Young about a valley in the Santa Monica Mountains of the *Los Angeles Basin*, an example selected from the number of American studies of old landscape history, uses the cross-section approach backed up by key vertical themes.[4] In a manner similar to British practice, the physical setting and the prehistoric scenes form the opening portions of the book. Thereafter, the topics pass in review in a manner as familiar to the student of Southern California as Emery's selection of chapter titles is to the British reader. Young's vertical themes of the tangled disputes over property ownership (produced by the rapid changes in political status and a clash of cultures), and the 'booms' and 'busts' of real estate speculation reflect the focus upon the past century of history for these scenic acres. The choice of themes leads to a notable concern on the part of Young with individuals as movers and doers shaping a physical landscape, and the tenure changes and real estate operations reflect the idea of the individual as the channel through which political and economic forces mould the land through successive changes in patterns of rural and urban land-use. The resulting shapes given to the built environment are a dominant element in Young's book, and the arresting and often eccentric visions of suitable forms lend to youthful Southern California some of the regional character imparted by Britain with its country houses set in parkland and its fields bordered by hedgerows.

For *Denmark*, which also boasts many studies of historic landscape evolution, we have selected a suitable illustration from a national handbook series. Viggo Nielsen, who deals with the history of agricultural practice up to the seventeenth century, and Aage H. Kampp, who covers the topic from that point onwards, together describe changing agrarian and settlement patterns for the nation as

Table 11 ILLUSTRATIONS OF PREFERRED TOPICS IN RURAL LANDSCAPE HISTORY

(A) Britain, Oxfordshire	(B) United States, California, Los Angeles Basin Rustic Canyon	(C) Denmark, Starreklinte, NW Zealand, Sønder Vestud, Møn	(D) Denmark as a whole
Outline of topics			
Making of the English landscape in terms of episodes and topics	Historic geological background	Starting with the first historical record, c. 1315, describing number of villages and farms, amounts cultivated	Prehistoric settlements
The earliest landscapes: natural, Prehistoric and Roman	A place in the sun: Californian Indians 25,000 B.C. to A.D. 1542	1370–1591, continuity and change	Types of traditional Danish villages by morphological groups
English settlement: primary and Saxon survivals	Arrival of the Spanish: 1542, 1602, 1769	1500–1800, reconstruction of field and cultivation patterns on the basis of the 1688 Tax Survey	Single farmsteads
Medieval expansion: Domesday landscape, colonization of the waste, forest landscapes	A tale of two ranchos: Spanish and Mexican California. Anglo California, post–1848	Eighteenth-century changes, Enclosure (c. 1800) and resulting reconstruction of field patterns	Manors and manor farms
Landscapes in transition: village desertion, texture of early Enclosure	The 1860s and 1870s Los Angeles and Santa Monica Canyon resorts	Great changes 1800–1974:	Coastal settlements for fishing and trade
Landscape by design: country houses and parkland, Parliamentary Enclosure, new routeways	Forestation with Eucalyptus 1885 to 1914	Subdivision of farms	
	Potential port development 1880 to 1920	Dispersal of farms	
The Victorian Countryside: changing villages, disappearing forests, conquest of the Thames, railways in the landscape	Turn of the century private homes built in Rustic Canyon	Establishment of a new type of manor farm	
	The theme of progress:	Small-holders and subdivisions 1921	
	e.g. the Uplifters in search of the Land of Oz, 1913–47	Decline of small-holdings	
	e.g. the Upper Canyon: visions of	New replacement land-use:	

Table 11 — (contd.)

	(A) Britain, Oxfordshire	(B) United States, California, Los Angeles Basin Rustic Canyon	(C) Denmark, Starreklinte, NW Zealand, Sønder Vestud, Møn	(D) Denmark as a whole
Towns in the landscape: types of towns and their functions				
The contemporary landscape		Utopia, 1924–66 e.g. the Lower Canyon: West Coast bohemia, 1913–50s e.g. community action, from 1926 onwards e.g. Architects Alley, 1923 onwards	summer residences, gravel works	
Examples of emphasis on specifics				
Visible landscape relics		Individuals as agents of landscape change	Changes in patterns of settlement	Changes in agricultural practices
Processes which shaped landscapes and left visible relic features		Real Estate and land tenure changes	Changes in field patterns	Changing field patterns
Transportation lines		Land use changes		Changes in agricultural technology
Field patterns		Estates and built structures		Changes in morphology of rural settlement
Built structures				Changes over time in function of settlements
Parks				

Sources: (A) Frank Emery, *The Oxfordshire Landscape* (London, 1974).
(B) B. L. Young, *Rustic Canyon and the Story of the Uplifters* (Santa Monica, Calif., 1976).
(C) Frandsen, Kampp and Morgenson (1975); Kampp and Frandsen (1967 and 1968). See notes 7 and 8 to this chapter.
(D) Hansen (1970); Kampp (1970); Nielsen (1970). See notes 5 and 6.

a whole.[5] A temporal cross-section approach is employed, and the illustrative examples are based on detailed local studies. Viggo Hansen, by contrast, looks at the evolution of the form and pattern of rural housing and settlement as these have characterized the landscape through time, in combination with changes in agricultural practices.[6] Together, these three studies cover all of Denmark with (like Emery and Young) emphasis on the topics of changing agricultural practice, field patterns and the form and function of settlement.

Unfamiliarity with Danish landscape may be overcome through the study of an individual village and its farms. The Starreklinte example from Northwestern Zealand is notable since it can boast a continuity of data from 1315 onwards and thereby can illustrate the nature and extent of the six major changes in agricultural patterns which occurred in rural Denmark during the last six centuries.[7] The narrative is divided into time periods for ease of handling, and the successive changes in both field patterns and settlement forms are described for the townlands of Starreklinte. Additional depth is provided by the study of Sønder Vestud, located on the island of Møn close to the south coast of Zealand, which reconstructs the open field pattern of 1688 and the pattern resulting from enclosure in 1800.[8] Here Kampp and Frandsen have added a dimension to the narrative history of rural landscape, when they use Sønder Vestud to illustrate the history of a single farm's experience of the two major chapters in the visible history of Danish rural lands. The elements stressed within these Danish examples were the physical changes in settlement and field patterns and not the political-economic factors which actually produced such different farming landscapes.

Design Elements Characteristic of Historic Rural Landscapes

So far we have considered what the rural landscape actually consists of and which features or developmental episodes are used by geographers, historians and local historians to illuminate their descriptive studies. Our next step is to describe the design elements which are characteristic of historic rural landscapes and thereafter to see how this list compares with that actually used by landscape historians, whether they be archaeologists, historians or geographers.

Participants in the American historic preservation movement have published lists of *design elements* or relic features which remain from past rural landscapes and represent their present-day visible history. Table 12 which is divided into two sections, contains

Table 12 DESIGN ELEMENTS OF THE RURAL LANDSCAPE

(A) Objects or relationships of importance to the *cultural resources* of a setting	(B) *Design resources* characteristic of rural landscape
1 *Natural Features* which have a place in the history of the community. Includes items such as hills, geological formations, water bodies, and vegetation, which, because they are striking and familiar characteristics of a community, impart a special character, historic identity, or aesthetic setting.	1 *Viewpoints and Landmarks:* forms which dominate or symbolize, prospects, vistas.
2 *Paleontological and Archaeological Sites,* yielding information about the prehistoric activities of Man, and give evidence of earlier cultures which once inhabited the area.	2 *Land and Plant Forms:* topographic features, groups of trees, exotic plants.
	3 *Single Forms:* artistic, utilitarian or curious objects or structures.
3 *Cultural History Sites and Structures* important in the history of the community, and including items associated with literary or political figures or events, or with religious or ethnic groups and individuals.	4 *Developmental History and Industrial Archaeology,* including unusuals.
	5 *Historic Districts* include groups of or individual buildings, historic neighbourhood transitions or boundaries.
	6 *Visual communications:* street signs.
4 *Developmental History and Industrial Archaeology,* including surviving sites, routes or structures important to the early settlement, economic origins or technical development of the locale, e.g. mines, factories, trails, canals, depots, harbours.	7 *Rural Open Spaces:* unbuilt upon land in the countryside, and within settlements.
5 *Historic Districts* include groups of or individual buildings, historic sites, natural features or items of landscape architecture which together create an exceptionally rich historic or cultural ambiance.	8 *Historic Sites:* sites of single events, associated with personalities, recurring events.
6 *Architectural History,* representing as many styles and as much diversity as possible, and including famous as well as anonymous buildings.	9 *Social Activity Sites:* recurring events or activities associated with major groups.
7 *Community Design and Aesthetic Features,* such as local building materials, street furniture, and other items which contribute to the look and feel of a community.	
Source: (A) California, *Historic Preservation Element Guidelines* (1976).	(B) Doylestown Borough Planning Commission, *Design Resources of Doylestown* (1969).

a summary list of *Cultural Resources* typical of the rural landscapes of California and a suggestion of the types of *Design Resources* which landscape architects have attributed to rural settlements and their surrounding fields.

Portion (A) of Table 12 enumerates leading elements of cultural resources, and, in keeping with conventional geographical practice, begins with the *Natural Features* which have a place in the history of a community because they have contributed to the development of its special character, historic identity or aesthetic appeal.[9] One thinks of streams, scarp lines or marshy areas which have helped to produce and shape field patterns, settlements and place names.

The separate identification of *Palaeontological* and *Archaeological Sites* reflects the North American propensity to treat as a separate category the remains produced by prehistoric Native Americans using resources and habitats to promote their material and non-material needs (Fig. 23). In both North America and Northwest Europe the landscape survivals from prehistoric times constitute a group of well recognized and cherished fossil features. American Indians receive much attention in Young's study of Rustic Canyon and prehistoric landscapes are stressed in traditional Danish descriptions, although British historical geographers find this period already well occupied by archaeologists. One result of this latter division of labour is that most British landscape histories either invite archaeologists to participate as contributors or depend upon concise summaries of the archaeological materials.

Category 3 in Table 12(A), *Cultural History Sites and Structures*, includes the expected and recognizable relics of the historic, recorded past with which the historian and the geographer may both feel comfortable. The narrative history of a community may be reflected or the lives and achievements of particular groups or individuals may stand out. For the North American, as an example, the preserved Colonial era meeting house with its hand-crafted benches and tables would represent the democratic customs associated with the New England village meeting and the Founding Fathers of the Republic. In England the place where the Magna Carta was signed would hold similar significance.

Category 4 requires the student of landscape history to seek places and structures which traditionally have been considered irrelevant to the history of the flowering of rural England or of the rise of the plantation system in the American South. The study of old mines, tip heaps, workers' housing, abandoned quaysides and canal locks is now more often emphasized as we seek to achieve a

Fig. 23 The secrets of the non-European rural landscape are illustrated by this scene of ridge-and-furrow fields from the lower Magdalena Valley of northern Colombia in South America. Here in 1965 J. J. Parsons and W. A. Bowen located and studied a extensive occurrence of pre-European Indian fields which may have been sufficiently productive to support a dense rural population. The preservation of a representative portion of this field pattern would assure its future availability for study by agricultural historians and intrepid tourists.

better understanding of our contemporary industrialized society. In the three national studies summarized in Table 11 the industrial and urban revolutions have been introduced as topics but are not fully developed in terms of their ultimate impact upon the modern urban world and its scenery.

The fifth category in Table 12 concentrates on single or grouped buildings which produce a landscape alluring to the architectural enthusiast or the architectural historian, and intriguing to the students of rural or urban areas. The concept of the *Historic District* is new to many; its intent is to broaden our historical concerns so that we move from individual buildings to entire village streets or suburban quarters which preserve relics of the rural community amid the bustle of the modern town or city. The idea of an historic district is best known to landscape historians seeking a workable solution to urban preservation. In the rural landscape, the concept of such a zone or designated area may equally serve the cause of preservation of the social or physical milieu in expressing concern for the venerable farmstead or ancient farming village (Fig. 24).

Architectural History, Category 6, on the other hand, finds its design data among the details of a Georgian country house or a half-timbered and thatched-roof farm building in a Danish or German village. The modest cottage which survives today from the rural past will not receive the same degree of attention as will a country house, but neither should the former type of building be discarded as unworthy of serious architectural study. Category 7, *Community Design and Aesthetic Features*, combines natural resources and local culture with vernacular architecture to produce an amalgam of landscape features long popular for study by landscape historians. The attempts to divide England into building-type regions according to the ground geology and its role in shaping site selection or construction materials is a well recognized exercise in the analysis on a national scale of community design characteristics. The landscape architect is the professional who may feel most at home here, but others can and do use this particular design element to describe specific cultural responses to environment or the characteristic regional patterns which have resulted.

Part (B) of Table 12, an inventory of *Design Resources*, is derived from the working vocabularies of the landscape architect and the architectural historian.[10] *Viewpoints and Landmarks* may be part of a grand design executed for an English country house or may refer to the peculiar quality imparted to the Danish skyline by groups of Bronze Age burial mounds. Regional character is the result of either of these two examples, and such character constitutes a landscape resource which may be enjoyed and exploited for its entertainment potential. The *Land and Plant Forms* category concerns the vanishing English hedgerows and farmstead woodland of North America which traditionally have imparted so much visual delight and ecological variety to their respective countrysides. *Single forms*, as a category of characteristics, includes follies dotting English landscape gardens as well as the gigantic nineteenth-century homes built by timber barons in the small towns of coastal Northern California.

Among the categories entitled *Architectural Examples* and *Architectural Combinations* the design analysts of the Doylestown countryside have placed rural and urban examples of particular building styles, period-based uses of building materials and the historic associations of buildings encountered in a farming hamlet of Elizabethan origin or in a Danish railway town (Fig. 19). *Visual*

Fig. 24 The Fosse Way and the Somerset countryside near Lydford and Hornblotton, about 10 km (6 miles) southeast of Glastonbury, illustrates a field pattern inherited from the process of enclosure by agreement. The Roman road majestically bisects the photograph but two deserted medieval villages and one shrunken example are less obvious. These are but hints of the many historical legacies which the English rural landscape contains. North is at the top of the photo. (ST 5833).

Communications take place through street signs or facade decorations which announce the inn or the baker and the market cross which represents the institution of the church. The group of features included within *Rural Open Spaces* represents portions of undeveloped land which may occur in the form of parks, meadows or fossilized remnants of old field systems. The intent of Table 12 is to include both built-up and open areas, in short, the village with its buildings surrounded by its fields and meadows.

Historic Sites and *Social Activity Sites,* which include birthplaces

of the famous, battlefields and explorer's routes, all receive attention from preservationists as well as from landscape historians.
Additionally, the colourful perambulation of Laxton's village fields
which occurs each year is a living relic from medieval England, and
the American Indian ceremonies celebrating the maize harvest or
the autumn hunt commemorate an equally arcadian past. These
ceremonial observations are tied to special places, and as such also
command the serious attentions of landscape historians and preservationists. Places of significance with arresting and ancient ceremonies serve both to instruct historically and to entertain holiday
makers. An entire library of published examples exists to tell us
what landscape history can and should be, and with the rise of the
preservation movement as an effective agency for the planned use
of the past, guidelines and lists of design and cultural resource
elements have been produced. With the assistance of these theoretical and practical suggestions, the next section of this Chapter
will be concerned with the design of an historic park to preserve and
display landscape relics from an important and scenic era of the
British rural past.

A Proposed Outdoor Historic Site Illustrating British Field Systems – Wormleighton, England

The deserted medieval village site at Wormleighton, Warwickshire
is well known among historical geographers thanks to the efforts of
the late Harry Thorpe, when he was Professor of Geography at the
University of Birmingham (Fig. 25).[11] Here one sees visual evidence left by four historic processes which have shaped the British
rural scene as we know it today. At Wormleighton the impact of
enclosure in around 1500 on the existing settlement and field pattern produced a new agricultural system and an associated estate
village. A fortunate combination of land tenure and agricultural
practice has allowed impressive landscape features to remain, and
these can assist the visitor who attempts to reconstruct the agricultural history of this site, which is set in very attractive countryside.

One of the main rules for dealing with a complicated relic landscape such as Wormleighton specifies that there be comprehensive
documentation of the site and of its significance.[12] Among the
general works which provide a background for an appreciation of
the variety of old field remnants to be found throughout rural
Britain, one may start with H. C. Bowen's *Ancient Fields* or
Christopher Taylor's *Fields in the English Landscape*.[13] The signifi-

Fig. 25 An aerial view of the medieval deserted village site at Wormleighton, Warwickshire (SP 4453) made well known by the research of Harry Thorpe. The Oxford Canal of the late eighteenth century crosses the village site which was depopulated in about 1500 as a result of enclosure. The old manor house foundations, the stewponds and large fishpond and the house platforms remain as do the survivals of medieval ridge-and-furrow and the later estate village which dominates the site today.

cance of old fields to a deeper understanding of the village and its agricultural pursuits is made clear by Joscelyne Finberg in *Exploring Villages* and by Nigel Harvey in his *Fields, Hedges and Ditches*.[14] For information about the appearance of the traditional open field system of land-use, one may turn to an illustrative source like Beresford and St Joseph *Medieval England* and for the specifics of West Midland systems to Baker and Butlin *Studies of Field Systems in the British Isles*.[15] The particulars of ridge-and-furrow in this area of England are discussed by Harrison, Mead and Pannett in 'A Midland Ridge-and-Furrow Map.'[16] Parallel to the story of the rise and fall of the open fields, is the history of settlement abandonment from Medieval times onward, and K. J. Allison's *Deserted Villages* provides an introduction which can pave the way to the more comprehensive work published in 1971 by Beresford and Hurst.[17]

For Wormleighton itself, the available studies depend upon the researches of Harry Thorpe into the abundant documentary and cartographic materials, augmented by his energetic field work at the site. Thorpe's 'The Lost Villages of Warwickshire,' (1959) is an early survey work which mentions Wormleighton, and his monograph entitled 'The Lord and the Landscape, illustrated through the Changing Fortunes of a Warwickshire Parish, Wormleighton,' develops in fullest detail the history of this particular place through a period of landscape transition.[18] A concise description of the site which would be very suitable as a guidebook is Thorpe's 1975 contribution to a Council for British Archaeology Research Report.[19]

Thorpe has assembled sufficient information to bring Wormleighton to life for audiences of school children or laymen, and the story of open field cultivation centred on a village subjected to enclosure, abandonment, agricultural changes, and the establishment of an estate is embodied in the green hummocks and ridges of the modern site. These historic episodes, which have given character to England's countryside over the past five hundred years, live at Wormleighton in relic form, and they could serve as visual evidence to convert an educational or recreational visit into a memorable voyage back into the nation's landscape history. Wormleighton is well suited to be made a living monument of English landscape history to commemorate the name of Harry Thorpe, its principal student.

Type of Site

Wormleighton seems to lend itself best to development as an *Open Air Museum* rather than as a *House Museum, Living Historical Farm* or *Re-created Community* unit, within the four categories mentioned by Hawes in his description of historical rural monuments built in North America over the last decade.[20] The Open Air Museum, well known in its original Scandinavian setting and more recently to be encountered on the Continent and in Britain, is defined by Hawes as being a site whose

> collections consist of historic structures in a representative setting, household implements and furniture, farm and craft equipment. Some

embody the folklife concept, seeking to preserve the physical remnants of regional or ethnic cultures. Others are formed on the agricultural life concept.

He goes on to say that:

Some open air museums have living history demonstrations of farm operations or household life, or maintain small demonstration plots of crops and some livestock. But there is no attempt to re-create a farming system or to give a sense of the processes of rural life.[21]

In summary, he notes that often the best results occur when several farmsteads are used to depict the interplay of agricultural development, urbanization and environmental change.

To consider first the relationships with the natural environment, the Wormleighton site straddles the boundary intersection between the Cotswold Fringe and the Feldon plain and is transected by the Oxford Canal which opened in 1778 (Fig. 25). Here a farming community developed which represented a dynamic ecosystem linking the inhabitants to their natural surroundings, and modern-day preservation has concentrated upon maintaining the resulting landscape. Any modernization of agriculture, on the one hand, or an attempt to reconstitute the original natural environment, on the other, would alter Wormleighton to the point that the fossilized ridge-and-furrow features, the medieval fishponds, the old field boundaries and the deserted village site itself would all be in danger of being lost to future visitors.

Site Interpretation

How much and what type of interpretative information would Wormleighton require in order to function as an outdoor museum illustrating the open fields system, enclosure and settlement abandonment? W. T. Alderson and S. P. Low in their *Interpretation of Historic Sites* make the obvious initial point that the less known about a given site by the visitor, the more need there is for site interpretation.[22] Although one may assume among those visiting Wormleighton at least a passing familiarity with the general facts about pre-enclosure agriculture and village abandonment, the specific details would need to be supplied and a summary provided (Fig. 26). The excellent sources already mentioned would fulfil this need appropriately. We must remember that the events represented by Wormleighton are distant in both time and experience from the world of the contemporary visitor, and more effort will be required

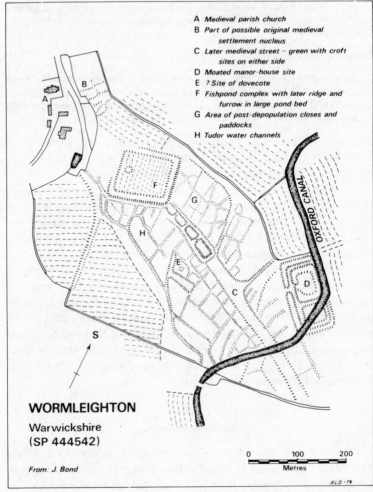

A Medieval parish church
B Part of possible original medieval
     settlement nucleus
C Later medieval street – green with croft
     sites on either side
D Moated manor-house site
E ? Site of dovecote
F Fishpond complex with later ridge and
     furrow in large pond bed
G Area of post-depopulation closes and
     paddocks
H Tudor water channels

OXFORD CANAL

WORMLEIGHTON

Warwickshire
(SP 444542)

From: J. Bond

0   100   200
          Metres

Fig. 26 Sketch Map of Wormleighton deserted village, Warwickshire, England. The village with the house foundations and street is bisected by the fishpond complex and surrounded by remnants of ridge-and-furrow. (Map by James Bond.)

to help bridge this information gap than would be needed if we were considering an outdoor museum site designed to represent Victorian agricultural practices or early industrialization.

Employing the terminology of Alderson and Low, one would describe Wormleighton as being a *Representative Site,* one meant to help us to understand a period of history or a departed way of life rather than a place which will increase our understanding of a specific historic person or event, functions of the *documentary* or *aesthetic site*. The representative site illustrates the characteristics of the society represented, such as family life, education, social life, making a living, the appearance of the homes and public buildings, and the uses of the contained furnishings, tools and equipment. Visitors to a representative site can enhance their understanding of the similarity of the basic needs of people of any age to our own, but also appreciate that the way they met these needs may have varied from our current practices. Visitors to Wormleighton might also be led to the realization that the way we think about certain issues today is influenced by the way our forebearers, including the medieval inhabitants of Wormleighton, handled similar problems. An appreciation of the verities of human experience which may reside in a piece of humanized rural landscape is a desirable by-product of a visit to a place like Wormleighton, and such an experience will enhance our appreciation of the relevance of the past to the present.

Use of the Site

Following additional suggestions of Alderson and Low, one is led to consider the interpretive objectives of a representative site such as Wormleighton and how these may be advanced when designing the site and its facilities. If the primary objective of the Wormleighton Outdoor Historic Site is to illustrate the landscape legacies which remain from the open fields, early enclosure and settlement abandonment, then we might propose 'wander-at-will' tours in preference to fully conducted ones. The use of *stationing* techniques, whereby limited amounts of interpretative information are furnished by guide-interpreters to roving visitors at specific spots at scheduled times, will provide a chance for the serious visitor to augment his own knowledge and that of his guide-book. The guide-interpreters would be able to enliven one's visit if they performed relatively uncomplicated craftsmanship demonstrations such as demarcating field strips or the proper use of tillage implements. The guide-interpreters could also check security and note attendance in addition to their normal crowd-control and site protection duties. These activities are part of any plan for general site management be it of a landscape park, reconstructed farmstead or country house open to the public. The use of park personnel to dispense information means that a visit can be much more enjoyable than it would otherwise be if people were left entirely to their own resources of imagination and learning.

If no arts-and-crafts displays or reconstructions of medieval farmhouses on the deserted village site are proposed for Wormleighton, to augment use of this complex site it might be advisable to provide posters, housed in a suitable museum, based on Thorpe's reconstructed period maps and any excavation finds. The addition of a living display, such as sheep grazing on the ridge-and-furrow undulations, would provide a striking and appropriate reminder of the landscape consequences of enclosure and village abandonment.

On-Site Teaching and Dissemination of Information

Our relative ignorance about people's motivation in visiting historic sites means that we have tended to concentrate our analysis on the controlled learning environment of the school tour, a subject which therefore has been well studied and has profited from innovative experimentation. Presenting and interpreting the site for a visiting class involves assessing the effectiveness of conducted tours as compared with discussion and suggests the use of the inductive method of assessment so as to arrive at general conclusions about the site and what it represents. In addition, one must consider the advantages of employing role-playing by the students to capture their attention, channel their energies, and encourage self-discovery whilst using an historic technique or tool. With the expectations of a school class in mind, design of an historic site to enrich the learning experience may be attempted with a greater degree of certainty.

My own experience at Wormleighton in 1973 with a small group of senior university students convinced me that, given the range and amount of documentary material available, this site would make an outstanding field laboratory for instructional work of various kinds suitable for several grade levels. Although the attempt to cultivate ridge-and-furrow with a reconstruction of a medieval wheeled plough might not be feasible, a tour on foot of the deserted village of old Wormleighton with maps and aerial photographs in hand, the measurement of ridges and furrows and some sampling with a soil auger would make student visits to this representative area of old English landscape an entirely worthwhile exercise (Fig. 26).

In the field of information dissemination, Britain still leads the way in making available to the visitor an *embarras de richesses* of maps, local history publications, inexpensive guides and instructional pamphlets. My suggestions about the literature on field systems and deserted villages, with particular reference to Wormleighton, illustrates this point. It should be a relatively easy undertaking to provide for a Wormleighton Outdoor Historic Site the appropriate maps and brochures so that both 'wander-at-will' visitors and school classes could be catered for at reasonable cost with sufficient materials to help bring to life this piece of beautiful and historically important landscape.

Further Details

For the sake of completeness tempered by brevity, the following details of site planning and construction are mentioned but not discussed in full. First of all, one must consider the matter of land ownership and the structure best suited to the administration of an outdoor museum proposed for the Wormleighton acres. They are currently held in private hands and, although visitors are welcome upon application, the site is not ready to receive casual day-trippers or busloads of school children. An outdoor museum may flourish equally well when operated by private, national or local authorities, since concern for the fabric of the site and its preservation transcend the details of ownership and tenure. Secondly, the financing of such a museum, although a matter of utmost importance in the practical scheme of things, is not within the scope of this book. Museum finance is a subject fraught with complexities and is closely related to the economics of running social service and cultural resources, whether by county, municipal or private agencies. A Wormleighton historic park would require money for its development and operation; for the moment we must be satisfied with our paper proposals. Lastly, site requirements for public access, visitor parking, toilet facilities, information and refreshment kiosks and site maintenance are issues best left for discussion elsewhere. The design of such facilities requires expertise in physical planning and landscape architecture, and the resulting solutions to the design problems will be as many and varied as are the park proposals themselves.

A hypothetical case-study of an outdoor historic site at Wormleighton has been used to illustrate existing site data and relevant design elements in order to show how a piece of historic rural landscape can be made to serve both recreational and educational purposes.

A complete inventory of all the varied field systems of the past, relics of which are yet to be found in odd corners of the world, as well as a listing of the many patterns of villages and hamlets which reflect ancient solutions to the problem of habitation and commun-

Fig. 27   South Field of Agri village in the Mols Mountains of east-central Jutland, Denmark. Dominating the scene is a field boundary laid down around 1800 when the lands of Agri were enclosed. The underlying open-field pattern of ridge-and-furrow extends from left to right across the bottom half of the photograph, and it is here bisected by the precise alignments of stellate enclosure. Since this rural scene illustrates both the facts of succession in agricultural practices and the role of the state as a maker of landscapes, it is good to learn that this portion of Mols is to be included within the bounds of a nature park. (Photo by the author.)

ity, would provide sufficient work to absorb the energies of many landscape historians for years to come. From the standpoint of planning theory and enabling legislation, we have an abundance of both to draw on when considering rural landscapes with historic attributes which lend themselves to educational and recreational use.[23] In seeking to preserve attractive and historic rural landscapes, we can bolster our arguments by citing the cultural and historic values in many such areas and their natural suitability for profitable outdoor recreation (Fig. 27).

The task is clear for those who have a high regard for cultural history within the rural environment. Mechanisms exist for making our inventories more complete, our analyses more clear and our proposals more sound.[24] Beyond this we have yet to agree on terminology or schemata suitable for the orderly classification of either field patterns or settlement forms.[25] In association with students of planned landscape management, we must give additional thought to the development of those landscape features which convey the story of developmental history and can communicate well with an audience of school children, laymen or professional historians of the countryside.

It remains to be seen whether we can move beyond the stage of the preserved farmstead and the outdoor museum to a more universal evaluation of entire rural landscapes as essential components of our cultural patrimony.[26] The contemporary agricultural landscapes of parts of England, France and Germany are rich in durable fossil forms which delight students of landscape history; the challenge is to retain the essential elements and overtones of history while at the same time agriculture is modernized for the benefit of rural producers and urban consumers. Our windows into the agrarian past should not be built into decaying land-use facades; our vistas are better preserved within the economic and social edifice of modern agriculture.[27] Primitive rural landscapes may fascinate the visitor, but their inhabitants deserve a better fate than to be a permanent tenant of an historic agricultural preserve.

7

Historical Remains within the Urban Context

Introduction

Los Angeles is characterized by a number of architectural gems from the past scattered through a mass of undistinguished and frequently outrageous buildings. Architectural critic Art Seidenbaum has listed ten outstanding buildings in Los Angeles and includes three erected before 1920. The Hollyhock House in Hollywood, built by Frank Lloyd Wright between 1918 and 1920, has been restored by the City of Los Angeles and today serves as an art gallery and conference centre. The elegant Gamble House, built in 1908 by Henry and Charles Greene, remains delightful, with its subtle lines and exquisite craftsmanship, notwithstanding the urban renewal and smog of Pasadena. Downtown Los Angeles takes pride in the artistry of brick and wrought iron and the interior atmosphere of Victorian entrepreneurial self-confidence achieved by Louis Bradbury and George Wyman in the Bradbury Building erected in 1893.

Such buildings as these attract the appreciative enthusiast who seeks them out for closer study. Visitors picnicking at Barnsdall Park, where Hollyhock House is located, may find their meal more enjoyable when taken within the shadow of one man's inspired solution to the problem of housing design. Downtown Los Angeles on a Saturday afternoon offers all the confusion and variety of a Latin American street fair around the ground storeys of nearly sixty buildings, which are worth study for their arresting façades and innovative decorations. People shop and promenade amid these buildings, unaware of the historic dimensions of the scene about them. Reactions to and uses for remnants of urban history range from mere appreciation of their handsomeness to practical plans for investing them with new life.

142

This chapter builds on three generally accepted opinions about the city. First, civilization and cultural advancement are considered to be intimately connected with the historic development of the city where, as recorded by Berry and Vance, the achievements of man are thought to reach their highest development.[1] J. H. Chambers has expressed the second opinion, noting that:

> Buildings and their grouping and assemblage are more than the shelter of our activities; they represent us beyond our life, they interpret us to posterity and they illustrate our past to us . . . It is in this context that the preservation of examples from the past acquires enormous importance in a culture.[2]

The structures we build express in a tangible way the evolution of a civilization, and we seek to conserve them as symbols of the continuity of human purposes and institutions (Fig. 14).

Our third opinion concerns historic preservation within our fast-changing urban environments and whether preservation should be a priority. The city is a place of work and residence, and we must ask ourselves whether it should endure and develop as a Museum or a Metropolis. Within the urban context the conflict of past, present and planned future finds expression in a most visible, dramatic and consequential manner. What can or should be retained from the past in order to enrich urban life in the present and future is the issue considered in this chapter.

The historic rural landscapes of the world have traditionally been those most studied by historians, geographers and archaeologists. It is in rural areas that relics have survived most successfully, whether as old field patterns, farmhouses or villages. Although the vast majority of geographers, including those who concern themselves with landscape history, actually reside in the city, only recently have they begun to address themselves to the considerable academic challenges presented by historical urban geography.[3] We now realize that worthwhile academic research may be done in old industrial complexes, within the walls of worker's quarters or under the shadow of a railway viaduct. The long record represented by our urban environments is used by students of visible history to depict the historic city as a theatre which presents lessons from the past which may instruct and entertain.[4]

It comes as no surprise to find that resources are available to planners and urban preservationists when we recall the concern expressed in so many quarters about the perplexing urban problems of law and order, mass transportation, and environmental quality, to name but a few. The immense energies invested in the study of these problems have stimulated interest in historic urban preserva-tion and have initiated a search for better uses of individual old buildings or entire districts which can be made to live again within the functioning body of the modern city. It is no longer the standard reaction of planners or architects to suggest that a municipality must raze and rebuild in order to revitalize its decaying urban core. It is necessary, however, to assess the extent of the erosion of history in a city before attempting the recycling of old buildings.

The Erosion of History within the City

In his book *The City in History*, Lewis Mumford introduced histori-cal urban geography to many people. His talents as an academic raconteur and his ability to marshal a staggering amount of detail about the urban environment from its origins to its contemporary complexity were among the reasons for the book's critical success.[5] The city as habitat, in the sense of a built environment, became an acceptable topic of study. In learning more about the contemporary city in the light of its past, the way was opened for the cultivation of a heightened appreciation of this history in planning studies and in recreational and teaching programmes. Parallel to this broader appreciation of the city as an historic arena came a realization of the threats posed to its fabric by urban growth, renewal policies and benign neglect.

A sharpening of professional consciousness concerning the urban environment with its historic manifestations was produced by the Ministry of Transport in the famous Buchanan Report on *Traffic in Towns*.[6] This alerted many people to the deleterious impact of motor vehicle traffic upon the old towns of Britain, particularly in the example of Norwich. Carolyn Heighway's *The Erosion of His-tory* summed up in dramatic fashion the impact of traffic plus renewal and expansionist forces at work within the dynamic fabric of today's towns and cities.[7] Buildings are vulnerable to damage caused by alterations to their structure, changes in functions and neglect. A new lease of life may occur, however, when a structure is restored and rehabilitated to serve as part of a new shopping pre-cinct. These British experiences have been duplicated elsewhere in the world, often in stronger and more arresting form.

Interactions Between Historic Buildings and their Environs

Figure 28 is a summary of the dynamic interchanges between an historically significant structure and its environs. The arrows point-

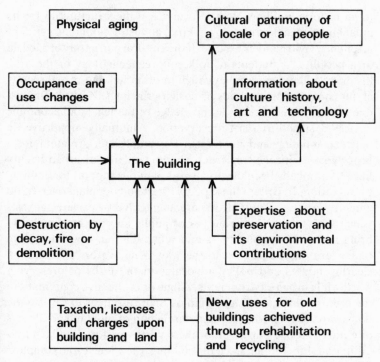

Fig. 28   Interactions between an historic building and its environs.

ing towards the building represent the positive and negative external factors which impinge on the structural shell and its functional contents. Ageing of the physical building is obviously inevitable, as are changes in its occupance and use, and eventually the very life-span of the building may be terminated by decay, fire or demolition. More subtle but equally dangerous to the building and its functions are the threats posed by rising costs for the materials and labour necessary to keep the structure sound and usable. Another negative influence on the building depicted in Fig. 28 is posed by the legal interventions of state and local authorities in the interests of extracting the maximum taxes from the building and the land it occupies.[8] There are numerous examples of obsolescent buildings and factories which have been unable to continue functioning and are becoming derelict purely because they cannot continue to function economically given the taxes, service charges and other costs levied by various authorities.

We have sketched the negative things which the environs can do to an historic building. What, in turn, can the structure do for its areal and human surroundings? First, an historic building can represent in a vivid manner aspects of the cultural patrimony of a locale or a people. To students of folk culture, technology or the arts, historic buildings can convey much information and reveal secrets about construction methods or design principles. If interest in visible history is matched with knowledge of the legal and economic devices designed to assist preservation, a mutually supportive tie between building and public can be established. Amateur local historians or citizens concerned about standards of urban beauty have traditionally been the organizers of public support for building preservation. In Britain these people staff and populate over 1,200 amenity societies. Their efforts are augmented by private agencies which seek to channel resources of public and private finance to bring about structural repairs and rehabilitation. Local and state bodies are often able to lead the way as innovators, information clearing houses and policy advocates in the tasks of preserving worthwhile urban environments. Alone or in effective combination, the preservation groups may employ their resources to reverse the downward spiral into decay and dereliction of individual buildings or entire districts. The result of these positive efforts can be a new utilitarian life for an ancient building or an historic complex. Beyond preservation as a house museum or mere cosmetic restoration of the structure, lie exciting possibilities for a building to be refurbished or modernized and thereafter recycled in its use within the city centre or a suburb.[9] Recycling may mean involvement in functions distant from the original concept and design of the structure, but the intended idea is for the building to survive, in altered form, and to serve new functions rather than ignominiously to perish beneath a motorway or housing estate.

Recreation in Historic Cities: Principles

The travel sections of newspapers constantly remind tourists that big cities and towns are notable for their architectural monuments, scenic old quarters and historic places commemorating notable events. Travellers to the United Kingdom cannot miss the history lessons visible in her towns and cities. Britain realized £1,300 m. from tourism in 1976, and this was due in large measure to her historic urban heritage and her skills in merchandizing it. Throughout Europe, indefatigable tour groups, following programmes laid out in guidebooks, are channelled by the hundred into such places as the Tower of London, the Sacre Coeur and the Uffizi Gallery. With the coming of these seasonal hordes, a full range of ancillary enterprises flourishes, including set-meal restaurants, shops selling Scottish woollens and the manufacture of plastic models of the Eiffel Tower.

Promotional materials indicate which historical urban features are thought to be strong tourist attractions. The *New York Times* praises Vienna for its musical life, cuisine and art museums, each of which is, in its way, a contemporary manifestation of historic traditions, practices and achievements. The noble buildings of central Vienna house these tourist attractions and themselves provide a portion of the 'Viennese experience'. Chester, according to the *Los Angeles Times*, is a slice of Roman history embedded in a visible medieval town fabric which endures as part of a functioning, modern market town, whilst historic Tucson, Arizona is a New World example of the brochure-vision of antique urban resources.[10] Leaving the high-rise hotel in the centre of new Tucson and guided by his Convention Bureau brochure, the visitor can find his way to the carefully maintained John C. Fremont House which dates from about 1858. This attractive adobe building, furnished according to its period, is flanked on the west by vast parking lots belonging to the Community Centre complex and is separated from the central business district on the north by a sunken motorway. Consequently, the ancient fig tree and the old well head in the patio of the adobe appear as incongruous relics from a long-distant past. Five hundred metres to the south is the Barrio Libre historic district. Here one wanders along streets and back lanes through a section of Tucson which has many buildings dating from before 1880 in the Spanish–Mexican architectural style. The Free Quarter faces an uncertain future depending upon planning decisions affecting the preservation of city structures and the urban activities which will be encouraged there. One hopes that its human scale and residential character will endure, so that it can continue to provide a pleasant and instructive urban history tour on foot in the heart of this bustling American city.

These three examples of the recreational use of old cities have several features in common. First, enough of the visible urban past has survived and is cherished so that tourists can easily find urban relics to enjoy. Secondly, it is clear that a great deal of time and effort have been expended by urban planning departments, city councils, groups of concerned citizens and interested business groups to ensure that historic tourist attractions have been preserved and developed to make them congenial and accessible. A third factor has been the serious promotion of such attractions by both public agencies and private industry so that knowledge about old Vienna, Roman Chester and historic Tucson has penetrated far into the tourist and travel business and widely among the travelling public.

Since urban tourism is a popular leisure activity which makes money, we should study the preferences of urban tourists so as to be better able to guide the development of the recreationally relevant portions of old cities.[11] We assume that tourists who visit historic cities are interested in seeing buildings or particular areas which enjoy an historic reputation: the Tower of London is a prime example of such an attraction. A building may also be associated with the life of a notable person, and Shakespeare's cottage in Stratford comes to mind as an illustration. A building or urban district may be a tourist attraction because it is unique or peculiar – thus one goes to see the oldest public house in London or the historic sewers of Paris. A fourth common reason for viewing old buildings is that the scenic properties of the structures and their environs may be sufficiently picturesque to command the special attention of the visitor. London overflows with examples of this latter category, including Smithfield Market and Old St Bartholomew's Church, the Chelsea Hospital and its grounds or Westminster Abbey.

Recreational enjoyment of buildings and districts such as these requires available information about them and their significance. All visitors will consider St Paul's Cathedral to be a building of note, but the outline of its architectural history, its historic significance as a building and the minutiae of its structure can be communicated to the visitor only by the printed or spoken word. This informational background need not be exhaustive, especially if the visitor's short stop at St Paul's is sandwiched between brief stops in the City and at the Tower. To be successful, the brochure writer must distinguish between what constitutes the entire cultural history of a complex building, such as St Paul's, and what will suffice to convey the necessary minimum of information. Layers of detail will escape the attention of the rapidly moving traveller but they are of great significance to the visiting architectural historian or the student of building technology. This is, of course, the general challenge facing those who attempt to disseminate an appreciation of the past among a broad audience.

The time spent at the site is also an important variable in the recreational equation. A tour group with only thirty minutes to spend at St Paul's is a different proposition from the visitor who intends to spend half a day studying and photographing the building for its visual revelations about an important historic district of London. A balanced approach to site management is essential if these two disparate groups of customers are to be accommodated.

School parties may enjoy educational recreation in the course of an excursion to an historic complex such as the Tower of London. The academic requirements facing the students and the instruction of the teacher mean that longer exposure and a higher level of appreciation may be expected from this type of visit. Brochures and field trip syllabus materials for students may complement the verbal resources of the teacher and local guides. If the school outing is an all-day affair, the experience may be enhanced by a park picnic within the shadow of a cathedral spire or castle battlement; this would also be an entirely acceptable recreational use of historical open space.

A final point concerns the informal recreational use of a city site such as St Paul's by those whose daily affairs take them near the cathedral hill. In this case, the historic building and its environs function as an urban amenity, an interest-point within a designed, contemporary urban landscape. Passers-by enjoy the building and its surroundings as they would any environmental amenity which makes one's journey to work more relaxing and tolerable.

Two Examples

There is little about the tourist's Oxford which is secret any longer. A person visiting this city on a guided tour can see collegiate Oxford at a fast trot. With more time at his disposal, and helped by courteous guidance from a representative of one of the local history groups, the traveller can enjoy a leisurely conducted walk through the colleges and other old parts of the town. From this type of experience, supplemented by detailed information, may come a more lasting impression of the place. If one delves further into the visible history of old Oxford, selected building exteriors can serve to illustrate the origin and growth of the city from medieval to modern times.[12] The deeper insights into Oxford's past offered by archaeologists, conservationists and geographers are accessible to the inquiring visitor in publications which recount the evolution of the city through ten centuries to its present status of a living architectural monument encapsulating much of England's history.[13]

Through the media of the excavator's trowel and the old town map, the persistent visitor may penetrate close to the roots of buried ancient Oxford to make his tour educational and more enjoyable.

In sharp contrast to world-famous Oxford, the hundred inhabitants of Locke, California are living out an obscure but fascinating chapter in the settlement history of the Sacramento–San Joaquin Delta.[14] Preservationists in California, concerned about husbanding the visible history of their state, have mounted an effort to assure a future for the fifty or so two-storey clapboard buildings which make up modern Locke. Its significance resides in the fact that it is the last surviving rural community built by Chinese, for Chinese and which is still predominantly occupied by them. Founded in 1915 by Chinese farmers on land owned by George Locke (an old-time resident in the area), the land was dyked, truck crops planted and the little settlement built. Although ethnically and culturally deeply Chinese, the craftsmen–architects erected the town according to local building styles. The resulting picturesque collection of wooden buildings with balconies overlooking the narrow streets is highly valued as a surviving example of California ethnic and vernacular architecture (Fig. 29). The town's development came to a peak during the Second World War when 1,500 people lived there, and their numbers were sufficient to support a variety of urban services as well as facilities (such as a temple, restaurants and gambling establishments) peculiar to the Chinese community which dominated the place. Subsequent out-migration by the young Chinese in search of superior economic opportunities has meant that the population remaining in Locke is mainly composed of aged Chinese who made up 28 of the 38 households resident there in 1974.

For nearly a decade there have been discussions on the future of Locke. The community, as a unit, is on the National Register of Historic Places, and plans have been advanced for the installation of adequate fire prevention equipment to protect the town against its chief physical enemy. The future of the town as a viable community is much more difficult to plan for or to assure. When the last of the surviving Chinese has passed from the scene, the cultural individuality of historic Locke will disappear. The current planning effort in Locke is directed to the twin goals of minimal disruption of the physical appearance of the town and no forced displacement of its elderly residents. If Locke can be converted in the future into a living historic town, its attraction for most Californians will still be in its quaintness and architecture. Should the considerable California Chinese community become committed to maintaining the

Fig. 29 A view along the main street of Locke, an historic Chinese settlement in the California Delta area. The two-storey, balcony style of construction is typical for the area around the turn of the century, but the store names and a majority of the present inhabitants are Chinese. Proposals have been advanced for the preservation of Locke as a monument to the Chinese cultural contribution to the state. The exact form that this would take and the recruitment of new settlers for the town are matters yet to be resolved.

place as a cultural monument for the education of their children, a more varied, multiple-function might emerge for Locke. The purchase of the town in 1977 by a Hong Kong real estate firm has complicated the legal situation for the town, its buildings and its inhabitants, because additional plans have been proposed which will include a Chinese cultural centre and a floating restaurant.

Oxford's future would seem to be as a thriving university town connected to a bustling industrial city. The popularity of the place is itself a threat to the fabric of the old town, and the traffic which finds Oxford so accessible is a major disadvantage to its enjoyment. Locke, by contrast, is a simpler place, one of the many living relics which contribute to a nation's lineage. The town's survival is in question and the rationale for its preservation is under discussion. Both places, however, attract visitors, and both can be made to function as effective and diverting recreational attractions for people interested in the origins and peculiar development of urban places. The pursuit of an understanding of the facts and processes of change, so fundamental in the shaping of our contemporary urban environments, is recommended by Kevin Lynch as being an important undertaking for urban-dwellers who are, in the last analysis, responsible for the tomorrows of our cities.[15]

Planned Recreational Opportunities in Three Historic Cities

Cities rapidly evolving in terms of physical and social characteristics may, nevertheless, contain remains from the past which interest people and provide them with instructive recreation. The differences among cities and the great variety of relics available for enjoyment means that it is hard to enunciate universal planning guidelines. Many types of development are possible, and the recreational experiences which may result will vary according to whether planned preservation is attempted for individual buildings, historic urban districts or entire towns. The three urban examples which follow were selected to illustrate this range of possibilities: they cover a case of urban renewal, a proposal for an historic district within a city and an idea for the revival of an entire derelict city.

Krems an der Donau: an Austrian achievement

Sixty-five kilometres upstream from Vienna, Krems and its sister town, Stein, snuggle into a south-facing pocket of level land which lies between the Danube on the south and the cultivated lower slopes of the Weinberge to the north. Settlement has been recorded here for the past thousand years, and as a town located at an important junction of the Danube with a north–south routeway, Krems enjoyed prosperity over the centuries. As a legacy from its past, the modern town of over 20,000 inhabitants contains an ancient core area 20 hectares (50 acres) in extent which recently contained 441 buildings inhabited by 3,250 people. Survey data by Kühnel indicate that 51 per cent of the buildings in the old core were built prior to 1800, and 35 per cent are from the sixteenth and seventeenth centuries alone. Stein, which arose as a patrician suburb one kilometre west of Krems, has an area of 17 hectares (42 acres) and this old core recently recorded 239 buildings housing 1,472 people.[16]

Considering the redevelopment possibilities within these two old core areas, Gattermann and associates suggest that the decline in population in Old Krems between 1961 and 1971 could be reversed by a thorough renovation of 300 structures to produce housing for an additional 1,700 people.[17] The population decline in Stein could be stemmed by the improvement of 170 units to provide adequate

Fig. 30 A view to the south from the old town centre of Krems an der Donau, Austria reveals the mixture of architectural styles and the complex building pattern which challenge the urban preservationist. This portion of the town, about the Pfarrkirche, has undergone successful renovation and rehabilitation since the 1960s.

housing for an additional 1,500 people. The detailed analysis of these two core areas proposes an improvement of the street pattern, the provision of more public open space, and the complete renovation of the best of the old buildings and the replacement of the most decayed (Fig. 30). These enlightened proposals will have to be carried out in urban areas in which, over the centuries, buildings have become encrusted with architectural modifications so that the original features of the town have disappeared.

The first task of the restorer is to see through these structural accumulations and to visualize the old buildings at the core. At Krems and Stein quite unsuspected revelations occurred when, for instance, an entire wing of a monastic cloister emerged from beneath baroque plaster and brickwork. The early Gothic Dominican church in Krems provided a dramatic example of such an unveiling when the physical evidence of its secular existence since 1785, which included service as a factory, a theatre and a cinema, had been carefully removed to reveal a noble structure underneath. Ten years' work and ten million Austrian schillings went into this single restoration, and in 1971 the church building housed a splendid retrospective showing of a thousand years of art in Krems.

With such architectural resources to work with, the possibilities for redevelopment within the northwest sector of the old core of Krems appear attractive. The restoration of a number of old buildings to provide housing and business premises would be accompanied by tree planting and the construction of play areas and pedestrian precincts which should stimulate a new life for the old district. In both Krems and Stein individual buildings of great historic interest and beauty have been restored. With these successes to build upon, ambitious proposals have been forthcoming for entire blocks. Whether or not these projects are ever fully realized and bring about physical restoration and social rejuvenation, the visitor to either town can see and appreciate the visual and utilitarian gains possible from the restoration, rehabilitation and recycling of attractive old buildings within the heart of a modern urban community. The recreational possibilities held out by the old Dominican church are complemented by the attractive and living neighbourhoods which surround it and through which the visitor may wander.

Trondheim's Ilsvikøra: a Norwegian proposal

Moving on from individual buildings scattered throughout a town, the next example of utilitarian preservation is the historic district.

As efforts have progressed within urban areas to spare the relics of the past and give them new life, more attention has been given to establishing historic districts. These consist of related groups of historic buildings preserved in their original space and activity envelopes within the larger body of the city.[18] The idea is to keep the district socially and aesthetically viable while at the same time attempting to prolong the life of individual buildings by improving them and their surroundings. The regulatory mechanism of land-use zoning laws can be brought into play in harmony with neighbourhood renewal programmes designed to improve housing quality and public spaces. The power of the town council and its regulatory devices are used to promote optimum improvement in such a district consistent with its traditions and within the bounds of economic feasibility. If business can be encouraged to flourish again and life return in renewed form to the streets, rehabilitation can be counted a distinct success.

As an illustration we draw on a proposal put forward in 1977 for the historic preservation of an old fishermen's quarter, called Ilsvikøra, near to the core of modern Trondheim, Norway.[19] Fewer than thirty houses comprise the district, and, although over a hundred years old, it continues to house people who represent five generations of a working-class milieu tied to traditional fishing and harbour activities characteristic of pre-industrial Trondheim (Fig. 31). Other small districts such as this one are still to be found in Oslo, Fredrikstad and Stavanger, but all of them are being subjected to pressures from industrial expansion and harbour development. Recognition of the intrinsic historic and social values of the Ilsvikøra district came some time ago, and by 1972 there was in existence a proposal by the town office of building registration for the preservation and rehabilitation of these homes. A reduction in residential density was suggested, with minimum floor space standards to be introduced. The average cost of rehabilitation per residential unit was estimated then as being 70,000 Norwegian kroner. Quite clearly, for a city of 130,000 inhabitants, the 2·5 million kroner needed to carry out this plan for a corner of the harbour area had little budgetary appeal, and the Ilsvikøra Plan was laid in a file marked 'Desirable but not Pressing'.

Fortunately for the proponents of a preserved and renewed Ilsvikøra, support was found for the project by reference to the successful effort undertaken in a similar type of settlement, Footdee, in Aberdeen, across the North Sea. About twice the size of Ilsvikøra, the historic and architectural merits of Footdee have long been

Fig. 31 The harbour district of Ilsvikøra in Trondheim, Norway is an historic fishermen's settlement over a century old. Private initiative has been successful in persuading the city council to fund restoration and rehabilitation of this neighbourhood unit in the interests of both physical and social preservation. One of the telling arguments advanced pointed out that modernization of this robust housing stock would be far cheaper than demolition and replacement.

recognized, and today this historic district, a fishermen's town for over a century and a half, provides an attractive and acceptable environment for its inhabitants who are very much a part of the life of a thriving community of 200,000. Valued as an example of early Scottish experiments with council housing, Footdee was still basically a fishermen's quarter, a fact reflected in its layout and construction. The past contacts developed and maintained between Aberdeen and Trondheim meant that these two 'Fish Towns' had much in common, just as their present-day problems of survival and planned preservation are shared. Since 1968, when Footdee was declared a conservation area, it has received funds for the preservation and modernization of its one hundred houses. A slum no longer, modern Footdee reflects the problems of relative affluence which arrive when property values climb as a result of renewal and conflicting claims for funds arise between preservationists and those insisting on improvements in housing standards to match the rise in family incomes.

Footdee, is an example of the gains and losses characteristic of planning efforts devoted to historic district preservation and management. The city council of Trondheim could compare the mixed success of Footdee when further considering the future of the Ilsvikøra district. Late in 1977 the council accepted the proposal for the preservation and rehabilitation of the district with a resoundingly positive vote. The cost of the project is now reckoned as three million crowns or more, but to construct thirty new houses on this site would cost twice that much, and the resulting housing project would lack the sense of historic community and the compatability of design which are features of the genuine and historic fishermen's quarter itself.[20] One result of the Ilsvikøra project and the earlier advances in Aberdeen is that a discerning visitor can still see something of the traditional seafaring way of life preserved by practitioners who live amid the bustle and business of a modern harbour. Relatively inexpensive housing has been provided for people who continue to value the social milieu of the fishing community, and we are all the richer for this preservation.

Suakin on the Red Sea: a Sudanese challenge

Whereas Petra, the ancient city hewn into red stone cliffs in southwestern Jordan, survives to attract the more adventurous tourists of our day, there is a type of Islamic city characteristic of the coasts of the Red Sea which has not yet realized its potential as an urban museum and which could also attract tourists. Suakin, a decayed port on the Sudanese Red Sea coast about 65 kilometres (40 miles) south of Būr Sūdān, the old Port Sudan, is at present a romantic relic of a mercantile era which produced an arresting style of domestic architecture. Built on an oval island 500 by 400 metres in extent (1,500 by 1,200 feet), Suakin until quite recently was a nearly intact example of a small Turkish port town which thrived from the sixteenth to the early twentieth century (Fig. 32). A town of almost 300 structures of residential, commercial and institutional types, Suakin has enjoyed a well-earned reputation for its scenic placement on a flat island as well as for the marvellous silhouettes it presents to those approaching by land or sea. The buildings themselves were designed to maximize air circulation and to provide protection from the hot shore winds and the glare of the midday sun. Built over a period of many years by rich merchants, the two- and three-storey structures were ornamented with handsome teakwood casement windows and decorated with lintels and cornices in styles permitted by the canons of Islamic art. In describing the visible remains of Suakin as it appeared in its recent prime, in about 1900,

Fig. 32 Suakin, Sudan on the Red Sea: an aerial view across the island and the surrounding coastal channels. This historic port for Islamic trade and commerce is today in a ruinous state, its multi-storey buildings having been robbed of their handsome wooden fittings. The irregular street pattern, the silhouettes of the buildings and the exotic locale would all have tourist appeal if rehabilitation were undertaken by means of Sudanese or international financial resources.

Greenlaw notes that the European visitor is attracted by the compact shape and stylistic unity which the town displayed.[21] The impact of Suakin is twofold, for, when viewed from afar, the walls and towers are as impressive as when one walks among them. From either vantage point the presence of the past is strong and palpable.

As an example of a particular type of port city along the Red Sea coast, embodying as it does examples of historic Islamic architecture, Suakin is a significant item in the historic patrimony of the Republic of the Sudan. In contrast to the preservational programme in Krems which focused upon individual buildings or that in Trondheim which involves a district within the mass of the city, in the case of Suakin we move up the preservational scale to consider the entire island-city to be a fit candidate for restoration and rehabilitation. One of the first questions to be answered concerns preservation for whom and for what purposes. A single building of historic interest or an historic district are expensive but feasible undertakings within the limitations of a municipal budget; the historic preservation of an entire town requires budgetary resources from the central administration of a nation.

The great amount of documentary and pictorial information collected by Greenlaw in his work for the Government of Sudan might already be sufficient to allow structural reconstruction on the durable building foundations of the city as it appeared in 1900. A restored Suakin could once more assume the role of a staging area for pilgrims bound for Mecca. Those who broke their journey within the shelter provided by restored buildings which symbolized the historic greatness of Islamic vernacular architecture might find their spirits doubly refreshed. Clearly, such a role for a renewed Suakin would need to be acceptable to Sudan's neighbours along the Red Sea coast. An alternative role for a reconstructed Suakin might be to develop it as a theme-park featuring the Islamic past. Within such a setting travellers would be welcome to pause, rest and reflect while also enjoying the resources of a well-managed seaside resort.

A planned use of this single portion of the Sudanese past would require the commitment of fiscal resources which the nation might be able to use better elsewhere. International capital, however, might be attracted by a plan for a theme-park and resort. In the event that Suakin became the Petra of the Red Sea coast, better housing and employment would become available to the population of squatters who inhabit Suakin Newtown, the ghost settlement of makeshift habitations which now occupies the ruins of historic Suakin. If, however, nothing is done for this historic town, then it will soon find itself sharing with many other ancient settlements an existence as a town site of interest only to archaeologists.

The preservation and recycling of historic relics within the urban context greatly interests planners and presents economic opportunities to modern cities. Threats to the urban patrimony originate with the processes of change which characterize the modern city, and urban inhabitants need to be on guard to ensure that useful relics from the past are not sacrificed needlessly in the interests of urban renewal. One should not be misled, however, into thinking that such preservational efforts can be easily or cheaply won.

Cities are rich lodes of information about both the pre- and post-industrial urban experience. Single buildings may function as museums containing exhibits illustrating this historic evolution. The historic district is used to combine individual structures into a whole unit which can illustrate a period from the urban past while it continues to serve the present as a place of business and habitation. An entire town preserved as a scheduled historic place is much less easy to develop and administer. Ancona, an Indian pueblo in New Mexico, still inhabited after nine centuries, is an unplanned example of a pre-industrial urban settlement which tenaciously survives. Norwich, by contrast, is a modern city with a valuable medieval core which has enlisted skilled urban planners and preservationists to make certain that its physical heritage is given its chance to survive the impact of modern development.

As a factor in public concern about the environmental quality of urban places, the remains from the past may be pressed into service to give design perspective and temporal balance to dynamic neighbourhoods.[22] In Britain the prehistoric and historic legacies of towns are becoming more exposed as a result of current research work, and the positive contributions to the contemporary urban fabric made by preserved old town remains are being accorded more positive recognition.[23] In addition to the formal preservation effort, an informed individual can readily appreciate the diverting history of the city simply by strolling through its streets and lanes in search of the drama and lessons revealed by the urban past.[24]

8

Old Landscapes Bearing the Imprints of Industry

Introduction

The historical legacy of the mining industry in Britain is visually represented by ancient tip heaps and pits which together produce an undulating topography. High up on the grassy summit of the Mendip Hills is an irregular surface which is the site of Charterhouse, a Roman lead and silver mining centre. Roman roads centred on the mining camp which developed here, and some indication of the widespread trade in metals is indicated by the lead ingots bearing this smelter's mark found in Hampshire and on the Solent. Swells and hollows and a disturbed pattern of drainage now commemorate this ancient mining activity. A second British field example is the astonishing collection of tip heaps which commemorate the birth of the Industrial Revolution. Up the hill from Ironbridge lie the remnants of Madeley Court, nestling among rolling, green slopes. These verdant hills are in reality tip heaps reclaimed nearly two centuries ago to produce more fitting surroundings for the great house of Abraham Darby. A different impression is created when the busy lanes of the A30 motorway through central Cornwall direct one to an arresting lunar landscape of white and light grey cones. These made-made sand hills glisten in the sunshine, and their hundred-metre summits impart to St. Austell a mini-alpine landscape which commemorates 200 years of activity in the Cornish china-clay industry. Each of these examples of mining history visible upon the contemporary landscape is threatened. Were their historic implications better appreciated, their message about the history of industry might be more clearly received and cherished.

Table 13 summarizes the process of historic Industrial Revolution, its impact on the fabric and functions of its supporting society

161

Table 13   INDUSTRIAL REVOLUTION – PROCESSES AND INTERPRETATIONS

Inputs
Technology
Economic resources
Labour
Organizational talents

Landscape impacts
Expansion of urbanism
Improved transportation
Migration from country to city
Agricultural changes associated with feeding the cities

Interpretative viewpoints
The great cultural-social watershed between agricultural and industrial societies
A key from the past to help understanding of the present, and a guide to the future
A phase in a scheme of history which may evolve in a cyclical form or according to
an inevitable evolutionary pattern
An infatuation with the high technologies of steam and steel of the past as powerfully
expressed in physical machinery

---

and four interpretative viewpoints on its significance. Students of
the Industrial Revolution in its historic dimensions, whether
devoted to event or process description or whether trying to come to
grips with interpretations, have a common point of departure. This
appears in the table under 'Inputs' and includes four general pre-
requisites. Firstly, a sufficient level of technological achievement
and productive talent must be available for the transition from
workshop craftsman to factory. Thereafter, suitable and sufficient
economic resources must be on hand so that machinery, plant and
raw materials can be assembled and production commence. Next,
with a change-over from intensive to extensive forms of agriculture,
brought about in Britain and Denmark as the result of enclosure,
labour should become available to serve as a human resource essential for industrialization. Lastly, the organizational skills needed to
bring raw materials, technology and labour together into a functioning whole, should be evolved by the skilled inventer-craftsman to
produce the full-blown captain of industry.

The impacts made by the Industrial Revolution are well summed
up by Allan Pred.[1] He discusses four principal impacts of this
process on its home environment, the growing urban-industrial
landscapes of Europe and North America. One result of this shift
from workshops to factories was the expansion of the city and its rise
to dominance over the land. Improvements in transportation
reduced transit times and permitted the movement of greater volumes of raw materials and finished products at reduced costs. The
transformation of agriculture was a response to the heightened

demands of a growing urban population. Pred's last thematic point concerns the increase in the movement of population from the land into the cities and the greater degree of social mobility through improved transportation linkages. His main argument is that the parallel rise of mine or factory as a place-of-work and the city as a place-of-residence produced closer ties between raw material and processing activities, processing activities and markets, and agricultural hinterlands and dependent urban concentrations. The close ties between modern industrialization and urbanization are sufficiently well recognized at the theoretical levels, but case-studies of individual cities or of industrial complexes are needed if the discreet facts are ever to assume understandable patterns. The operation of this general scheme within the sphere of influence of a primate city is well depicted in E. A. Wrigley's model of the growth of London during the onset of the Industrial Revolution in Britain.[2]

Viewpoints About the Industrial Revolution

The impact of industrialization on rural and urban landscapes and the resulting alterations in human life within these environments represent one of the great watersheds of cultural history whose significance to the post-industrial experience is more fully appreciated by geographers and planners, whereas its symbolism as a 'loss of innocence' has been a popular and abiding theme in literature and art. Many have tended to view this watershed as the equivalent of an expulsion from the Garden of Eden. There is a good case consequently for studies beyond the narrative or descriptive which focus on the landscape impacts of industrialization in seeking to trace the devolution of Eden into a scene marked by Satanic mills, wretched workers' housing and black, polluted waterways.

A second reason for making this study is to place ourselves in a better position to understand present and future trends of industrialization in the light of what has gone before. If we find that our society and our cities are unsatisfactory, one line of reasoning suggests that if we could unravel the processes and decisions which created our cities, we should be better able to make new plans for the future of an urbanized society.

The legacies of the Industrial Revolution are important from a third point of view: that assumed by students of historical cycles or inevitable historical patterns. Followers of Arnold Toynbee look for evidence to clarify the role of industry and the urban way of life in the rise and fall of modern societies, for, if such cycles within cycles can be demonstrated for the past, the future lifespans of existing nations and peoples can be predicted. On the other hand, the same evidence will be fuel for the Marxist who seeks to demonstrate the inevitability of the rise of capitalism as contrasted with the eventual triumph of the proletariat. Rather than searching in the past for keys to the future, this third group of scholars with an interest in the Industrial Revolution are seeking data from the past which supports their respective intellectual schemes.

A fourth category of interest, also shown in Table 13, regards the Industrial Revolution and its historic impacts on the landscape as the victorious conquest by technology, Prometheus unbound, of difficult challenges posed by energy conversion and locomotion. At the heart of this viewpoint lies an infatuation with the techniques of construction and the machinery itself: the conversion of heat to mechanical energy, the conveyance of this energy to tracked wheels or propellers, and the appurtenances associated with such activities or designed to house them. The appearance of the railway buff, the steam traction engine specialist, the canalboat restorer or railway timetable authority is manifested in a romantic and expert fascination with polished brass handrails, stainless steel connecting rods and handfinished wooden dashboards. This concern with physical relics reflects an appreciation of the time and effort invested in the technology which harnessed steam to mass production and rail transport.

The Field Evidence of Industrial Revolution

With industrialization, new and complex geographical patterns result, manifested physically by buildings, factories and lines of transport. These hallmarks of historic mining and manufacturing, whether dating from before the Industrial Revolution or after, are the focus of this chapter, and our particular emphasis is on the preservation of these remnants either as recycled structures or recreational attractions. Darby's *A New Historical Geography of England* deals with the impact of industry on the English landscape from earliest times through the Industrial Revolution up to the situation in 1900.[3] The theories of the rise of significant industries from the days of cottage production to factory systems and the development of regional patterns of industry with concentrations by specialization or groupings of industries are recounted in detail in his book. The schemes of Pred and Wrigley, for example, are hereby supplied with substantial examples and clarifying data.

The contemporary realities of this great, geographic change are strikingly suggested in *Man Made the Land* where the vivid word-pictures of writers of the time are supported by illustrations which depict the wonders of new machinery and the canals and rails which served it.[4] The co-operative effort of the BBC and Professor W. G. Hoskins in producing for television a series on English landscapes made it possible for many viewers to obtain a visual impression of the 'landscape of transport', with its canals or railway engineering and the great nineteenth-century expansion of mining, manufacturing and transportation activities.[5] The focus of the British experience may be further sharpened by reference to an interesting and readable local study of industrial history and archaeology by Frank Booker in his description of the rise and fall of the mining industry in the Tamar Valley during the last century.[6] Moving on from descriptive and analytical treatments of the processes and spatial patterns characteristic of mining and manufacturing, what are the actual things and structures which arrest our attention through the vivid manner in which they represent these historic changes?

Artifacts of Interest

A representative of an historic industry disappeared when the factory which for so long produced 'England's Glory' matches in Gloucester closed in 1976 as the result of a production rationalization scheme. By contrast, the original but surplus clock from Victoria Station in London is now safely preserved as a commercial attraction at one of the Victoria Station restaurants in Los Angeles. Other glories of the recent past have in some cases faded fast, as indicated by the surplus-property sale of the structure at the NASA John F. Kennedy Space Center at Cape Canaveral, Florida, from which the historic US Apollo flights to the moon were launched. This example of the transitory nature of some technological achievements can be contrasted with the enduring light from the past still cast in a fire station at Livermore, California by a light bulb which has burned nearly continuously for seventy years. Todays' students of the Industrial Revolution can find a bewildering array of rare and interesting books dealing with railways and their equipment, roads and vehicles, canals and boats and dozens of industrial specialities, as well as a growing library of books on industrial archaeology with their lists of scores of preserved or derelict mining engine houses, watermills, steam engines and harbour facilities.[7] Great numbers of antique steam trains, automobiles, airplanes, machinery and hand-tools exist, many safe in museums and private collections to the delight of the enthusiast. In America, the Smithsonian Institution in Washington, DC is probably the centre of such collections, much as the Kensington complex of museums in London fulfills the same role in Britain. The British Transport Trust will open the doors to over sixty collections which deal with the history of transport, and the Kew Bridge Engines Trust and Water Supply Museum will welcome admirers of nineteenth-century steam powered beam engines, the true dinosaurs of the high period of steam technology. How many of the 25,000 museums in the world are devoted to technological displays is not known, but it must be a rare example which does not contain at least some items representing man's efforts to harness science for technological purposes.[8]

Buildings and Structures of Interest

If the machines which ran on rails or through the waves or which turned wood or shaped metal fascinates us, do the built structures which housed or served them have a similar attraction? Most would agree that we are less enthusiastic about the structures of wood, brick or concrete which represent the age of the factory, even though the buildings themselves frequently are striking examples of good design (Fig. 19). However, with our heightened general interest in our built patrimony a greater concern is being expressed about such relic features as medieval English lead mines, Cornish wheelhouses, Danish workingmen's housing and early American office buildings. Recently, as an example of this concern, in Broxstowe, Nottinghamshire, 200 nineteenth-century miner's cottages were restored at a cost of £6,000 per cottage. Clearly this amounted to many times the original costs of such houses, but the work was given impetus by the fact that D. H. Lawrence was born in one of them in 1885. Beyond these more obvious relic structures, what is the opinion about the preservation and potential use of stretches of Roman roads in England, old Indian trails in eastern Canada or overgrown sections of abandoned French canals?

The pages of *America's Forgotten Architecture* (1976) illustrate the variety and state of repair of the relics of America's industrial past.[9] These physical remains, existing today within the contemporary built environment of American cities, span the centuries from colonial village to pioneering efforts in mass production manufacturing. The Gruber Wagon Works in Pleasant Valley, Pennsylvania, which date from 1882, are recorded by the National Park Service.

The age of railway steam is memorialized in today's Gandy Dancer Restaurant in Ann Arbor, Michigan which occupies a railroad station built in 1886 in the massive, Richardson-Romanesque style. Lastly, and quite fittingly, the Second Ward Savings Bank of Milwaukee, Wisconsin, a handsome beaux-arts style building erected by local captains of industry between 1911 and 1913, today houses the Milwaukee County Historical Center within its splendid, ivy-covered walls.

Publications such as *America's Forgotten Architecture* which are devoted to industrial archaeology and architectural history, illustrate architectural details, entire structures and groups of buildings which still convey to us through their utilitarian beauty and technological finesse something of the outlook, drive and capacities of the men and women who brought the western nations into the industrial age. Such remains from the urban-industrial past provide a more immediate and accessible method of reflecting a way of life than do equally familiar agrarian relics. The geographer attempts to order these data about buildings, furnishings and other details according to differences in their geographical location and their designed functions. Within the contemporary urban scene we can find and study examples of relic industrial zones, with their associated quarters devoted to worker's housing, and the transportation arteries which served to bind together work, residence, markets and supply areas. The industrial zone itself, located in a city, may include colourful remains from the brewing, baking and wholesale commodity trades. In the countryside we may find old source areas for raw materials with their tip heaps or quarries, dating from early times and served at one time by an adjacent old canal or railway siding.

Problems with Preserving Industrial Revolution Relics

Given the wide variety of objects and structures of interest within the context of the Industrial Revolution and their rural or urban-industrial manifestations, what can be said about the specific needs and problems associated with their presentation and usage?[10] Firstly, we can assume that a preservationist is interested in *events* associated with the Industrial Revolution. In this category we include the monument plaque at Coalbrookdale which identifies the area where Abraham Darby perfected the use of coke to smelt iron. Physical *constructions* associated with the coming of industry also interest the preservation planner. Buildings, factories, mining sites or a complex of canal locks all qualify for inclusion within this category: the twenty-nine locks of the Kennet and Avon canal at Devizes, Wiltshire being an outstanding example of such a construction. Lastly, there are individual *objects* which were built for service or use during the early periods of modern industry. Here one might think of the justifiably famous preserved colliery winding engine at Beamish, County Durham.

In thinking further about these objects and constructions, several general points need to be made on the problems associated with their preservation and eventual reuse. Firstly, the *acquisition* of a site or piece of machinery requires sufficient financial resources for purchase or lease. In order best to apportion such financial resources, one must have enough inventory information to give a balanced judgement regarding the preferability of a given feature for preservation over other competing items within its class or category. Frequently the legal aspects associated with such an acquisition may be very complex and unravelling this particular knot can be a costly and frustrating experience.

Once acquisition has been achieved, the *preservation* of the physical object or its environs emerges as the next step. Technical skills of a high order are required if one intends, for example, to rebuild and restore to operating order a derelict Cornish beam engine. If knowledgeable professionals are lacking for such meticulous work, the dedicated amateur may be called upon to attempt to breathe life into a steam traction engine or a rural railway station. If acquisition is frequently a costly matter, the unlimited appetite for labour and parts which machinery restoration can present is truly amazing.

Perhaps the most complicated problem to solve in this general area of industrial preservation is how to make *recreationally useful* and *attractive* to the visitor a site such as a St Austell china-clay pit or the historic Fulham Gas Works in London. In dealing with deserted medieval village sites or with medieval York one can take advantage of the aesthetic pleasures for the eye which such historic locations provide. Very few individuals among even dedicated social historians can wax eloquent about decayed miner's cottages in rural County Durham or the Fenland's Great Sluice on a raw spring day! The initial impact made on the lay observer by a number of monuments to industrial history is weak and contains less to charm than does a vista of fields and hedges of a landscape of parliamentary enclosure or the Georgian terraces in old Bath. One may be best served, as practice already suggests, by taking a page from the London Science Museum where working models and abundant textual materials serve to convey the wonders of complicated machinery to both children and adults. To make industrial archaeology approachable and understandable usually requires a guided presentation so that the message of the past will come through sufficiently clearly and impressively. Some have argued that our depiction of the Industrial Revolution should be broadly based so as to include the preservation of a block of fully restored, Victorian miner's cottages in South Wales and a weaving shed adapted for the use of juvenile labour. It is questionable whether a museum devoted to perpetuating such stern images could attract people as a recreational goal. One characteristic common to most relics of the industrial past is that machines are made to operate, and something which moves and does a job or produces a product is guaranteed to captivate an audience. If the machine requires tending and its tenders are appropriately costumed, the resulting impact may be splendid and entertaining even if the product is as mundane as the peat brickettes produced at the Hjerl Hede Outdoor Museum in northern Jutland, Denmark. If, on the other hand, the product is as traditional and attractive as that once produced at the historic Glengoyne Distillery within the shadow of Ben Lomond, so much greater will be the visitor's delight and instruction.

The *funding* of exercises promoting the recreational and instructive uses of a preserved industrial past stands on an equal footing with general preservational efforts in both the rural and urban settings. Starting with private funding or evolving from a firm's investment in preservation for promotional or public relations purposes, a local society which concentrates on the study and care of railway locomotives, municipal waterworks pumps or canal boats and locks may be able to take a lead in organizing the necessary funding and broader-based preservation or restoration campaigns. Increasingly, as more trained economic historians, industrial archaeologists and geographers with an historic bias become involved with public planning agencies, the amount of effective leverage by preservationists develops and can be used to shape and present financial requests. The attractions of many of the showy items salvaged from the industrial past assures them of a good chance in the competition for funds. Other categories of relics, however, must be promoted in the same way that hedgerows in remote country areas and slum-quarter lanes dating from the medieval history of a city must be promoted, namely, vigorously and with no apologies made for the fact that these items could never win a popularity contest with a working example of a coal mine or one of England's scenic villages.

The next question concerns *preservation for whom?* The chain of 'Victoria Station' restaurants in the Los Angeles area exploits genuine relics of the industrial past derived from its steam railways. Whether or not one is jarred by the peculiar combination of a British name with prime ribs of beef consumed within American railway freight cars, this clever use of railway nostalgia coupled with the selection of excellent locations readily accessible to a motoring public means that at least these portions of the industrial past are made to serve the hungry present. At the other end of the scale, railway history enthusiasts eagerly visit each museum which boasts appropriate displays and they revisit sections of operating track noted for their technological ingenuity, even if only modern-day diesel engines use them. The wide range of interests between technical specialists and the general public means that old steam locomotives can serve either as museums or as restaurants, but both groups will patronize and enjoy the same type of relics from the industrial past. Whether audiences arriving to tour Coalbrookdale, the cradle of English industrialism, are composed of school children alone or include bus loads of visiting Canadian or Japanese tourists will depend on how interested the site is made to be and how well its historic attractions are publicized. The short answer to the question of preservation for whom, therefore, is nearly anyone you care to include if you are willing and able to restore and promote the attraction in an appropriate way.

The last question to be posed here concerns *preservation at whose expense*. That is to say, not only the question of who will shoulder the funding of the project, but whether people will be displaced from jobs or dwellings in order that an historic building may be preserved or restored and alternative uses be instituted. When considering the preservation of a deserted medieval quarry or a derelict building located beside closed-off railway sidings, the actual displacement of people and jobs will be nil. On the other hand, if one considers metropolitan railway stations, a category of large buildings unsuitable for most other uses and apt to come under great pressure because of their real estate value, any of three contrasting preservation–displacement results can be anticipated.[11] In New York City, Pennsylvania Station, built between 1906 and 1910 and designed on the model of the Baths of Caracalla in Rome, was lost to the real estate market in 1963 and demolished, the site to be developed for new office-building space. The Grand Central Terminal station in New York, built in 1913 as an elegant beaux-arts monument to the passenger railway age, has been defended in the courts by aroused preservationists seeking to fend off the construction of a fifty-five storey building complex on this valuable piece of property, once the present building was demolished. In Baltimore, Maryland, the Mount Royal Station of 1896 was converted in 1966 into attractive and suitable quarters to house the College of Art of the Maryland Institute. In summary, municipal railway stations which have lost their function in the age of the automobile and which sit upon extremely valuable ground close to urban centres, may either disappear, live on amid litigious court actions or be recycled to house completely different but compatible uses. In the first case, jobs are lost and physical displacement of the urban fabric takes place. In the second, jobs continue but at reduced levels as rail traffic declines and salaries increase. In the third, jobs are lost but replacement employment occurs and the new activities thrive within the preserved shell of a monument from the early days of the transportation revolution.

Planned Preservation of the Industrial Past for Public Recreation

Three concrete examples will serve to illustrate the planned use of relics from the industrial past for the entertainment and education of the public. One is an American commemorative re-enactment of an historic event, and is, consequently, a transitory example. The British success in providing windows on the industrial past in the form of museums accessible to the public is our second case-study. The third example is a monument to the Danish industrial past which, when completed, will pronounce its message from the arena provided by a provincial market town of some 50,000 inhabitants.

Re-enactment of an event from the industrial past: the Last Spike at Lang Station, California

Amid the agitated observance of the United States Bicentennial in 1976, a re-enactment of an important event of one hundred years before in the history of railway construction in California was commemorated at Lang Station in September. The decisions made on the routing of railways and their subsequent construction have been as significant in the settlement history of the western United States as has been the case in the United Kingdom. Thus it was that a turning point in the history of the sleepy town of Los Angeles was reached on 5 September 1876 when a golden spike was used to signify the completion of a segment of railroad which would henceforth tie the little town to the transcontinental route via San

Francisco. On the same date one hundred years later, a re-enactment of the original scene brought this important historic event to the attention of the public, and people were able to relive vicariously a great moment in the history of rail transportation (Fig. 33).[12]

By calling this a planned event it is intended to indicate that interest had to be awakened, a programme laid out and a schedule of events for an afternoon co-ordinated. A dozen organizations sponsored the event, including the Southern Pacific Railway Company whose tracks would be used, the Newhall-Saugus Elks Lodge whose members would usher the visitors about the site and the Santa Clarita Valley Historical Society which worked with railway history experts to produce a commemorative brochure.[13]

With all preparations in hand, on a hot Sunday afternoon some 500 people collected at a visually undistinguished site in the Transverse Ranges north of the Los Angeles Basin. The station building at Lang had been demolished in 1971 when passenger service on the line was ended, and the original structure from 1876 which had early fallen victim to fire had also left no visible reminders. The visitors met amid the dust and bright sunlight between the dry river bed and the surrounding hillsides to see static displays of modern railway engines and to follow the practice for the actual re-enactment of the spike driving, the whole time being serenaded by a high school brass band. With the salute to the flag and the arrival of the Southern Pacific Centennial diesel engine and the special caboose numbered 1776, the commemorative speechmaking could begin. The California Gold Rush was represented by the local chapter of E Clampus Vitus – an appropriate appearance since it was gold, in great measure, which had attracted the iron rails to the American West Coast. The Chinese Historical Society, accompanied by a Lion Dance, unveiled a plaque which monumentalized the largely unsung contribution made by Chinese labourers to the construction of this demanding piece of railway engineering. A matching bronze plaque was placed by the historical societies to mark the historic achievement of completing this line and what it meant for the future of Southern California. Finally, it was time for the driving of the Golden Spike, and a replica of this important Victorian device was delivered to the exact spot by a crew aboard a vintage handcar. Then, while the assembled notables drove the spike into the rail plate and the rail engines hooted, the band played, cameras clicked and applause rolled back from the surrounding hills (Fig. 33).

The observances marking the half-century celebration in 1926

Fig. 33   The centennial celebrations commemorating the driving of the golden spike at Lang Station, California in September 1876. With this historic completion of a rail link to San Francisco, the sleepy town of Los Angeles became linked by land to the rest of the United States. A dozen organizations sponsored this historic recreation of a triumph in the saga of the steam railway in North America. Such exercises in living history allow public participation and call forth expressions of expert knowledge of obscure varieties. The replica of the original golden spike is brought, fittingly, by handcar to the spot where the assembled dignitaries will see it properly driven into place. (Photo by the author.)

and the centennial in 1976 were much more modest than the original spike driving in 1876 when dignitaries, present in numbers to celebrate the triumph of the railway over the barrier presented by the Tehachapi Mountains, consumed a nine-course Victorian banquet held at the Union Hall in downtown Los Angeles. Costumes and steam locomotives were featured in 1926, but 1976 saw the commemorative plaques being unveiled to provide a permanent monument to the epic link-up at Lang Station. Enactments of this type, when carried out with such a degree of attention to historic detail, when executed with such full co-ordination among representative organizations and when so well attended by a broad cross-section of the public, succeed well in commemorating significant events in the history of industry and technology. In addition, an historic site is hereby invested with deserved recognition, and the vital public participation ensures that episodes and achievements from the industrial past will be accorded their appropriate level of significance in local and national history.

Windows on the industrial past: museum preservation in Britain

Although relics of the Industrial Revolution are apt to be large and difficult to display in all of their complexity, their attraction for the general public is well recognized.[14] London's Science Museum in South Kensington was the second most frequently visited museum during 1977. Nearly one out of every four visitors to museums in the UK in that year went to this museum where mechanical principles are clarified and models illustrate the operations of individual mechanical engines and entire industrial processes. Museum displays tend to stress the craft industries in terms of their required tools and their particular products. In addition, static displays or considerable collections of large machinery may be housed either indoors or outside. Preference is usually given to transportation equipment in this case, acknowledging the enthusiastic interest of the public in steam locomotives, carriages and marine craft. There are certain limitations on the conventional house museum specializing in the technological and industrial past depicting either an industry as space-consuming as iron and steel production or a regional industrial complex or grouping of industries, such as the extractive mineral industries of Cornwall or the clay-products grouping of the Potteries.

As an example of the industrial museum complex designed to illustrate a complex of activities and technological developments, one cannot improve upon the Blists Hill Open Air Museum near Birmingham in the West Midlands[15] (Fig. 34). Here the Ironbridge Gorge Museum Trust has contributed to the planned restoration of this old and over-used landscape, the birthplace of the Industrial Revolution. If Telford Newtown is designed to provide a framework within which new life and a revitalized economy may

Fig. 34 The site of the Blists Hill Open Air Museum near Ironbridge and Coalbrookdale as it appeared to a group of visiting geographers in 1964. The Ironbridge Gorge Museum Trust has been instrumental in furthering the planned restoration of this monument to the birth of the Industrial Revolution in England. At the site a constellation of industrial exhibits serves to remind the modern visitor of the skills and venturesome spirit of the inventors and artisans who became involved in this great technological saga. (Photo by the author.)

function, the clever masters of industrial innovations, machine-building and mass-production techniques will have their monument at Blists Hill. Coalbrookdale provides an unparalleled record of the Industrial Revolution with its legacy of Abraham Darby smelting iron with coke by 1709, the building there of so many early innovations in iron such as locomotives, rails, boats, and the construction of Ironbridge itself in 1779, which is the culmination for most visitors. At the Blists Hill site there are exhibitions and reconstructions of blast furnaces, coal mines, steam engines, tile works and transport canal engineering. Within a reasonable circuit the actual places of invention and fabrication can be seen, and one should leave the scene better informed and with clearer appreciation of what was achieved here by these engineers and artisans of such skill and ingenuity.

At Beamish in County Durham, the North of England Open Air

Museum succeeds in conveying the architecture and atmosphere of a regional industrial development visible in its historic lineaments.[16] In contrast to the Blists Hill complex where so many items are viewed within their original surroundings, at Beamish the stone engine house and the headstock have been moved from coal-mine sites to the museum. The row of colliers' cottages has likewise been re-located here. What results is a skilful and impressive reconstruction of the regional industry of coalmining as it developed and was traditionally practised in the north of England. If the epic innovations represented by Coalbrookdale are absent at Beamish, by contrast the visitor comes away with a better understanding of how local people, pursuing a harsh trade, adapted to its demands and fashioned local improvements in their tools and dwellings.

The railway system of Britain as it has evolved over 150 years is probably the most popular item of industrial archaeology. The imagery and drama of steam powered trains pounding across the countryside on steel rails are highly valued in these days of technological sophistication. The recording of engine numbers by schoolboys continues as a practice, but the less polluting diesel locomotives compare in a pale way with their predecessors. Enthusiasts dip into such reservoirs of information as the David & Charles series of monographs on the history of construction and the details of engineering characteristic of British railways. The histories of many individual rail lines make good reading, and an abundance of guidebooks serves to direct students to historic sections of surviving track, viaducts of note and commanding railway bridges. The Transport Trust of London is willing to provide directions to over sixty transport history displays throughout the country, including railway preservations. It is, however, difficult and expensive to preserve anything like an entire railway system, and the interested visitor must be content with visiting and inspecting relics in the landscape or viewing railway technology captured within a museum. The opening in 1975 of the National Railway Museum at York has served to consolidate in one place the collections of rolling stock held by British Rail. In addition, the museum itself has been specifically constructed, using a turntable design, to display at their best locomotives and carriages of historic importance or special technological interest. If the walls of a handsome museum cannot contain the romance of the age of steam railways, nevertheless the fine technological innovations associated with this industry will find there the shelter necessary to assure their preservation and the public will continue to enjoy them in the future.

Preserving the Industrial Revolution in a town: the Horsens, Denmark Project

With a quickening interest on the part of architects, urban planners and urban historians in the contribution by the Industrial Revolution to the shaping of our modern cities, the preservation and re-use of structures in factory quarters or areas of worker's housing has been encouraged. In looking through Kenneth Hudson's guide to the relics of the industrialization of Europe one finds listed many distinctive separate buildings and industrial facilities.[17] Except in the form of an outdoor museum, conservation, recycling and exploitation of the industrial history of an entire district of a city is seldom attempted. Hudson, for instance, mentions only few undertakings of this kind, such as the Swindon railway industrial estate, the saltworks at Arc-et-Senans in France, the ironworking village of Kauttua, Finland and old industrial Leningrad.

Our third example here of the re-use of the visible relics of the industrial urban past for purposes of commerce, housing and recreation is drawn from the Horsens, Denmark Project, based in an attractive town on a fjord mid-way along the east coast of Jutland. Since autumn 1973 and under the stimulating guidance of Otto Norn, a professor of art history at Aarhus University, Denmark, a comprehensive study has been mounted of the documented and visible history of the Industrial Revolution as it shaped this town between 1850 and 1914.[18] Although the economic history and architecture of industrialized Denmark have been studied actively, this is the first comprehensive investigation of the impact of the era upon the fabric of a single community. The project is designed to allow the efforts of individual research workers to be focused on detailed facets of the general topic. Clearly, the impact of industrialization on housing and public services and home and social environments has many dimensions.[19] The understanding of the buildings and functioning of individual firms and their premises also requires lengthy study. The third part of the project concentrates on the official actions of the local municipality in response to alterations in the rate rolls and demands for public services. In short, it was anticipated that the Horsens Project would be able to reflect in miniature the processes and impacts characteristic of the coming of industrial revolution to an urbanized market town.

In order to reconstruct the modern industrial history of a provincial market town such as Horsens, Danish scholars have learned to understand and interpret many types of documentary materials.

The building codes applied to factories and residences may be examined along with descriptions from topographic and local history publications. The local photographic archive is not to be overlooked, and the records of the town council are a fruitful source. Town plans, contractors' sketches and an entire succession of town directories dating from 1832 onwards provide abundant cartographic documentation. In addition, fire insurance records, newspaper files and records of building and contracting firms provide the raw materials needed to trace the physical growth of the built fabric of the town through changes in building practice and fashion.

The Industrial Revolution in Horsens was reflected in the new economic impulses and managerial initiatives which impinged upon the town's business life when, in around 1860, Moritz Goldschmidt and A. P. F. Crome joined their talents to establish what was to become a large and flourishing cotton textile business. The firm of J. P. Møller and S. J. C. Jochumsen incorporated about the same time for purposes of manufacturing machinery. The coming of the railway in 1868 and the founding of the Bastian timber products firm shortly thereafter equipped Horsens to lead the way among Danish cities in forging a solid industrial base for its economy (Fig. 35).

Associated with the economic and financial developments in Horsens was a parallel physical expansion of the town to enable it to embrace both factories and the railway. With the rapid growth in numbers of industrial workers employed in the town's industries, the demand for workers' housing also increased. The building trades and real estate interests responded, and from the 1870s a distinctive working men's quarter of the town grew up to provide housing, and even today many of the techniques and details of this early brick construction remain in active use and may be studied.

Workers' housing is still in use, but the large weaving hall of the textile works is derelict. By contrast, Bastian has survived nearly intact and continues today in the wood products business and by providing storage space. Møller and Jochumsen is still in the machinery manufacturing business, and many of the original buildings and some of the original machinery has survived. The pressures on parking space and the interest in urban renewal are felt by these industrial relics, but only the empty textile mill urgently requires recycling as either off-street, enclosed parking space or storage room. A recent planning competition has produced some viable ideas for the refurbishing and recycling of part of this urban heritage as a step towards the fashioning of the Horsens of the future.[20] An additional step is being taken to preserve within a museum format machinery and objects which reflect the skills and uses associated with the early industrialization of Horsens. By incorporating a handsome example of urban industrial architecture – the 1906 brick-built electrical generating plant – into the scheme, an appropriate link with Horsens' past has been fashioned neatly.[21] Built by Otto Norn's father, a civil service architect, this building illustrates what may be achieved when part of the built fabric of the past is allowed to serve educational and recreational purposes in the present by housing materials and exhibits which cannot be brought before the public in any other way than by becoming part of a museum. The hope is that the inspiration of the museum and its contents will stimulate the interest of Horsens' citizens in their town's industrial past and encourage the town policy makers to take into consideration the legacy from the immediate past when planning the town's future. As an attraction for visitors, the Workers' Artisans' and Industrial Museum in Horsens can serve to remind people in an entertaining and instructive manner of the accomplishments and sacrifices of the past, made in order to lay a solid foundation for the economic prosperity which the nation enjoys today. A thoughtful appreciation of this period in the history of a single provincial town can lead to a deeper understanding of what took place elsewhere in the course of the Industrial Revolution.

In contemporary Western nations the legacy of the Industrial Revolution is a determining element in the shaping of our daily lives. As an event of great importance in cultural history, the interpretation of its origins, achievements and promises can add much to our search for solutions to current social and urban problems and can furnish guidance to our plans for the future. To a lesser extent, its familiar physical relics can provide a degree of enlightenment. If one examines the fabric of the modern city, much of its present form and functions are products of the revolutionary industrial past. The fact that old factory buildings or rows of workers' cottages do not charm us to the extent that straw-thatched cottages or green roads do, suggests that we cling more to a rural, arcadian aesthetic tradition than to one which stems from the true patrimony of our contemporry daily lives. In attempting to describe and interpret our surroundings, we must account for the impact produced by mining, transportation and manufacturing on the land itself and on human settlements. The objects and constructions which represent the industrial past are many and varied, and they may be grouped so as to produce various categories of landscapes. Thus, it is possible to

Fig. 35 The imposing brick monument to the Industrial Revolution in Horsens, Denmark. The home of the original Bastian wood products manufacturing plant, the quality of bricklaying visible in this chimney has been exceeded few times, and it stands as a handsome monument to the coming of industrial enterprises to this Danish town during the latter half of the nineteenth century.

describe an area as devoted to the extraction of raw materials, as knit together by lines of transportation, or, within the city, as composed of zones or districts which combine manufacturing with workers' housing.

In terms of the problems, from the preservational and recreational points of view, which characterize old landscapes bearing the imprints of industry, they are basically the same as those which typify the agricultural and urban scenes. Acquisition to preserve sites or objects requires money, and certain legal instruments must exist to assure effective husbandry in the public interest. In part, the field of industrial archaeology has bloomed in response to the awakening interest in and demand for precise information about the industrial past.[22] The rehabilitation and conversion of urban industrial sites into useful and attractive recreational or commercial properties seems easier to achieve than the renovation of rural, agricultural remains. The metamorphosis of an old chocolate factory in San Francisco into an attractive and highly successful shopping and entertainment complex in Ghirardelli Square is a renowned success story. The financing of such an undertaking can often be managed with private capital, although the public money available to local municipalities frequently must also be tapped. Whether the resulting preservation will serve leisured visitors as well as indigenous residents, is not always clear to see. Too often, some believe, urban renewal and preservation result in the displacement of the area's previous residents to less desirable quarters, for once the rehabilitation is complete, the well-to-do alone will come to monopolize this revitalized part of the city. This question of preservation and usage for whose benefit is not peculiar to historical industrial landscapes, since equitable solutions are universally sought in schemes for historic preservation and redevelopment.

9

Old Landscapes Bearing the Imprint of the State

Introduction

After crossing Knag Burn, a short walk up the slope across the old cultivation terraces and past Housesteads Farm brings the visitor to the excavated ruins of Vercovicium, the Roman fort located atop the Whin Sill with its vistas reaching far to the north beyond Loughs Broomlee and Greenlee. This is Hadrian's Wall at its most impressive and commanding. The complex structure of this masterful military frontier in Northern Britain lies spread out before one. The stone-built wall with its towers and milecastles is impressively intact along this stretch, and the two hectares (five acres) occupied by the ruins of the fortified camp display an intricate pattern of building foundations and streets revealed by excavation. The sweeping grandeur of this imposing natural site, topped by the Wall with its appurtenances, admirably displays the skills of the Roman military planners and engineers; and here on the Wall a vivid legacy imprinted by the state upon the land is clear to see and can be enjoyed by daytripper and student alike.

Landscape Evidence of Political Geography

By reference to a standard text on political geography a list can be assembled of significant, visible manifestations of political entities on the surface of the Earth.[1] The nation state itself, a self-conscious entity, expressive of both group and individual identifications, exists in geographical space, possesses a unique location and encompasses area. The boundaries and frontiers of the national territory are important topics for study, and even the restless oceans of the world have been allocated as national space. The actual

182

landscape manifestations of these dimensions of the state are some of the most arresting and easily interpreted visual features contributed by political geography to the earth's surface. All types of symbols, including flags or statuary favoured by an incumbent regime, are used to identify and establish the existence of the nation state on the landscape. Location and area are both mappable quantities, and their cartographic depiction in atlases, schoolbooks and newspapers reinforce in the minds of the public the position and extensiveness of a state. National boundaries are the clearest and most frequently encountered manifestations of the concept and practice of nationalism. Passport inspection, a change in the colour and style of uniforms, and the presence of fences, walls or fortifications all clearly indicate to the traveller that he or she is crossing one of those lines on the political map which indicates where one state ends and its neighbour begins. Although the demarcation of maritime boundaries is not as easy to see as the terrestrial ones, nevertheless, the trespassing herring or tuna fisherman is quickly made aware of the power of the state by armed fisheries patrol vessels.

The contents of the space which makes up a particular nation state interests the political geographer. Population, raw materials, the settlement pattern and the foreign ties are all characteristics for any evaluation or understanding by him of this institution. The size and effectiveness of a given nation, its people and its resources are not readily visible. The estimates of travellers as to whether a nation is densely populated, whether the people are patriotic and industrious, and whether their lives and activities are centrally directed often depend on mere accidents of daily contacts and on whether the stranger is conversant in the local language. It is less difficult to collect opinions about core areas and capitals via the television news, the press or personal travel. The political geographer is also interested in the internal and international relations which characterize a particular nation. Such relations may be quite clearly visible on the landscape since conflicts among states produce strong impacts on the land, overlapping claims to territory may be reflected in contrasting styles of vernacular architecture, and variations in settlement forms or urban street patterns may signal a complex political history. Finally, political activity both in the past and present may be concentrated about the ownership or exploitation of raw materials which transgress boundaries. Water resources which originate in one nation and are intensively used in an adjoining country provide a classic illustration. The conflicts over extensions of national sovereignty onto the world oceans or into space are both old and new, and the result is that a student of historical political geography may find it profitable to search for the visible relics of the nation state beside the seashore or within the depth of a star-filled night.

Examples of Visible Historic Relics of the State

The statement attributed to an Apollo astronaut returning from the Moon that the Great Wall of China was the first terrestrial, man-made feature discernable upon the surface of the earth from deep space is apocryphal and in error. What was actually first visible from space in this category of objects was Lake Nasser which stretches for 450 km (270 miles) upstream along the Egyptian Nile where it is impounded behind the Aswan Dam. Here the stupendous size of the feature, its nature as a strongly contrasting land-water feature, and the atmospheric clarity of that part of Africa will tend to enhance its visibility and identification from space. Lake Nasser is an excellent example of a feature of the cultural–geographical land-scape which has been produced as a result of political decisions, and as such it fits well into any collection of objects visible on the earth's surface which have historic–political and geographic roots. The Great Wall of China, certainly one of the political–geographical wonders of the world, is also visible from space, if not from the Moon. A LANDSAT satellite orbiting at an altitude of over 900 km (570 miles) records the Wall clearly.[2] Another aerial vista some-what nearer to our daily experience is Palmanova in northeast Italy (Fig. 36). It was founded in 1593 by Venice as a fortified strong point on her eastern flank against the encroaching Turks. What resulted was a monumental exercise in town planning for state military purposes carried out on a portion of the low-lying Venetian Plain and with good access to both Venice and Udine. In much the same way that form and function are so closely related in an exca-vated Roman camp in Britain or in a British cantonment built in Imperial India, the internal lay-out of Palmanova was prescribed in both its geometric and functional dimensions as clearly as its exter-nal fortifications with their intricate Renaissance ramparts and ditches. Today a municipality of about 6,000 inhabitants, Pal-manova was perhaps twice as populous during its zenith as a military city. That it survived in a frontier backwater of modern Italy is itself a marvel, and from both the air and the ground its regularity of plan and intricacy of design provide an impressive insight into just how

Fig. 36 Palmanova, in northeastern Italy, represents the high point of Renaissance military city design and is a remarkable surviving example of the impact of the state upon the land. Founded by Venice at the end of the sixteenth century as a fortification against the Turks, this planned city and its geometric defences endure as a modern if small town. North is at the top of the photo.

profoundly the political process can shape terrain, habitations and street patterns.

Table 14 summarizes the categories of features which have their origins in political decisions, and, furthermore, in the table there is a differentiation between those features which result from the direct impact of political processes and those which owe their existence to indirect political influences.[3] An item which reveals the obvious and direct state design is the ancient Roman fortified frontier zone, relics of which are still visible stretching across the desert areas of the Middle East. Paris with its magnificent pattern of boulevards and massed public buildings is a notable example of a great urban settlement which has been patterned politically and on a grand scale. Religious sites, including the Stonehenge complex, Carnac and its avenues of standing stones or a medieval cathedral which forms the heart of a North European town, reflect the strong influence which an organized religion may exercise through its role as an arm of the state. Social and educational facilities such as hospitals, schools or universities may possess an institutional layout which leads one to suspect state intervention in their construction.

The things which can be shown to have had political roots without these connexions being directly obvious represent the large collection of visible features listed in part (B) of Table 14. The arresting regularity of the rectangular land survey system of the American Midwest shows even the casual visitor the influence of the state as land surveyor and colonizer, whereas the British landscape of parliamentary enclosure is best interpreted by the skilled student of agricultural history who is less likely to be diverted by the scenic attractions of the large, regular fields and hedgerows so as to overlook their historic, legislative significance. Settlement patterns which reflect state policies of land redistribution, such as those visible in Danish yeoman farmers' properties dating from the 1920s, cannot be interpreted alone on the face of their appearance. In contemplating reclamation projects of the size of the Zuider Zee or the English Fenlands, it is safe to assume that direct state involvement has occurred. On the other hand, the origins of the small reclamations visible along the shores of the Limfjord in Northern Jutland, Denmark are more difficult to interpret having been undertaken by individual entrepreneurs seeking an outlet for their talents and fiscal resources. In this case the mark of the state does exist, but the precise degree of political involvement is not obvious from the visual evidence alone.

The category of political boundaries listed last in part (B) of

Table 14   VISIBLE LANDSCAPE FEATURES RESULTING FROM POLITICAL POLICIES OR
PRACTICES

(A)*Features directly recognizable as having political roots:*	
Military constructions	Fortifications, castles, military installations and settlements
Patterned settlements	Grid-plan cities, frontier settlements, settlements in areas of reclamation
Religious features	Prehistoric barrow fields, stone circles and alignments, temples, cathedrals, cemeteries, monastic settlements
Transportation features	Road networks, some railways, harbours and docks
Public institutional features	Schools, hospitals, monumental assembly places, exposition sites, national shrines
(B) *Features whose political roots are not visually obvious:*	
Land survey patterns	The results of Enclosure, land apportionment schemes, land surveys in newly settled areas
Patterned settlements	Occurring in frontier areas or reclamation schemes
Natural resource development	Some cases of forest and coastline usage
Irrigation and reclamation projects	Patterned landscapes of various sizes and geographic locations
Transportation features	State-financed railways, canals, motorways
Boundary lines	Frequently difficult to see and usually requiring additional information for interpretation

Source: the author.

Table 14 is frequently only indirectly comprehensible as being the result of politics at work upon the earth's surface. Although boundaries may be the result of clear changes in terrain texture or culture, without a supplementary data source such as a map of boundary lines, it cannot be certain whether one is looking at an example of the delicate interplay of physical and cultural features upon the land or at a surgical scar resulting from two political entities sharing, over time, a common boundary. As seen from the air, for example, the dramatic landscape changes which occur along the Canadian–US boundary in the vicinity of Alberta and Montana are well-known examples of differences in national practices of landscape development. Political boundaries can and do produce arresting pattern differences of this type; for the state, through its devious influences upon cadastral systems, crop patterns and settlement forms, continues to profoundly shape our world.

Preservation of Visible Relics of the Impact of the State on the Landscape

Having considered the physical manifestations of the state on the surface of the earth and having cited some examples, we now turn to the types of features which have been preserved and are used for public recreation. Hadrian's Wall, mentioned in the Introduction, is an outstanding example of a relic from the political past of Britain which is visited by members of a wide public. This complex frontier work is majestically sited and solidly built, and its location on what was a distant perimeter of the Roman Empire enhanced its chances for survival to the present time. The fact that the Wall is located in a nation much given to the study and preservation of its antiquities means that this monument to past politics is readily accessible to the visiting public and that abundant brochure material is available. Coaches filled with schoolchildren arrive for instructive day-trips, bus-loads of tourists are brought to view the scenic and archaeological wonders and the solitary traveller may also enjoy Northumberland's unique blending of nature and human history displayed here to such advantage.

The preservation and public use of such relics from the nation's political past is designed to bring something of the past to life through visits to national shrines, battlefields or landscapes displaying the nation's heritage. The purpose in attracting visitors to these places may be to cultivate patriotic sentiments or to establish or re-enforce a sense of national identity through a greater familiarity with the nation's historic past. Powerful emotions are involved and powerful interests may be active whether they represent the motivated individual, the patriotic organizer or the party propagandist. The shrines of nationalism rival those of religion in the strength of their popular attraction and in their potential for arousing easily manipulated public sentiments. Hence, the recreational usage of the political past is a sensitive arena for the preservationist and planner to enter.

Table 15 lists nine sites, chosen from the variety available in Britain, Denmark and the United States, to illustrate, in turn, national shrines, battlefields and rural landscapes shaped by the state. The national shrines which have been selected promote national consciousness and a feeling for national roots, and they are suitable for use as recreational facilities. The enshrined battlefields are thought of as promoting feelings of patriotism in the citizens who visit them, whilst the third category of features in Table 15 suggests examples of rural landscapes which are representative of a particular national spirit or character. During the formation of these landscapes, debate and law-making have together and over time produced a rural scene which today can be identified as being a physical signature of a particular people or nation. The specific sites

Table 15   EXAMPLES OF GEOGRAPHICALLY VISIBLE POLITICAL RELICS ACCESSIBLE
FOR PUBLIC RECREATION

Site category	Political quality being promoted	National site example, present ownership and preservational status
National shrine	National consciousness	England: Blenheim Palace. Private estate open to the public
		Denmark: Roskilde Cathedral. State-owned national monument
		USA: Lincoln's birthplace, Hodgenville, Kentucky. Federal ownership, National Parks Service
Battlefield	Patriotism and awareness of an historic watershed in national history	England: Hastings battlesite. Acquired by British Government in 1976 from private owners
		Denmark: Dybbøl Mill, Southern Jutland. Preserved Danish national property and a national park
		USA: Gettysburg Battlefield, Pennsylvania. Gettysburg National Military Park. Partly private and partly federal land. Partly administered by National Parks Service
Rural landscape representative of a nation	Sense of national heritage and national identity	England: early enclosure along the Fosse Way, Somerset. No specific preservation, private lands
		Denmark: Parliamentary enclosure, Eastern Jutland. No specific preservation, private lands
		USA: the Visible Rectangular Land Survey System, American Middle West, no specific preservation, private lands

Source: the author.

listed in the table are roughly equal in their political and historical implications for each exemplifying country, and their present day preservational status and recreational development are similar. The national shrines and battle fields are, consequently, all well recognized places accessible to the public, even though they are under various types of preservational control, and guidebooks and maps are readily available to the visitor. The additional, contemporary uses to which these individual buildings and places are put, over and above their recreational use, vary, and this fact reflects the different policies for preservation and site administration currently in force in Britain, Denmark and the US.

The sites representing national rural landscapes differ from the two other categories in that they are integral parts of dynamic contemporary countrysides; the political heritage is embedded within the present-day rural scene. The selection of historic field patterns for discussion in this connection reveals the bias of the geographer who views them on the same level as battlefields and shrines in terms of what they can reveal about regional or national politics in the recent or distant past.

National shrines

Roskilde Cathedral on the island of Zealand in Denmark is outstanding as an example of a national shrine which serves to reenforce national consciousness. Having served as a repository for the royal Danish dead over the past 550 years, the nation's consciousness of being a political entity finds a focus within the walls of this cathedral which dates from the early eleventh century. The building itself has great architectural merit and as a national symbol together with the royal tombs placed in chapels added over time to the main cathedral building, it complements in a powerful way its additional present-day functions of cathedral church, visual focus for a city and major tourist attraction.

Blenheim Palace, originating as a royal hunting lodge in the twelfth century, is a state monument and reward to a particularly esteemed national hero. Queen Anne conferred the manor on John Churchill, Duke of Marlborough, in 1704 and the building of this great house and its landscape gardens reflect the powers of decision-making and the financial resources which characterized the English nobility in the eighteenth century. That fact that Sir Winston Churchill was born here, invests the site with additional notoriety which further stimulates national consciousness. Privately owned but preserved and open to the public as a national monument, Blenheim Palace attracts tourists from abroad as well as Britons who share an interest in visible national history.

Sinking Spring Farm near Hodgenville, Kentucky, houses the Abraham Lincoln Birthplace National Historic Site which consists of the crude log cabin in which the sixteenth president was born in 1809. The cabin, which dates from the early 1800's, was eventually dismantled and moved to this site where it is today sheltered within a Neo-Classical Revival memorial building which is complete with columns and porticos. Visitors, who find their way to this area of federal land administrated by the National Park Service, can view the physical evidence which gave rise to the national myth that an honest politician could ascend from a log cabin to the White House as he sought fulfilment in political service to his country.

Battlefields

The site of a battle is a popular type of patriotic historical monument for the citizens of the winning side. Since many of these sites have not been built upon subsequently, their acquisition and maintenance is more easily accomplished than in the case of a national cathedral, a country house or a fragile log cabin. The battle site at Hastings represents a national monument to an event which profoundly changed the course of a nation's history. The land, which includes the actual battleground, was owned by the church from the Conquest until the Dissolution, when it passed into private hands until the British government, with financial help from America, purchased it in June 1976. This acquisition directly involved the government in the preservation and maintenance of a piece of the national patrimony. In past years recreations of this famous battle have done much to popularize this particular chapter in British history.

Gettysburg National Military Park in Pennsylvania represents for Americans the patriotically inspirational but appalling events in July 1863 when the armies of the Union and the Confederacy, numbering upwards of 160,000, met here in battle during which an infantry charge was turned back and the battle was thereby won and a political union was saved. Today, the visitor who looks beyond the kiosks, the diorama building and the viewing tower may ponder America's national history among the monuments to regiments and batteries spread across the acres of private and federal land which together make up this impressive site. In celebration of the US Bicentennial in 1976, the Battle of Gettysburg was re-enacted with help from some 2,000 participants for an audience of 30,000 onlookers and the millions watching their televisions. This careful recreation of the past could be said to have made the battlefield site come alive for many citizens.

In sharp contrast, it is a battlefield of defeat at Dybbøl Mill in Denmark's southern Jutland, enshrined as a national property and a national park, which serves to remind Danes of the subsequent national greatness which arose from the ashes of their defeat here by Prussia in April 1864. With the loss of one-sixth of present-day Jutland from 1864 until the Versailles Treaty when territorial restitution occurred, Denmark and its citizens made a conscious decision to use their resources of courage and hard work to redevelop the heathlands of Jutland by way of compensation. When Southern Jutland was reunited with Denmark in July 1920, a good part of the disgrace of the defeat in 1864 was erased, and today the restored windmill, set amidst earthworks and battlefield mementos, is imbued with a great spirit of patriotism. It has become such a hallowed spot that even visiting foreigners are impressed, and its tale of national defeat and subsequent revival transcends language differences.

Rural landscapes representative of a nation

The variety of possible changes which the state can produce in landscapes using its arsenal of laws, edicts and police powers, can result in equally varied landscape features. Public works projects, intrusive urban land-use patterns and monumental designs for human settlement worked into the countryside are illustrations of state-sponsored landscape planning. Specific examples include the remnants of a medieval hunting park fossilized in an estate and walled off from the public. A defunct canal which today leads nowhere may have been a piece of early nineteenth-century military engineering designed to deny powerful foes the capability of cutting off important coastal traffic. The decaying shells of industrial housing which reveal low standards of amenity design may reflect the use of parliamentary influence to establish favourable housing and building codes for speculative builders. These examples of state sponsored landscape design are not as easy to interpret as would be a hero's birthplace or his field of victory. The amount of time and money required today to interpret such sites for the visiting public may be much greater than that demanded by a Blenheim Palace or Gettysburg. It is consequently difficult to exploit, for purposes of patriotic tourism, a piece of countryside which reflects in its present-day configurations the long and twisting history of state decision-making. The following three examples have been chosen to illustrate the spirit and outlook of national groups, who used political instruments to shape their land.

For many foreign visitors and Britishers alike, a countryside composed of small, irregularly shaped fields each surrounded by verdant hedgerows forms the typical, English landscape. Such a scene as that along Fosse Way in Somerset in the vicinity of Lydford (Fig. 24) symbolizes centuries of forest clearing, private and parliamentary enclosure and agricultural policies, all of which manifest state influence in the countryside.[4] Our Danish example illustrates the impact of the state at one moment in the nation's history when, in about 1800, the countryside of the entire realm was enclosed according to a royal scheme which used four basic designs. One of the patterns was a stellate design by which individual farmlands were laid out so as to radiate from the village nucleus with the farmstead located at the apex of the triangularly shaped and now consolidated agricultural parcel. This rigid geometric solution to the problem of enclosing open fields and replacing them with individual farms illustrates the strong hand of the state at work reshaping the rural landscape and the patterns of its inhabitants' lives. Although today this stellate pattern is often difficult to appreciate from ground level unless one walks field boundaries and takes sightings along them, a map or aerial photograph clearly reveals the intriguing geometric patterns which resulted from the work of state land surveyors who, nearly two centuries ago, reshaped the economy and society of rural Denmark at the behest of the King. The American rectangular land survey system, which so impresses anyone flying over the Mid-Western states, resulted from a political decision made in the context of a federal policy for wilderness settlement in support of national territorial expansion. The result was the dictating of the configuration of the cultural landscape which developed during the next century and a half across half a continent, and as a programme it must rank as being one of the world's most impressive examples of the State as a shaper of the earth's surface.[5] Great squares, six miles a side and oriented with the cardinal points of the compass, impart a remarkable rectangularity to human patterns of work and residence.[6] Along the international boundary separating Canada and the United States, the contrasts between the US survey system and the Canadian one are dramatically revealed even from a satellite orbiting in space. The recreational potential of these historic landscapes is greater for their being a part of national resources of open lands. If, however, one wishes to learn more about their political background, one must seek guidance from historians of the rural scene. The recreational and educational opportunities residing in historic rural landscapes are not as widely recognized as they should be, but then it is not easy to monumentalize the fields and hedgerows of an entire nation nor to construct living museums which adequately tell the story of Denmark's enclosure, Britain's fields or America's rectangular Mid-West.[7]

Exploitation of Visible Relics of the Impact of the State upon the Landscape

As is well recognized, visible images of the State and its leaders can be created and manipulated for purposes of political gain or retribution. The foregoing discussion of national shrines, battlefields and landscapes has avoided comment on the use of these features for specific political purposes. The following Table 16 lists examples of

Table 16   VISIBLE LANDSCAPE RELICS EXPLOITED FOR POLITICAL PURPOSES

Political Purpose	Site Example
1 To establish national political identity	(a) Albania and the Illyrian tradition. A nation-wide programme to establish cultural roots, included archaeological excavations
To establish national identity as a separate group within a nation	(b) Ayers Rock, a cult place of the Australian Pitjandjara aborigines. Accessible under the Australian National Parks
2 To provide a rallying point which will strengthen public patriotism	(a) Masada, Israel representing an inspiring national resistance against the might of Rome. Accessible, under National Parks Authority
	(b) The Alamo, Texas, a regional rallying point which symbolizes victory in defeat. Texas-owned National Historic Landmark, accessible
3 To provide a rallying point against external foes and a symbol of indigenous independence struggles	(a) Zimbabwe African Iron Age ruins in Rhodesia representing indigenous African achievement. No apparent preservation, accessible
	(b) Voyage of the Polynesian canoe *Hōkūle'a* from Hawaii to Tahiti and return. A Pan-Polynesian/Anglo archaeological experiment in 1976
4 To represent the contrasting historic perspectives of winners versus losers	(a) Heroic Anglo defeat at the hands of Indians, Battle of the Little Big Horn, 1876, Gen. Custer v. Sioux. Custer Battlefield National Monument, Montana, accessible
	(b) Tragic Indian defeat at hands of US Troops, Battle of Wounded Knee, 1890. National Historic Landmark, South Dakota, accessible
5 To further revision of the national past	(a) Achievements of pre-Hispanic Indian civilizations in Peru as evident in the Nazcan desert remains and Incan mountain fortresses at Cuzco and Machu Picchu. Partial preservation, accessible
	(b) Relocation centres in California used to intern Japanese citizens during World War II. California Historical Landmarks, accessible

Source: See Notes 8 to 13.

well recognized historic relics which have been publicly exploited for political purposes. The examples are arranged according to the type of political aim they have been made to serve, and the current preservational status of each site is noted. The examples have been selected so as to stress geographic dimensions or historic happenings which are specific to one place or which reflect landscape alterations. The mere casting down of statues representing the previous head of state or the conquest of new territories have been neglected in favour of cult sites, battlefields and cultural monuments whose two-sided historic implications have been used to further or to reverse definite political policies.

The most ambitious of these examples is the effort of the current Albanian regime to identify and develop, in a politically conscious undertaking, a national cultural identity for the modern Albanians which will serve to build state unity and a sense of national purpose.[8] After 500 years of foreign domination there was a large accumulation of non-Albanian cultural artifacts and traditions in the country. By going back in time to the Iron Age Illyrians who dominated this part of southeastern Europe prior to the imposition of Greek control, c. 500 B.C., the regime was able to recover a satisfactory national 'role'. Since World War II the official emphasis in Albania has been upon happenings 'before or after our era', and in an effort to develop as much as possible of the physical remains from Illyrian times great encouragement and support has been given to archaeological excavation and restoration. These relics retrieved from the Albanian soil represent a people who flourished 2,500 years ago, and their legacy is being used to help fashion a national identity for modern Albanians.

The Navel of the Universe located at Ayers Rock in Central Australia represents a physical legacy and a cultural tradition which are perhaps still able to establish an identity for a group of aborigines emersed within the greater culture of a modern state. This enormous, dome-shaped monolith of gritstone stands 400 m (1,100 feet) above the surrounding desert (Fig. 37). At its base, amid tumbled boulders and sheltering caves, the Pitjandjara people occupied and exploited a fertile ecological niche for a very long time.[9] They constructed an entire cosmos of beliefs and traditions about Ayers Rock, and the totems and cyclical observances resident in this mysterious place gave form and substance to their lives. Since 1873 Europeans have visited and reported on the spot, and today its cultural relics in the form of rock carvings and paintings as well as its natural geological and zoological wonders are administered by the

Fig. 37 Ayers Rock, the Navel of the Universe, located in Central Australia, rises some 335 metres high and 3 km long (360 yards by 2 miles) as a gigantic and mysterious totem from the surrounding plain. The cosmos of the Pitjandjara aborigines, it is today a powerful attraction for tourists who come to admire it; it still needs a small man even for the most casual visitor.

Australian Parks Administration and well appreciated by visitors. The Rock is a passive reminder of the intellectual and artistic accomplishments of a group of hunters and gatherers, and its political message is that diversity and separate identify have a place within a society and a nation predominantly shaped by and functioning under European ways.

Turning next to the conscious cultivation and moulding of public patriotism, the excavated heroic defence site at Masada in Israel is an outstanding example. On this commanding mesa with a wide view over the Dead Sea, Jewish zealots defended impressive fortifications against the might of Rome in the first century A.D. When on the point of being overwhelmed, the defenders chose self-destruction over surrender, and a smoking, corpse-filled ruin was all that the Roman army won. In the post-World War II era, the state of Israel has benefited greatly in terms of public relations and propaganda from the revelations produced at Masada by a state-supported scientific investigation and excavation.[10] People from many Western nations participated in the dig, and state support assured that the inspiring revelations received prompt and arresting dissemination in print and film. This ancient Jewish resistance, within the grim shadow of a modern holocaust, has been dramatized in order to promote the concept of a nation which is united and therefore better able to face a hostile world. In addition, the circle of fellowship binding Jewish and Gentile 'Masadaites', those who participated in the excavation and those who visit it, works to the national advantage in fashioning sympathetic ties between Israel and other nations at times when national programmes and goals need the widest possible support.

The Texan defeat in 1836 at the hands of General Santa Ana's thousands who finally overran the venerable adobe fortress called the Alamo has become a world recognized symbol of victory in defeat. The stirring cry of 'Remember the Alamo!' symbolizes the American tradition of independence and survival under six different flags. The Alamo itself, which occupied a Spanish mission dating from 1718, was renovated in 1849, and today the site is owned by Texas. As a registered historic landmark, the Alamo is cared for by the Daughters of the Republic of Texas, and it is promoted as being a hallowed spot for patriots past and a source of inspiration for those who visit it today.

The search for symbols of identity which may also serve as a rallying point is also part of indigenous struggles for independence. In East Africa the imposing stone-built fortress of Zimbabwe fulfills this role, and claims for its African authenticity as well as challenges of its age and origin have been aired and debated both within parliamentary walls and the pages of archaeological publications.[11] Dispassionate investigation has revealed an African origin for Zimbabwe and 150 related forts, habitations and religious structures spread over the highlands of East Africa. Dating back to the Iron Age, Zimbabwe was built during two periods of activity within the span from the fifteenth to the early eighteenth centuries A.D. Some have sought to derive this technical masterpiece from Phoenician or Portuguese influences whereas others have made good of the point that it is an indigenous African accomplishment. Although not preserved or developed as an accessible tourist attraction, the name and symbol of Zimbabwe have figured prominently during the years of contest for political supremacy in Rhodesia.

An ephemeral experience in the assertion of indigenous political identification took place during the US Bicentennial year when *Hōkūle'a*, a twin-hulled, two-masted Polynesian voyaging canoe, was sailed from Hawaii to Tahiti and back.[12] As originally planned, the trip was to be made in a vessel built according to traditional patterns in use in the Eastern Pacific 600 to 1,000 years ago. This ancient design was modified as the result of experience, and a mixed crew of Polynesians and whites sailed to Tahiti in thirty-five days and returned to Hawaii in twenty-two. From its beginnings as an exercise in experimental archaeology, the voyage of the *Hōkūle'a* developed into a testing experience for the two racial groups involved, and it stimulated a measure of self-awareness among native Hawaiians of the accomplishments of their forefathers. In the celebratory year of 1976 and given the American bias toward ethnic separateness, the experiment in seamanship aboard *Hōkūle'a* became invested with nationalistic sentiments, and the voyaging canoe carried a significant cargo of Polynesian political self-consciousness across the Pacific.

The fourth category of political exploitation of the past as depicted in Table 16 concerns the contrasting historic perspectives of winners versus losers in confrontation politics. Two distinct chapters from the book of the American Indian wars serve to illustrate these contrasting viewpoints. The Battle of the Little Big Horn took place in Montana in the summer of 1876, and under the redoubtable Chief Sitting Bull the Sioux Indians annihilated the Army Cavalry forces under the command of Lt. Col. George A. Custer. 'Custer's Last Stand', as this defeat is known, may either be viewed as an heroic sacrifice in the face of great odds, or as retaliation by the aggrieved Native Americans. The site, the Custer Battlefield National Monument, is on the national register of historic places, and under administration of the National Parks Service its displays and cemeteries are accessible to the public.

The opposite of Little Big Horn occurred at the Wounded Knee Battlefield in the winter of 1890 when Sioux warriors and their dependents, who were participants in the Ghost Dance Rebellion, were slain by US troops. Today, from the viewpoint of the Native Americans this site represents the duplicity of the white man and his unjust treatment of the Indian; a technical win for the whites becomes a moral victory for the vanquished. As a national historic landmark on private land, Wounded Knee, South Dakota, is accessible to the traveller. Its symbolism, in the continuing American discussions about Indian rights in the light of historically unjust treatment, provides 'strong medicine' for the political debating chamber and the courtroom.

The subject of historical revisionism is a big one, but in connection with our discussion here I wish to cite two examples wherein the national past is being changed to fit new modes of thought, and these changes are represented by visible historic sites. The achievements of pre-Hispanic peoples in what is today Peru have been dramatically underlined in order to assert national identity and to apportion more historical honour to Indian civilizations. The mysterious figures and geometric drawings produced over 1,000 years ago by the Nazcan culture on the desert pavements of coastal Peru are admired for their mysteriousness as well as for their suggested connection with flying saucers! In the mountainous portions of the country, the Inca fortresses at Cuzco and Machu Picchu after nearly five hundred years have not yet lost their fascination for North American or European visitors. Partially preserved against attack by nature and man, these native technical accomplishments are accessible, and Peru can exploit them for what they say about pre-European achievements to people seeking an identity on the contemporary Latin American political map.

Our last example concerns the recent and painful chapter along the West Coast of the United States when Japanese were interned during World War II.[13] The ten camps or re-location centres became home for over 100,000 internees from early 1942, in the shadow of Pearl Harbor, until the end of 1945. Considered a prudent defence measure at the time, the consequent abridgement of constitutional rights and the economic victimization under the guise of national protection have both subsequently come in for hard criticism. Revision has come full circle at Camp Manzanar and Tule Lake in California with the installation of a commemorative plaque which describes their ruins as representing concentration camps, monuments to hysteria, racism and economic exploitation. Today in public ownership and listed in the state inventory of historic landmarks, these visible landscape relics of the recent past have been pressed into service as instruments to serve contemporary programmes to revaluate and reinterpret the public past. For those who assume that historic preservation is an apolitical activity and that the recreational use of the past is not intended as a lesson in values, a rude awakening awaits!

Three Historic Political Geographic Sites With Recreational Potential

The US Bicentennial celebration in 1976, which ranged in content from the promenade of the Tall Ships in New York harbour to beer cans in the national motif, and the British celebration of the Queen's Silver Jubilee in 1977, from its striking chain of hilltop bonfires down to its emblazoned plastic shopping bags, both illustrate exercises in the merchandizing of the past for the entertainment and inspiration of the present.[14] These two national celebrations provide guidance to anyone who contemplates exploitation of the political past for present recreational purposes since the full range of possibilities, from the sublime to the ridiculous, was on display. In such an undertaking a definite focus must be available to serve as a rallying point for any commemoration: a central theme helped the Silver Jubilee to succeed but lack of one hampered the celebration of the US Bicentennial. However, it is not easy to find a sufficiently general theme which can be interpreted without involving distracting contraditions and wasting divisiveness. Moreover, it is now clear that disciplined pageantry will win out over disorganized presentations. The British genius for displaying the past in glorious colour should be the model for all others attempting celebrations of national historic accomplishments. Finally, for any historical political site to function in a recreational context there must be abundant information in the form of maps, brochures and background literature available to visitors. With these guidelines in mind, I shall next consider three examples of historical political sites which are suitable for development as recreational attractions.

A developed site: Hadrian's Wall

The outer marches of the Roman Empire were fortified, and this construction is particularly impressive along the German Rhine and monumentally imposing through the deserts of the Levant. In terms of accessibility to the modern tourist, however, it is Hadrian's Wall which must rank as the best example. Its natural setting is most attractive and conducive to field walking. With the information available from excellent Ordnance Survey maps (1:25,000 scale) and R. G. Collingwood's *A Guide to the Roman Wall* as augmented by G. D. B. Jones, the visitor is free to select from its 117 km (70 miles) the outstanding sections such as the *vallum* in the east where the Wall itself is visible, or Housesteads where excavation has exposed much for us to ponder on.[15] The preservation and maintenance of the Wall by the Department of the Environment and private owners is admirable given the many feet which tread it during the course of a year. The Wall continues to reveal more of itself as indicated by Robin Birley's book on Vindolanda, so that the instruction to be gained from a visit, complemented by its scenic splendours, will assure active future enjoyment of this relic of the imperial Roman past.[16]

An existing site with recreational potential: the Los Angeles Memorial Cemetery

The thought of a cemetery becoming a recreational attraction for the general public in search of its national past is not so difficult to accept if one recalls the popularity with survivors from the World Wars of the military cemeteries on the Continent. When meticulously maintained by national commissions and private organizations, the green lawns stretching to the horizon and dotted with markers remind us of the great costs of the periodic defence of national liberty. When a national cemetery offers in addition a pleasant green oasis in the heart of a bustling urban area, then its recreational potential is more clearly evident.

The Los Angeles Memorial Cemetery, located in West Los Angeles adjacent to the giant University of California campus and only a stone's throw from one of the region's most busy motorways, is an impressive example of the national past in the turmoil of the city. Established in 1889 and today containing over 68,000 interments, this cemetery provides a democratic roll-call of America's wars from the 1846–8 conflict with Mexico, to Vietnam in the 1970s.[17] Its 45 ha (116 acres) come alive on Memorial Day when 68,000 flags mark the graves, and relatives arrive with bouquets of flowers to decorate the memorials (Fig. 38).

My proposal is that this memorial park, within a densely built-up

Fig. 38 The Los Angeles Memorial Cemetery, California, with its 68,000 veterans' graves decorated for Memorial Day 1977, represents a patriotic and reflective imprint of the state on an urban landscape. Spanning as it does 130 years of American military conflicts, it represents for many citizens an appropriate last resting place for kin who have served in the nation's military services. During a few days of the year it comes alive with thoughtful visitors, and one wonders whether this green park might not offer other recreational possibilities to hard-pressed citizens of this great metropolis. (Photo by the author.)

urban landscape, could serve a broader use than that of being a repository for the nation's honoured dead. With a roll-call of names and nationalities displayed on the tomb markers providing an encapsulation of 130 years of national military history, it would seem possible that a recreational park could be established here within an attractive landscape of entombed patriotism. Such a public park would provide a respite from the traffic, noise and confusion produced by modern Californian urban life while at the same time contributing to the spiritual and physical betterment of noontime picknickers and weekend kite flyers. Clearly, such a proposal would require a simplification of the overlapping areas of responsibility for the cemetery, an increased staffing for park maintenance and an acceptance of non-traditional activities within memorial parks. Whether the public would accept and then avail itself of such an open space in sufficient numbers to justify the increased maintenance costs cannot be answered. However, when one notes the shortage of safe and accessible parkland in this part of the Los Angeles Basin, combined with the inspirational impact which a democratic national cemetery might have, it becomes an attractive proposition to develop this land reserved for the dead as a reflective retreat for the living.

A potential site: Royal Land Reform in Denmark

The imprint of political decisions, via an historic land survey, on contemporary landscapes can be illustrated by a third, potential site in Denmark. In the Mols Mountains of East Central Jutland there occur remnants of field patterns which date from the times of open fields and enclosure (Fig. 27). They have survived because the area has very poor soils, with the result that modern intensive cultivation has not been practised and thereby obliterated them. Secondly, these relics of agrarian history occupy land which has been proposed for inclusion within a Danish Nature Park so that their future preservation appears certain. The Mols Mountains are formed of glacial moraines which rise to an elevation of 137 m (450 feet). Contemporary cultivation is intensive on the relatively fertile flat lands, whereas forest plantations, heathland and grass dominate the poorer soils of the hills.[18] Notwithstanding the existence of poor soils, the pre-enclosure tax records of the 1680s indicate that there was no land which was not allocated and very little of it which was not cultivated even if the rotation sequence might specify fallow periods for as long as 20 years. The fossilized ridge-and-furrow remains which are still visible in Mols date from this open field period.[19] The later, state-sponsored enclosure of the open fields, which occurred in about 1800, also shows up very clearly on the contemporary agricultural landscape in a pattern of striking field boundaries which run across hill and dale.

Both of these sets of relic field patterns occur in a portion of eastern Jutland which, because of its scenic and historic resources, is a prime candidate to become a Danish rural park.[20] The scientific and educational resources of the area's 2,700 ha (6,700 acres) are useful to many disciplines, and day-trip picnickers and ramblers would also find it to be a spot worth patronizing. Access roads with parking facilities should be built so as to support the system of trails which already laces the area. Within the park perimeter the continuation of normal rural activities and land utilization would be encouraged, for the Danes prefer that these parks incorporate as much of the local contemporary life as possible in order to avoid the production of yet another static landscape museum. The archaeological treasures of the Mols Mountains would be protected within a nature park accessible to an interested public, and the churches and old houses of the villages would continue to serve the inhabitants as well as being living history on display. Fossil field relics of both the medieval common field pattern and later enclos ure should also be accommodated as cultural history features within a nature park. With appropriate trail postings and the publication of brochures and pamphlets, self-guided tours of the area could be made available to the energetic public as well as to the solitary walker and the school class. If the megalithic and Bronze Age tomb of prehistoric Mols reflect the impress of religion upon the land scape, then the geometry of enclosure reflects the imprint of the secular state in an equally indelible manner.

The nation state is one of the greatest human forces which shape our landscapes. Statues, public monuments and official building abound, national boundaries exert their subtle effects, and martial history, social programmes and land-use policies often impinge directly upon the land. Not all national sentiments or achievement are worthy of preservation, perhaps, but time presents us with an astonishing variety of features to choose from when we consider the recreational development of sites which accentuate aspects of national identity or ethnic achievements. Since opinions regarding the meaning of a site or monument often conflict, an approach may be preferred whereby a general recreation function may be used to defuse what otherwise might be an unacceptable flaunting of state power or the celebration of a now discredited regime. Although the management of historic landscape relics representing the political past is a difficult and sensitive undertaking, the financial resource available for development are often considerable, and the positive impact of the results upon the public may be such as to make the enterprise worthwhile.[21]

Part III

Summary and Conclusions

At this stage it is necessary to sum up the case for planning the past. The contemporary concern about preservation of the collective past has grown out of a realization that the fragile fabric of old buildings and landscapes is very susceptible to being damaged or destroyed in the course of present-day activities. The destruction of the past is not always intentional, and frequently damage is a by-product of well-intentioned and necessary agricultural modernization or urban renewal. Concern over these developments has found articulate expression and a concrete programme among a wide spectrum of people in many countries. Part I of this book discusses the technical methods and legal instruments which have been developed to help protect the past and to make it useful and economically productive for a contemporary world. In Part II four distinctive groupings of historic features are described and analyzed in terms of their preservational peculiarities and recreational potentials. The countryside and the city, the industrial complex and the landscape-shaping activities of the state are all discussed in turn. There remains now the task of viewing the landscape as an entity which, through the techniques of landscape analysis, can become better understood by planner and preservationist in order that more effective and economical efforts may be undertaken to preserve as much of the puzzling and varied visible past for the instruction and entertainment of as many people as possible.

10

Landscape Analysis: a New Tomorrow for the Visible Past

Introduction

Planning the past to serve the present and the future is a demanding undertaking which requires a sense of balanced design, an expertise in execution and an ability to unify conflicting points of view. In addition, it is necessary to anticipate future uses for the past in order that present projects will continue to be appropriate. Newgrange, a megalithic passage-grave four and half millennia old, built of large stone slabs covered by a circular mound of cobbles and located in the Republic of Ireland, is an outstanding example of this procedure. This remarkable ancient burial site in the valley of the Boyne has been studied extensively and recently restored by the Irish Office of Public Works, National Monuments Branch. Not all planning at Newgrange is of modern origin, however, for here an eerie legacy from the past was discovered by M. J. and Claire O'Kelly.[1] The roof box, a structural feature built over the entrance to the passage-grave, at the time of the winter solstice admits a beam of sunlight which sweeps the length of the passage and on into the end chamber to reach the front edge of the basin stone resting there. As this band of light moves through the tomb it dramatically illuminates the carved reliefs which embellish the walls and corbelled roof. We must assume that solar illumination at a specific time of the year fulfilled an essential role in the symbolism of Newgrange. One message which this discovery conveys to us is that we must not only conserve and study the visible heritage of the past but also search out the hidden features of inspired design which are dramatic legacy from unknown minds.

Newgrange represents both the substance of the visible past and the process whereby that past is developed for contemporary

recreational enjoyment. Not content to have this magnificen‹
megalith languish as a mere static item decorating a very histori‹
area of Irish landscape, the tomb has been restored and is preservec
as both an object and a site of great cultural significance. Its relativ‹
accessibility and notoriety will assure its drawing power among th‹
public. What visitors will anticipate and what impressions they wil
carry away afterwards are, however, difficult to estimate. The soli‹
nature of the past and the pragmatic requirements for its preserva‹
tion and use are well illustrated by Newgrange. If the perception›
which it fosters are difficult to define or describe, as a landscape i›
can be studied by means of landscape analysis in the service of th‹
geography of recreation. This promising technique will be the topi‹
of this chapter.

The study of the artistic and aesthetic impact of a scenery ha›
unfolded over the past two centuries whilst modern, commercia›
tourism is already a hundred years old, but research into the geo‹
graphy of tourism and recreation has only become popular withi›
the past fifteen years. Leisure-time resources among the affluen‹
populations of Western Europe and North America have fuellec
the development of a huge travel industry with all its satellit‹
activities.[2] The amount of investment in the industry and its notabl‹
impact upon the landscape commend its study to both planners an‹
geographers.[3] When tens of millions of Northern Europeans holi‹
day in the Mediterranean lands and their expenditure there consti‹
tutes up to a fifth of the foreign currency earnings for the hos›
countries and when Canada and Mexico welcome millions of U$
day-trippers, the magnitude of the travel industry and its involve›
ment with mass transportation, the hotel business and resulting
pollution problems can readily be appreciated. The impact which i›
makes upon the rural landscape has been well studied in Britain by
Coppock and Duffield and within a broader European and Nort‹
American context by Simmons.[4] The role played by the physical an‹
cultural peculiarities of British landscapes in attracting and enter‹
taining tourists is less clear but has been covered in Burton's stud›
of Cannoch Chase in terms of its carrying capacity, its physica›
limitations and the spatial concentration of tourist activities.[5] Row›
ley and Breakell have taken a close look at the historic resources o›
the landscape using the archaeological inventory along with a›
analysis of site attractiveness, whilst the recovery of the histori‹
rural heritage of Britain's landscapes and its presentation t‹
interested visitors is discussed by Aston and Rowley.[6]

What the future holds in the way of research work on histori‹

landscape resources is suggested by the bibliographies compiled for the Council of Planning Librarians and by examples of topics pursued in recent American doctoral dissertations.[7] Certain features and images of the rural and urban past command the interest of tourists and this knowledge can help to guide development of the recreation industry. Historical geographers may apply themselves to the task of illuminating the past in this connection in order that its messages may be made more accessible to contemporary travellers and tourists. The UK research trends along these particular lines are suggested by the fact that twelve individuals listed in a recent directory of historical geographers declared themselves to be engaged in active research which dealt with the recreational use of the past.[8]

The application of landscape analysis is an attempt to solve a number of recreation planning problems and to achieve optimum balances between resources and goals. Necessary labour and the money to operate public parks are made available by fiscally conservative legislative groups and automatically reduced by economic inflation which skims off a good percentage before the project managers receive it. An additional problem concerns the presentation of the most satisfying recreational environment to a public which grows in numbers but whose expectations change and whose tastes are fickle.

As an example, the National Park Service (NPS) of the United States strains today to meet its assigned task of maintaining natural and historic features for the use and enjoyment of the nation's citizens.[9] The NPS maintains and administers 290 separate facilities which include 100 new units added during the expansionist phase since 1960. There were 113·7 million visitors to these many attractions in 1965, 228·9 million in 1975 and an estimated 280 million in 1977. The budget of the NPS has increased by 200 per cent between 1970 and 1976 but even so only 74 pence was spent by the park system for each visitor in 1976. Even with such a modest expenditure per visitor the NPS continually seeks to cut costs while maintaining services, and in this endeavour budgets must be closely inspected and some unpleasant decisions made. In order to improve the efficiency of parks' management one may study the facilities themselves and investigate the ways in which they are promoted and operated. In addition, studies may be undertaken which will reveal public preferences relative to the park facilities so that park management may support the more popular attractions at the cost of the less popular or seek to channel patronage so as to promote a more even usage of the facilities. The assessment of public preferences and patterns of use requires feedback from public opinion to guide future planning. It comes as no surprise, therefore, to learn that much work is currently underway which concerns the recreational preferences of the public with later application of these findings to more general planning studies. The combining of information about public recreational habits with an analysis of the attractiveness of scenery together can provide the recreational planner with a sounder basis on which to predicate his economic and physical proposals.

Recreational Planning and Landscape Analysis

Landscape analysis is a sub-unit within the larger process of landscape assessment which has been adopted for use in planning studies in Britain and the US.[10] In order that we may produce a planned response to recreational demands or to environmental problems it is essential that we have more than offhand estimates of local resources and their potentials. An important element to be judged here is the attraction which a given landscape has for the public. Study of this environmental characteristic, landscape aesthetics, is difficult because there is no single, accepted technique for measuring either the aesthetic content of a scene or its aesthetic impact upon the visitor (Fig. 39). The methods which have been proposed and used fall into two groups. In measurement techniques the emphasis is on an objective evaluation of individual physical attributes of a landscape which may be regarded as being positive and attractive or negative and repellant. By contrast, preference techniques assess landscapes in a total way in terms of the impact which they have upon individual viewers. The preferential approach depends upon people's assessments of a number of landscape scenes as these may be simulated by means of photographs or questionnaires. Not surprisingly, these two methodological approaches have their champions and detractors. Since scenic merit is very difficult to describe in any precise manner and can produce misleading measurements, the student of landscape aesthetics will try many different techniques in the hope that one will serve his purpose, leading eventually to a better matching of landscape capacity to public demand.

The application of landscape analysis which interests us here became a possibility as the result of two separate lines of work, landscape planning at national and regional levels and the study of the environmental perceptions of recreationists, meeting in the area of recreational planning. The geographer becomes involved when

Fig. 39 The heart of Tilst, Jutland in Denmark, illustrates village morphology including the pond on the green, the encircling band of four-squa. farmsteads and infilling in the form of cottages. The eight-hundred-year-old village church stands just to the left of this aerial photo and the firs village school from the 1870s just to the right. An analysis of this fragile amalgam of physical and social legacies from the Danish rural past is necessary before any plan designed to promote its viable future can succeed.

the study concentrates on the evaluation of landscape vistas, the changes in land-use texture, and the visual impact of open spaces and water bodies weighed against closed fields or forest barriers (Fig. 40). At the same time, the geographer is interested in the perceptual preferences for specific scenes, categories of views or activity areas manifested by the public at leisure. If one combines the separate landscape evaluations of the geographer and of the general public, it should be possible to provide both the students of landscape aesthetics and recreational planners with information to assist them in shaping proposals for leisure landscape development and use.

The study of environmental perception as a way to analyze the man–land relationship has developed in geography over the past two decades.[11] Application of such psychological principles by geographers and others has resulted in studies of human perceptions of environmental hazards, particularly those associated with river plain flooding, and of the ways in which people view the urban milieu. Today, the study of the recreational use of open lands attempts, via perception analysis, to find out what makes some outdoor scenes so attractive and their leisure-time resources so heavily used in consequence. In the following pages I shall describe, with help from Danish examples, the way a proposed plan and the realities of environmental perception can be brought together, through the efforts of the geographer, to do a better job of planning the recreational uses of the past.

The Danish Experience

National plans and the resources of rural areas

As an outgrowth of reconstruction after World War II and of liberal support for central planning as an aid to regional development, the Danish Parliament enacted legislation proposing a three-stage organization for planning; efforts to fulfil these aims have been underway since 1960.[12] The national Zone Plan of 1962, although never adopted, nevertheless provided a graphic scheme for a more even distribution of economic activities and services throughout the 42,000 sq. km (16,000 sq. miles) of the realm. Existing laws for the regulation of economic and social development in both urban and rural areas were strengthened in 1969 by several pieces of supporting legislation. The Rural Zones Act divided the nation into urban and rural areas, with secondary summerhouse districts which

Fig. 40   This oblique aerial photo illustrates the pre-enclosure, ridge-and-furrow field remains belonging to Strandkaer hamlet in the Mols Mountains of east-central Jutland, Denmark. This landscape, which has been used by man for over 6,000 years, challenges the landscape analyst and the recreational planner with its wealth of visible history as it excites the enthusiasm of students of landscape history.

occupy some of the more attractive portions of the country. More related to our interests was the Nature Conservation Act which was designed to promote public access to the recreational resources of the countryside while at the same time protecting those delicate features and landscapes from damage or excessive use.[13] Further work in the Parliament resulted in laws concerning rural and regional planning and regional planning specifically in Greater Copenhagen in 1973. In anticipation of Denmark's entry into the European Economic Community, which occurred in January 1973, an important and far-reaching piece of legislation, the Municipal Planning Law, was passed, and it took effect in February 1977 with its requirements for genuine grassroots participation in the planning process. As a group, these bills represent the intent of Parliament that a new and comprehensive effort should be made to inventory national landscape resources, to measure present and estimate future levels of landscape usage and to promote planning at local levels in an effort to achieve a more equitable distribution of goods and services, social services, jobs and recreational opportunities for the population at large.

County landscape resource inventories

The Nature Conservation Act of 1969 opened the way for the production, by the efficient planning offices of the fourteen Danish counties, of a most impressive set of landscape inventories and analyses. As an example, by 1970 Ribe County had published a complete *General Landscape Plan* which, together with the elegant study produced in 1972 by its northern neighbour, Ringkøbing County, set the standard for a succession of similar reports.[14] Hardworking staffs of planners, foresters, economists, architects and geographers were able to accumulate a great amount of inventory material which was then plotted on maps which were in turn published in colour with explanatory text. Although predicated upon the same legislative act, each of these county studies has used a slightly different format and the topical emphasis has varied from one to another.[15]

The primary technique used in the county studies is an inventory of features which can form a basis for an estimate of open land recreational potentials. In the case of the 1972 Ringkøbing study one finds maps which show land use, ownership and preservational status, and the distributions of archaeological, historical, geological and biological attractions. With such an inventory in hand, the planner next looks at present-day recreational use of the county's rural areas and matches this against the limitations on further development imposed in the interests of pollution control, water purity standards and expansion of the built environment. It is then possible to define the areas within the county with the highest landscape values in the recreational sense and which have the highest tolerance for this type of use. Once these candidate recreational areas have been mapped, a proposal for the establishment of a county recreational preserve (a nature park in Danish terminology) may follow.[16] In Ringkøbing County such a potential park area, consisting of 52,000 ha (130,000 acres) and located adjacent to three major towns, was identified and circumscribed. Subsequently, a group of outside consultants was asked to give individual, disciplinary-based assessments of the potential park area; my own contribution to this dialogue being to identify and map eighteen occurrences of Iron Age field remains within the perimeter as representative of a visible and recreationally explorable element in Danish cultural history.

Nature park assessment: Mariager Fjord

An extremely attractive fjord landscape, combining hilly terrain with broad sweeps of water and a varied shoreline, was jointly proposed by North Jutland and Aarhus Counties as a national nature park. A professional forester, Niels Schou, working for these county preservation planning committees produced an attractive and effective analysis of Mariager Fjord and its recreational potential.[17] Once the 76,000 ha (190,000 acres) of the proposed park area had been singled out in the course of both national and county investigations of scenic and usable regions, the detailed proposal was based in an assessment of some thirty-seven recreational goals which could be satisfied in the area around Mariager Fjord. Nearly all of the proposed park area was of potential interest to research workers in archaeology, history, zoology and geology, and the attractions of the area for teaching and student field-work were also stressed. Such a multiple approach to recreational landscape analysis depends on the accumulation of many types of data derived from reliable sources. This inventory data is plotted on large-scale maps and areas of concentration are defined in terms of both elements and potential interest. When compared with areas of either conflicting or conforming land use, a further selection of the interest areas most readily accessible and untroubled by competitive land uses can be offered. A visual impact assessment of the area was also achieved by means of some 340 observations covering over half of the area of the potential park. The study concluded with a proposed plan for conforming developments along Mariager Fjord which would release and make usable areas of special scientific, educational and recreational interest whilst maintaining as much visual beauty and integration with the pursuits of traditional daily life as possible. If adopted and established, the Mariager Fjord nature park could serve to open up this portion of northeast Jutland to the holidaymaker, research worker and school outing group.

Park and people: the lake country of Central Jutland

In the interest of combining a park proposal with an analysis of recreational activity potentials versus actual practices in the Lake

Country of Central Jutland, a working group of geographers at Aarhus University completed a research contract for a consortium of three county preservation planning committees.[18] A national study in 1967 had already highlighted this portion of Central Jutland as a potential nature park, and the three county agencies were interested in receiving help with their study of the 1,000 sq. km (380 sq. miles) of scenic and popular lakes, rolling hills, heathlands and forests.

The two approaches most commonly used in the execution of a landscape evaluation in such a case depend, in turn, on defining sub-areas of potential recreational value in terms of what a group of scientific specialists suggest or, alternatively, in terms of a general rule which states that recreational areas shall be scenic, varied, contain water bodies, have culture history interest and be located near to metropolitan areas. The strength of the Framke study at Århus lies in the fact that a two-pronged research programme was executed which employed a theoretical evaluation of the landscape in the potential park as well as an active investigation and analysis of sample, personal evaluations. The results of the geographers' research could then be combined by the county planners with their conventional inventory of the area's landscape resources and with studies of tourist preferences among existing landscape attractions. The eventual product would be a blending of the actual with the potential to the end that a joint, county park plan could be produced.

The geographers' theoretical evaluation of the Jutland Lake Country utilized eleven site elements for each of the 331 quadrates into which the parkland was divided. The results were statistically analyzed and weighted before being mapped. The resulting maps depicted, for example, the relative relief quotient for each quadrate, the amount of surface irregularity and the amount of forest present. The second part of the study focussed on recreational use of the park and produced a spatial interpretation of the actual recreational patterns in the area. A third analysis which the geographers successfully executed used a verbal technique, the semantic differential, to evaluate sample landscape types from photographs and field observations in terms of factors contributing to scenic composition.[19] For example, a landscape could be evaluated as to whether it was open and friendly or closed and threatening, and numerical values could be set to these judgements. The Århus project in the Jutland Lake Country illustrates the methods which can be used to evaluate, in numerical form, landscapes and landscape components which carry a subjective connotation. If we can tally the contents of recreational landscapes and quantify their attractiveness to the holiday maker, then the planner will be equipped with potent data on which to base forecasts of levels of usage for existing facilities as well as to demonstrate the potential inherent in the undeveloped features of a park area. The end result is that scenic villages, forest glades, castle ruins and old fie d boundaries can receive fair representation in competition with the more usual recreational attractions of lakeshores, hiking trails and hilltop vistas.

Landscape Analysis and Historic Places

I have discussed within the Danish context the use of landscape planning to promote recreational use of rural landscapes containing relics from the past. Now I shall venture a broader approach to the question of landscape analysis techniques as applied to historic places and things. A pioneer statement in this topical area was Fieguth's observations on the authentic past as being a regional resource exploitable for both educational and recreative purposes.[20] As he sees it, Canadian public interest in the national past as a recreational attraction suggested a need to stress authentic historic features, and to promote the integration of natural scenery with meaningful, visible images from the individual and collective past. What may result from such an effort is a head count to assess the popularity of historic sites which are functioning as mass tourism attractions, and the results of such a survey were suggested in Frisbee's 1970 study.[21] The US Bureau of Land Management is well aware of its responsibility toward the care and use of the nearly 500,000 historic sites and features to be found on the lands it administers. The planned development of Bureau lands is supposed to include historic sites which are of popular interest in order that the intent of the Historic Preservation Act of 1966 be implemented.[22]

Landscape analysis on a national basis is well represented by the comprehensive and voluminous study on the physical and cultural resources of Australia published in 1974 in the *Report of the National Estate*.[23] In this ambitious summing up, Australian officialdom has sought to enroll the academic and technical planning resources of the nation in order, firstly, to evaluate the environmental damage to both nature and man's past and, secondly, to recommend future courses of action which will avoid a continuation of the destruction. The components of the National

Estate, including natural features, the built environment, aboriginal sites and historic cultural properties, are to be conserved while, at the same time, they are made available for public use and enjoyment. One suggestion in this study concerns the establishment of a heritage commission which could serve, at district levels, to oversee the opening up of rich and fragile places, such as Ayers Rock, to more intensive but carefully monitored public use.

A number of individual investigators have been seeking to analyze in a quantified way the recreational role which landscape features, as cultural history items, can play. Lindquist has used his experience with fossil remains of Iron Age settlement in Sweden to propose improved methods for the analysis of rural landscapes.[24] He has succeeded in tallying and mapping the visual contents of landscapes, with particular emphasis on features such as vistas and borders between landscape types. In addition, he has combined the advantages of the Swedish data grid with the flexibility of computer mapping in order to carry out research in human perception of landscape qualities and site accessibility which has provided quantitative and visual assessments of potential recreational complexes.[25] The question of what people really think about historic landscapes is extremely important to the park planner, and a start has been made on this topic by investigators working along a broad front. Prominent among these is D. W. Meinig who suggests that we must be aware that our perceptions of landscape involve impressions of its dimensions of nature, habitat, artifact content, ideology and history, place and aesthetics.[26] These perceptual qualities, singly or in concert, shape our impressions, sharpen or distort them, and, in the end, direct us to prefer one combination of features over another. Normally we are content to use attendance figures as the basis for budgetary planning of facilities and staff necessary for the management of a given historic attraction or park. If, however, we could quantify the public's impressions of an old field system, a battlefield site or an historic house, then our planning data and related budgetary negotiations could become more reflective of the true attraction value of a landscape and its legitimate claim upon scarce administrative resources.

My own experience in studying opinions regarding the attractions of the past concerned the rural environment in Jutland, Denmark. Here, in the course of a departmental research project for the local municipality, we sought viewpoints regarding the attractions of historic houses and the positive qualities of Danish village life among a sample of 1,400 inhabitants from 105 rural communities[27]

(Fig. 39). The results of this portion of our study indicated, as we had been led to expect, that a majority of people liked old, half-timbered houses as a landscape amenity at the same time that they expressed a preference to continue living in the particular type of housing they presently occupied, be that modern single-family home or thatched farm cottage. Secondly, the commonly accepted milieu enrichment features present in the traditional Danish village and its society were rated highly even as this way of life was presently on the rapid decline. Within an urban context, a similar type of study was carried out by geographers at McMaster University in Canada when they investigated the feelings which urban dwellers hold about old landscapes and visible relics of the past.[28] In the Toronto study over 1,200 urban inhabitants were asked to indicate their attitudes and preferences on a written questionnaire. The results revealed a general interest in the topic of old landscapes and an appreciation of them as constituting a part of one's cultural heritage. The more highly educated people had a greater appreciation of the past, but those from the lower socio-economic grouping, if they were long-term residents in an historic part of the city, also highly valued this element of their environment. The exciting prospects for preservational planning presented by the Canadian and Danish work suggest that additional studies along similar lines should be undertaken in other countries.

If attitudes about the visible past and its potential for recreational development are difficult to discover among the population at large, the opinions on the same topics held by preservationists and environmental planners are equally varied and difficult to isolate and measure. Travis defined a few characteristics of regional attitudes about the preserved past in the United States in a study which analyzed the National Register of Historic Places in terms of these particular variables.[29] In looking at regional concentrations of types of sites, he was able to identify a block of states in the northeastern US plus South Carolina, Texas and California, all of which shared a propensity for urban sites with an emphasis upon historic buildings, private ownership of the features and public accessibility. By contrast, in the southeastern and northwestern states the historic sites most frequently represented military events, were federally owned and accessible to the public. This use of a general data source such as the National Registry provides the preservation planner with a tool for keeping track of trends in site registration and for gaining insights necessary for the establishment of a regional balance in the types and numbers of preserved places and things to the benefit of the nation as a whole and its vacationing public.

Preservation of What, For Whom and Why

Given our basic solicitude for the visible past, guided by our efforts to produce accurate and comprehensive field inventories and using landscape analysis to improve our planning studies for the benefit of a leisured public, we are, however, faced with a number of fundamental questions concerning historic preservation and the planned recreational use of the past. These basic questions addressed to the preservation endeavour and the uses to which the results may be put are summarized in Table 17.[30] The seven, salient queries which have been raised are listed along with the extreme range of opinion or of solution which they evoke. As I hope to have demonstrated, historic preservation and the recreational use of the past encompass a great

Table 17 QUESTIONS ABOUT HISTORIC PRESERVATION: THE RANGE OF OPINION ON ASSUMPTIONS, GOALS AND METHODS

---

1 *Preservation of what?*
Types of landscape: Original natural or cultural examples or completely artificial, man-made scenes
Landscape form and function: Original form and function or preserve original form and accommodated new functions
How much to preserve: All relic features, only a representative sample or the best examples alone

2 *Preservation from what?*
Protect original environment from any further environmental impacts or only from incompatable or destructive land uses
Avoid both misguided preservation as a static museum and overly energetic reconstructions or theme parks

3 *Preservation for what purpose?*
To promote research and education or commercialized recreation

4 *Preservation for whom?*
The appreciative few or designed for mass appeal
To fulfil elitist values or to promote welfare of inner city minorities and Third World peoples

5 *Preservation by whom?*
Local groups using local ordinances versus centralized master plans guided by comprehensive legislation

6 *Preservation financed with whose money?*
Taxes, grants and private donors derived from the local level versus State and International funds and large foundations, all remote from the actual working level

7 *Preservation for how long?*
Stop-gap, emergency efforts designed to arrest imminent destruction or protection of national treasures for all time

---

Source: See Note 30 to this Chapter.

deal of variety and pose a broad spectrum of planning problems for which no single solution is sufficient. At this point it seems more profitable to search for guidance among varied generalizations than to pursue the myriad details characteristic of hundreds of individual case studies.

In addressing the question of what to preserve, three key issues arise. To start with a viewing of the entire landscape, involves asking whether we are interested solely in the untouched natural scene and the arcadian rural landscape or whether we have time to spare for the historic nuggets concealed in the technological landscape of the modern city (Figs. 14 and 23). A corollary to this is the proposition that we preserve the landscape in terms of both its original forms and functions. Such an approach would suggest that farmers continue to plough with oxen and dwell in thatched cottages. The opposite extreme, and a point of view more widely accepted today, is that our efforts are better served when we seek to preserve the original form but adapt it so that other and newer functions can be accommodated within these old fabrics.[31] The establishment of preservational priorities is further tested whenever we approach the thorny question of whether to seek to retain the total population of relic features or, perhaps more realistically, all examples of a certain type of feature. Standing opposite to this extreme view in our table is the proposition which says that moderation is preferable, and that only the best examples of a class or type of feature need rescue and careful handling. By example, present day Denmark bears the remains of nearly 70,000 earthen burial mounds which date from Bronze Age to Viking times. From this vast population only 20,000 have been scheduled, and a significant number of those have been badly used by time and man. It would seem that the Danes are so well supplied in this category of antiquities that a few examples sacrificed to road building, urban expansion or agricultural improvements would not be a national tragedy. The problem is, however, that the significance, contents and state of repair of the scheduled barrows are not fully known, and the consequence is that the decisions which will allow one example to disappear here so that two may remain untouched elsewhere is at best a chancy and subjective determination. A similar situation occurs in Britain with her thousands of deserted village sites, moated settlement remains or abandoned old farmsteads. The safest and most prudent course of action seems to be to attempt preservation of all known examples against the day when research can provide necessary data for quali-fied decisions to be made about their preservational and historic value. In the meantime, each suggested destruction of a barrow or moated site is met with resistance as the best delaying tactic in the struggle to retain as much as possible of the past for use in the future.

Turning next to the dangers faced by the unprotected past, the question arises as to what we are trying to guard against. Two varieties of threat exist, the one stemming from external forces which impinge on old remains and the other originating with the type of use to which the features are put (see Figs. 4 and 5). Absolute protection within a figurative glass case would preserve a building or field pattern from any intrusive environmental impacts excepting those originating in cataclysms of nature or man. In direct contrast, insensitive development may so alter the feature and its environs or be completely overwhelming so that only a shell remains which is of little interest to the historical planner or the holidaymaker. To take the English Fens as an example, a nature preserve which encompasses one of the last remaining areas of true fenland must by definition exclude all other activities and most of the public. Other fenland remnants detectable among contemporary farmlands and settlements reveal their landscape history to trained eyes alone, and even their most basic preservation is difficult to achieve. The internal threats result from the type of protective scheme which is adopted for a particular feature or landscape, as they are represented, on the one hand, by the dull, static house museum approach, and, on the other, by an all too energetic theme park exploitation. In both cases the physical fabric of a building or the atmosphere of an historic precinct will be weighed down by either too much or too little silence. A museum of rural life will fulfil its functions and be much more attractive if demonstrations of smithing or weaving accompany the static displays of the tools and equipment which those trades have traditionally used. By contrast, a popular battlefield site may be improved as a tourist attraction if fewer concessions offering swings and roundabouts, meat pies or souvenirs are licensed. Extremes of either overdevelopment or underdevelopment of historic relics deter potential visitors and reduce the chances that the messages from the past will get through to our overworked modern ears.

If we can surmount the difficulties associated with deciding what to preserve and how best to husband them, then a fundamental question presents itself, namely, preservation for what purpose? The range of potential customers is varied for an attractive and historically significant rural landscape as well as for a clean and historic urban district. On the one hand, enclosing a piece of medieval forest will best serve the interests of the research worker and the graduate field class in botany. By contrast, a Danish nature park is supposed to be designed so that resident farmers may pursue their daily rounds undisturbed by families on a picnic outing or by solitary landscape painters or bird watchers. The multiple-use approach to the leisure time enjoyment of rural or urban historic preserves is logically the ideal, but inhibiting conflicts of interests may easily arise. An example of such a conflict is illustrated by our proposal in Chapter 9 that the Los Angeles Memorial Cemetery might equally well accommodate the honoured dead and energetic youngsters on a school outing. If it is not difficult for the student interested in landscape history to steer a path between the Wicken Fen Reserve type of use and the Old New Orleans recreation at Disneyland, the preservation planner and the recreation developer must maintain a broader view since their task is to build and maintain facilities which depend on visible history to fulfil public demands for information and entertainment (Fig. 3).

Preservation for whom is a matter of considerable debate among preservationists who have begun to concern themselves with old buildings in the city core area. Traditionally the contest for allegiances has been between the museum-supporters and old house enthusiasts, on the one hand, and those wishing to convert the western ghost town into a public park and the outdoor museum of fine old houses into a multiple-use recreation complex. Relatively recently this question has been introduced into the urban socio-economic battle lines when it became apparent that the preservation of a cluster of fine Victorian houses in a given city centre would result in the displacement of the current black tenants and their replacement by well-to-do young professionals, few of whom are black. Some critics are of the opinion that funds spent on preservation programmes could be better used in rejuvenating downtown for the present disadvantaged population. The confrontation between supposedly élitist values represented by a white, middle-class outlook and those of greatly contrasting inner city minorities indicates that ethnic-based polarization in the city is now able to frustrate and financially penalize preservational efforts which many have assumed to be altruistic and non-political.

A lively indication of the complexities inherent in such an ethnic-based conflict over a preservation project is illustrated by the attempts to develop the historic city Plaza in Los Angeles, California (Fig. 17). Here the Spanish and Mexican traditions are physically most evident, but today the Hispanic community is divided within itself over the degree of aggressiveness which it should adopt in its attempts to promote a more representative picture of the Hispanic contribution to historic Los Angeles. Two nearby communities, the Chinese and Japanese, also have a commercial and historic interest in the development of the Plaza historic district. Added to these complexities is the conflict between the city and the state over management of the park, traditional differences which are now complicated by the several racial interests which impinge upon the proposals for the development and financing of this historic relic area in the midst of a vast and varied urban community. Even Third World politics may enter the historic preservation arena. A ruin which appears worthy of restoration to Western eyes may demand investment of national funds which the local government feels would be better spent on programmes to improve agriculture or village water supplies. Suakin, a romantic ruined city on the Sudanese Red Sea coast, might seem to the American to be a splendid candidate for restoration and development into an historic theme park. To the Sudanese national, however, programmes for improving housing for the present population of this old seaport and for developing local industries must receive a higher priority, and even if foreign investment funds were available for the construction of an historic preserve at Suakin, they would not be able to underwrite the improvements in local infrastructure which are so much more pressing.

Preservation by whom is a question of operational tactics which assumes unexpected importance by reason of state law and administration having become so closely involved in these undertakings. Traditionally, the campaigns to save old houses and to establish local historical museums have been initiated by local people interested in pursuing such time-consuming and marginally popular ventures. As indicated in Chapter 4, with the entry of state and local governments into the preservation business and with the impact of their great resources of law and money, the use of centralized master plans and of comprehensive programmes of preservational legislation has fundamentally altered the working environment for those interested in the visible past (Fig. 18). In terms of the seven questions posed in Table 17 and taking just the existing programmes in Britain, Denmark and the United States, there has developed an unexpectedly good balance because, although the impetus derives from legislation and funds made available by national or county authorities, the actual preservation efforts are carried out largely by interested and involved local people.

Who pays for the preservation effort is also an increasingly important and worrisome question to be faced (Fig. 32). If, in the past, private fund-raising, donations and grants have been sufficient to fill the preservational coffers, today state financial resources dominate the field. With this new prosperity have come all the headaches associated with bureaucratic accountability and the accompanying multiplication of professional consultants who are skilled in the writing of grant applications. If yesterday the Rockefeller financial resources were responsible for the reconstruction of Williamsburgh, Virginia, today it is the rate-payer who contributes to rehabilitation programmes within historic urban districts or to studies concerned with the preservation of rural landscapes. If more financial resources are available now for preserving the past and developing it for contemporary use, the negative consequences result from the very fact that tax money is employed in these pursuits and that people who oppose these debatable investments will attack the programmes at planning commission hearings. As a consequence, advocacy skills must be cultivated by the preservationist who seeks to campaign under law for the public funds and, in some cases, tax-relief private donations essential for programmes to be realized.

Preservation for how long is a question to which we seldom address ourselves, believing that if something is worth saving, then it clearly must be considered as being an enduring feature. Alert preservationists use stop-gap efforts to prevent imminent destruction and call upon emergency legislative action or the press in order to promote rescue digs on construction sites or to stop the destruction of a house. Their aim is to gain time so that a professional decision can be made either for preservation, re-location or a quick study and destruction. Preservation for ever, by contrast, has a noble ring about it, but is it a feasible proposal even for the national heritage? The British National Trust policy which requires funds for site maintenance to accompany the transfer of a property is a sound method of assuring preservation for the foreseeable future. But even with such foresight, is it ever possible for a national shrine such as Blenheim Palace to be allowed to tumble down into a neglected ruin, to become a latter day Angkor Wat for which preservation funds simply do not exist either in the host country or within the international community. Such things have occurred and still do take place.

Stop-gap preservation in the form of a staying order from the courts to prevent physical destruction and an accompanying appeal to the public for funds sufficient to assure a future for the threatened structure are familiar enough tactics. The idea in this approach is to make people and government bodies pause long enough to consider the historical merits of a site and for preservation funds or feasible proposals for resiting or alternative use to be developed. A good deal of the legal machinery in preservation law is designed to provide early warnings of potential damage or destruction to historic features and to suggest legislative alternatives to enforce a delay.

At the other end of the time-scale of preservation action the issues are much less clearly defined, the subject has been less thoroughly debated and the methods for achieving long-term preservation are less well developed. Even when we speak of our national heritages as being held in perpetuity, changes in public taste and in official history may promote destruction and consign to the historical dustbin a grave marker, a battlefield site or an entire landscape (Fig. 4). Counteracting this pragmatic treatment of the collective past is the grand conviction that the past matters both to the changeable present and to the unknown future. Site destruction is a serious step because it obliterates the genuine artifact and any later reconstruction or replacement is apt to be very costly and not very satisfactory. It has been estimated that to rebuild a single Danish Bronze Age barrow, for example one as famous as the burial mound where the oak casket of the Egtved Maiden was found in 1921, would have cost in 1974 about £170,000 or $350,000.[32] In our role as custodians of our collective past, we are obliged to finance its preservation and to administer responsibly this patrimony which we hold in trust for the future.

Public and Private Interests in Planning the Past

Convinced that our landscape patrimony is not passé, and certain that the rediscovery of our collective past should proceed hand in hand with the planning of our future, we must, nevertheless, admit that public and private interests involved in these undertakings are not always unanimous about either goals or means. Now adversaries, now allies, the line-up between the two groups shifts with the issue at hand and is modified by the specifics of each preservation challenge. A celebrated example of this situation occurred in June 1978 when the Supreme Court of the United States, in an important ruling, voted six to three that the landmarks preservation law of New York City was indeed constitutional.[33] This ruling meant that Penn Central Transportation Company, which owned a piece of land in central New York and the splendid Grand Central Terminal located upon it, could not carry out its plan to erect a 53-storey office building on this site. The railway company had sought to dispose of the air rights or vertical space above the sixty-year old terminal building so as to preserve it, a decision reached after acrimonious protest against the company's original plan to demolish part of it, while also realizing a needed economic benefit from this corporate land holding. The terminal still serves its original function as a railway passenger station for commuters to New York although at a reduced level of use, but its architectural merits are undiminished by either age or the encroaching steel and glass boxes which have come to dominate New York's skyline. Ten years of legal combat ensued between the private railway company, which badly needed fiscal rejuvenation, and an effective group of private individuals who were dedicated to conserving the best of the past while trying to make it a part of a better urban future. The public agencies in the city of New York and the courts provided the legal apparatus whereby an alternative to unsuitable redevelopment eventually won the day. In a concentrated form this is an example of the interplay between those who would keep the past and make it usable and those who would replace the past with alternative structures. In addition, the Grand Central Terminal case pitted private interests against each other, and the public or state sector was not, at least from the preservationist's point of view, playing the usual role of insensitive bureaucratic steamroller.

The usual confrontation of opposed interests occurs when either a private or state developer, working within the zoning laws and according to the guidelines of responsible economics, proposes to demolish a building or obliterate a rural landscape in order to carry out needed urban renewal or industrial expansion. Opposed to such a programme will be a veritable flock of private individuals and organizations which advocate retention of old buildings or rural landscapes with subsequent restoration, preservation, rehabilitation or recycling into alternative but conformable uses. A more complex situation arises when an outdoor museum of historic buildings is to be assembled at public expense and conflicts arise over which buildings are to be included and just how much popular entertainment needs to be provided.[34] The subjective balance of facility design and the competition of public parks with private entertainments are but two of the polarizing features involved in this type of debate. Lastly, a privately owned theme park which specializes in reconstructions of historic buildings or milieus may seek planning permission to demolish genuine historical features in order to accommodate its expansion. Here too the use of the past is being viewed from completely opposite points of view.

Such examples help us to visualize the varieties of conflict which may occur and the shifts in allegiances which may result. Table 18 is designed to clarify positive and negative aspects of public and private interests in preservation and thereby to contribute a measure of understanding about this tangled skein of planning and politics relating to the preserved past. Among the positive elements

Table 18   CONTRASTS BETWEEN PUBLIC AND PRIVATE INTERESTS IN PLANNING THE PAST

PUBLIC INTERESTS	PRIVATE INTERESTS
Positive aspects	
a continuity factor in the form of the professional civil servant	concerned citizens expressing their proprietary sentiments regarding historical relics
equipped with the legal powers to block destruction or to support preservation	experts in local history and museum operations and in playing the role of enlightened lay people
dispensers of public monies designated for preservation support	users of the preserved past whose patronage is essential
	the commercial firms involved in theme-park uses of the past
a force expressing the interests of the public at large	voters effective in mounting pressure campaigns in support of preservation actions or to raise funds
the opponents of special pleading	
Negative aspects	
sensitive and susceptible to political pressures originating from office holders or from public or private special interest groups	special interest pleaders
insensitive to needs and programmes which are out of the ordinary or which are not broadly popular with the public at large	not able to reflect all the public viewpoints or even a balanced scan of them
conservative about break-through approaches and about complex planning issues relating to urban or natural environments	characterized by group memberships which are volatile and shifting in numbers, which in fact makes a continuity of viewpoint difficult to establish or maintain

Source: the author.

which are present, that with the greatest importance is the subjective viewpoint regarding the past which is expressed by a public agency, an organization or a private citizen. In situations dealing with planned use of the past the individual or private interest is able to assume a more flexible stance than can a bureau or agency. On the other hand, a continuity of outlook and a steadfastness of purpose may characterize a public body, and most people would agree that it is well suited to the exercise of the legal powers which shape our collective dealings with the past. In these days of massive taxation and state-sponsored finance, official bodies are the providers and private citizens are the users of the buildings and activities located within historic districts or outdoor museums. Lastly, if private groups are more effective in expressing their varied opinions through the medium of the lobbyist, then it is the state or local agency which supports the general public interest through resistance to special pleading.

Turning next to the negative aspects of public versus private interests, we reverse the previous statement in noting the susceptibility of public agencies to political pressures designed to influence and shape their decisions and their functions. The special interest pleaders from the preservationist's lobby are, of course, one such group which attempts to subvert the dispassionate posture of politicians, bureau chiefs and department heads. Even if lamentable, the skilful use of pressure and influence is a recognized mode of behaviour in public policy making, and its presence seems to be an entirely natural characteristic of this human endeavour. The contrasting degrees of sensitivity to minority viewpoints, expressed currently in the volatile issue of central city minority population displacement for the furtherance of renewal projects, marks the negative side of the equation for both public and private interests. Lastly, if private groups are quick to seize upon innovative measures and public agencies are conservative by nature and design, the general lack of enthusiasm for complex plans which seek to combine the living past with the developing present results from tendencies toward conservatism on the public side and a degree of volatility on the private.

Current attempts designed to weld together public resources and an enlightened preservational outlook with the flexibility and individual scale of private viewpoints have produced a mixed bag of failures, half-successes and hope-filled beginnings. Among the failures we would have to include the Rochester House in Los Angeles (Fig. 11). Caught in the twilight zone of public and private efforts toward relocation and restoration, its future is held up by planning indecision and fiscal embarrassment. The half-successes might include a warming enthusiasm and a growing positive conviction within both the public and private sectors regarding the financial benefits which may be derived from the sound economic practice of historic preservation.[35] Opinion can be backed up with economic facts in order to convince many that imaginative utilization of old buildings within the city will create jobs at less cost than that demanded by demolition and new construction. In addition, preservation can be demonstrated to be energy saving and to have a beneficial impact upon local economies which are in need of stimulation. Although the figures and charts may convince us, a hard-headed case-by-case examination of each proposal is necessary to assure an eventual victory for preservation as a sound business practice. To achieve such a victory will require persistent effort from lay enthusiasts and civil servant planners alike before any general celebration can take place.

The launching of hope-filled beginnings on the part of public and private interests involved in the planned use of the past is best illustrated by the educational efforts which have been undertaken. The general public is, first of all, well served by an inventory of the past as it is recognizable upon the present surface of the globe or even within the confines of say a single Canadian province; let the public become aware of the treasures which it has inherited.[36] Guidebooks, financed by public funds and written by lay experts, show how to set the inventory into an historic regional perspective and provide a manual of how-to-do-it which will be useful to both local planning agencies and individuals or groups interested in preservation.[37] Such public education, undertaken as a combined operation by public and private interests, reaches down to the level of so-called bricks and mortar preservation and is illustrated by a fine publication, *Rehab Right*, which contains clear instructions for interested homeowners in both the affluent suburbs and the decayed urban core of Oakland, California.[38] Central city minorities are here invited to participate in the profitable hobby of home improvement as an effective type of historic preservation. Last and most hopeful is the introduction of preservation planning into education. Adult training in the form of national and regional meetings of preservationists serves to spread the word, disseminate references and establish contacts. Only now, in the United States at least, are training courses and workshops being offered to people of all ages who are interested in becoming knowledgeable and more effective in the preservation field.[39] Academic courses in the schools are not yet numerous, but the introduction of instructional packages dealing with historic preservation is becoming popular as a form of curriculum enrichment. British developments which are described in the pages of the monthly *BEE* are notable examples of this trend.[40] Regardless of the frustrations which characterize work with the planned preservation of the past and the budgetary uncertainties which plague the design and administration of programmes to promote its adoption, the overall effort is essential and worthwhile for both public and private agencies and individuals. Recreation, instruction and inspiration may be derived from well conceived and financed rural outdoor museums, working industrial museums and urban history trails.[41]

The Outlook

At present, the outlook for both historic preservation and recreational use of the past is for more intensive development which will cost more money and be controlled by more laws. The current public expressions of concern over the careless handling of our visible past mirror the well founded and well argued opinions of experienced preservationists. An identifiable programme is underway to increase public awareness of the nature and scale of the preservation challenge, and the impact of this expressed concern is greater since it can now command supportive legislation and mandatory funds. The goal is to produce an effective early-warning system which will first identify unrecognized historic features and then stimulate demand for the commitment of the resources necessary to carry out the inventories and any eventual physical restoration. The search goes on for more effective inventory techniques, for better ways of organizing local support for legislation and for assuring in general that long-term maintenance programmes for relic features are set up and funded.[42]

The other half of the equation, that which deals with the leisure time pursuits of affluent populations, is beginning to concentrate upon tempering this pursuit with environmentally responsible attitudes and practices. Some statements suggest that recreational pursuits can be made attractive learning experiences wherein the individual's rural roots, an ethnic group's achievements, or patriotic pride can be strengthened by a closer acquaintance with the historic processes which have shaped the land. Meanwhile, the recreation industry continues to expand energetically. The balancing trick for

the preservationist is to make certain that sufficient historical material, along with its supportive artifact scenery, is present so that
recreation has the potential to become a learning experience as well
as being a diversionary one. In order to advance this goal, the
student of the past seeks to develop a greater public awareness of
and an appreciation for visible history as well as a dedication to its
continuing preservation.

Throughout this book the positive side of the worth of the past to
contemporaries in their work and play is emphasized. In addition,
there is an abiding feeling of optimism regarding the feasibility of
preserving the past for present and future energetic, leisure-time
use. Our visible past is like a fire which was lit aeons ago, and if we
tend it carefully its flames will illuminate our pleasure and the
images in its coals will touch our imagination and our hearts.

Notes and References

Chapter 1 *The visible past*

1 National Geographic Society, *Visiting Our Past: America's History-lands* (Washington, DC, 1977).
2 A series of these were republished in A. R. H. Baker and J. B. Harley (eds), *Man Made the Land. Essays in English Historical Geography* (Newton Abbot, 1973).
3 *Los Angeles Times*, 29 March 1978; and 5 April 1978.
4 Nan Fairbrother, *New Lives, New Landscapes* (London, 1970; and Harmondsworth, Middx, 1972).
5 F. Sorlin, P. Gazzola and R. Lemaire, 'Rescue operation: the face of Europe', *Council of Europe, Committee on Monuments and Sites, Study Series*, No. 1 (Strasbourg, 1973).
6 Council of Europe, Committee on Monuments and Sites, *European Programme of Pilot Projects*, Part II, 'The national projects' (Strasbourg, 1973).
7 H. C. Darby, *Domesday England* (Cambridge, 1977); and H. C. Darby (ed), *A New Historical Geography of England* (Cambridge, 1973).
8 W. G. Hoskins, *English Landscapes* (London, 1973); and British Broadcasting Corporation, 'The making of the English landscape', Film. Producer Peter Jones (first transmitted in 1972); and *The Making of the English Landscape* (London, 1955).
9 Christopher Taylor, *The Cambridgeshire Landscape* (London, 1973); and Frank Emery, *The Oxfordshire Landscape* (London, 1974). Both in the 'Making of the English Landscape Series'.
10 Michael Aston and Trevor Rowley, *Landscape Archaeology. An Introduction to Fieldwork Techniques on Post-Roman Landscapes* (Newton Abbot, 1977).
11 Alan Rogers and Trevor Rowley (eds), *Landscapes and Documents* (London, 1974).
12 B. K. Roberts, *Rural Settlement in Britain* (Folkestone, 1977); and Christopher Taylor, *Fields in the English Landscape* (London, 1975).
13 See note 7; and Michael Aston and James Bond, *The Landscape of Towns* (London, 1976).
14 M. W. Barley (ed), 'The plans and topography of Medieval towns in England and Wales', *Council for British Archaeology, Research Report*, No. 14 (1976).
15 Peter Laslett, *The World We Have Lost* (London, 2nd ed, 1971); and Raymond Williams, *The Country and the City* (London, 1975).

234

16 A. R. H. Baker, 'Today's studies of yesterday's geographies', *Geographical Magazine*, 43 (1970–1), 452–3.

17 The National Trust for Historic Preservation in the United States, 'A place in time', Film (1977), made by John Karol and National Trust Education Services Division.

18 L. R. Ford, 'Historic preservation and the stream of time: the role of the geographer', *Historical Geography Newsletter*, 5, No. 1 (Spring 1975), 1–15.

19 Hugh Prince, 'Preservation, restoration and revival of the past in English landscape', unpublished lecture (Spring 1973).

20 R. M. Newcomb, 'Geographic aspects of the planned preservation of visible history in Denmark', *Annals, Association of American Geographers*, 57, No. 3 (1967), 462–80.

21 *The California Land; Planning for People. Report of the California Land-Use Task Force* (Los Angeles, 1975).

22 State of California, Office of Planning and Research, *Historic Preservation Element Guidelines* (Sacramento, 1976).

23 State of California, Department of Parks and Recreation. The Resources Agency, *California Inventory of Historic Resources* (Sacramento, 1976).

24 Grady Gammage, Jr., P. N. Jones and S. L. Jones, *Historic Preservation in California. A Legal Handbook* (Stanford, Calif., 1975).

25 W. T. Alderson and S. P. Low, *Interpretation of Historic Sites* (Nashville, Tenn., 1976).

26 California, Sonoma County Planning Department, *Historic Preservation Program. Sonoma County General Plan Technical Report* (Santa Rosa, Calif., 1976).

27 Millicent Hall, 'Theme parks: around the world in eighty minutes', *Landscape*, 21, No. 1 (Autumn 1976), 3–8; and J. C. Starbuck, 'Theme parks: a partially annotated bibliography of articles about modern amusement parks', *Council of Planning Librarians, Exchange Bibliography* No. 953 (1976).

28 Roy Christian, *Vanishing Britain* (Newton Abbot, 1977); and Ray Taylor, Margaret Cox and Ian Dickins (eds), *Britain's Planning Heritage* (London, 1975).

29 J. A. Patmore, *Land and Leisure in England and Wales* (Harmondsworth, Middx., 1972).

30 Karl Meyer, *The Plundered Past* (London, 1973).

31 P. A. Rahtz (ed), *Rescue Archaeology* (Harmondsworth, Middx., 1974).

32 Wayland Kennet, *Preservation* (London, 1972); Trevor Rowley and Mike Breakell (eds), *Planning and the Historic Environment* (Oxford, 1975), and see note 29.

33 R. W. Travis and J. A. Jakle, *Preserving Past Landscapes. Historic Preservation as Environmental Management* (Stroudsburg, Pa., in press); and Ann Falkner, *Without Our Past? A Handbook for the Preservation of Canada's Architectural Heritage* (Toronto, 1977).

34 Veit Koester (ed), *Bygningsbevaring. Vejviser i lovgivning, myndigheder, institutioner, foreninger, fonde og legater* (København, 1975).

Chapter 2   *Present recreational usage of the past*

1   W. T. Alderson and S. P. Low, *Interpretation of Historic Sites* (Nashville, Tenn., 1976).
2   Millicent Hall, 'Theme parks: around the world in eighty minutes', *Landscape*, vol. 21, no. 1 (1976).
3   J. C. Starbuck, 'Theme parks: a partially annotated bibliography of articles about modern amusement parks', *Council of Planning Librarians, Exchange Bibliography*, 953 (January 1976).
4   Freeman Tilden, *Interpreting Our Heritage. Principles and Practices for Visitor Services in Parks, Museums and Historic Places* (Chapel Hill, North Carolina, 1957).
5   Peter Michelsen, *Museerne og samtiden* (København, 1972).
6   *Aarhuus Stiftstidende*, (1 July, 1976), p. 19.
7   Kenneth Hudson and Ann Nicholls, *The Directory of Museums* (London, 1975).
8   Peter Michelsen, *Frilands Museet. The Danish Village Museum of Sorgenfri* (København, 1973).
9   Bo Bramsen, *The Old Town in Århus. The History of the Old Town Museum in Århus* (Århus, 1971).
10   Kenneth Hudson and Ann Nicholls, *The Directory of Museums* (London, 1975).
11   *ibid.*
12   *Los Angeles Times* (29 February, 1976), sect. VIII, p. 14.

Chapter 3   *The inventory and resource assessment*

1   Don Benson, 'A Museum, Oxfordshire', in Elizabeth Fowler, (ed), *Field Survey in British Archaeology* (London, 1972), pp. 16–22.
2   J. B. Harley, *Ordnance Survey Maps: A Descriptive Manual* (Southampton, 1975).
3   Ole Klindt-Jensen, *A History of Scandinavian Archaeology* (London, 1975).
4   *National Register of Historic Places* (Washington, DC, 1972 and 1976 2 vols.)
5   Department of the Environment, *List of Ancient Monuments: England* (London, 1974); Robin Fedden, *The National Trust. Past and Present* (London, rev. edn., 1974).
6   Rescue and Council for British Archaeology, *Archaeology and Government. A Plan for Archaeology in Britain* (Worcester and London, 1974).
7   P. H. Sørensen, 'Jysk oldtidsagerbrug – lokaliseret efter luftfotografier', *Kulturgeografi*, 120, 24 årg., no. 2 (1972–3), 337–354.
8   Kenneth Hudson, *A guide to the Industrial Archaeology of Europe* (Bath, 1971).
9   John Cornforth, *Country Houses in Britain: Can They Survive?* (London, 1974).
10   R. A. Buchanan, *Industrial Archaeology in Britain* (Harmondsworth, Middx., 1974); Arthur Raistrick, *Industrial Archaeology. An Historical Survey* (St Albans, 1973); Hugh Bodey, *Discovering Industrial*

Archaeology and History (Princes Risborough, 1975); see also chapter 8 of this book.

11   R. A. Buchanan, *Industrial Archaeology in Britain* (Harmondsworth, Middx., 1974).

12   State of California, Department of Parks and Recreation. *California Inventory of Historic Resources* (Sacramento, 1976).

13   R. M. Newcomb, 'The Århus, Denmark Village Project: applied geography in the service of the municipality', *Geographical Review*, 67, no. 1 (1977), 86–92.

14   Vivien Russell, *West Penwith Survey* (Truro, 1971).

15   John Bradford, *Ancient Landscapes, Studies in Field Archaeology* (London, 1957); M. W. Beresford and J. K. S. St Joseph, *Medieval England: An Aerial Survey* (Cambridge, 1958); D. R. Wilson (ed), 'Aerial Reconnaissance for Archaeology', *Council for British Archaeology, Research Report*, no. 12 (1975).

16   A. E. Puckett, 'Comments on the earth resources sensing and data acquisition program', in US House of Representatives, Committee on Science and Astronautics, *Remote Sensing of Earth Resources* (Washington, DC, 1972), 25–41.

17   N. M. Short, P. W. Lowman, Jr., S. C. Freden and W. A. Finch, Jr., *Mission to Earth: LANDSAT Views of the World* (Washington, DC, 1976).

18   Ralph Bernstein and G. C. Stierhoff, 'Precision processing of earth image data', *American Scientist*, vol. 64, no. 5 (1976), 500–8.

19   R. M. Newcomb, 'An example of the applicability of remote sensing: historical geography', *Geoforum* 2 (1970), 89–92.

20   David and Ruth Whitehouse, *Archaeological Atlas of the World* (San Francisco, 1975), which lists nearly 5,000 sites; Nick and Helna Mika, *Historic Sites of Ontario* (Belleville, Ont., 1974), which includes over 700 sites.

Chapter 4   *The law and the visible past*

1   Viggo Nielsen, 'Status for den Antikvariske Lovgivning', *Fortid og Nutid,* Bind XXIV, Hæfte 5 (1971), 475–98.

2   Grady Gammage, Jr., P. N. Jones and S. L. Jones, *Historic Preservation in California. A Legal Handbook* (Stanford, Calif., 1975).

3   *Preservation News,* XVI, no. 5 (1976), 8.

4   National Park Service, US Department of the Interior, 'The National Register', (Washington, DC, 1975), pamphlet.

5   National Trust for Historic Preservation, compiled by E. L. Kettler and B. D. Reams, Jr., *Historic Preservation Law: An Annotated Bibliography* (Washington, DC, 1976).

6   Robert W. Burchell and David Listokin, *The Environmental Impact Handbook* (New Brunswick, N.J., 1975).

7   R. M. Newcomb, 'Has the past a future in Denmark? The preservation of landscape history within the nature park', *Geoforum,* 9 (1972), 61–7.

8   Danmark, Miljøstyrelsen, *Miljøreformen og Borgerne* (København, 1974).

9   R. Taylor, M. Cox and I. Dickins (eds), *Britain's Planning Heritage*
    (London, 1975); Rescue and The Council for British Archaeology,
    Archaeology and Government. A Plan for Archaeology in Britain
    (Worcester and London, 1974).

10 *Report of the Committee of Enquiry into the Arrangements for The
    Protection of Field Monuments 1966—68*, Sir David Walsh, Chairman
    (London, 1969).

11 Royal Commission on Historical Monuments (England), *A Matter of
    Time. An archaeological survey of the river gravels of England* (Lon-
    don, 1960).

12 R. W. Travis and J. A. Jakle, *Preserving Past Landscapes: Historic
    Preservation as Environmental Management* (Stroudsburg, 1978).

13 J. J. Costonis, *Space Adrift. Landmark Preservation and the Market
    place* (Urbana, Ill., 1974).

14 Central Solano County Cultural Heritage Commission, *Our Lasting
    Heritage. An Historic and Archaeological Preservation Plan for Central
    Solano County* (Suisun City, Calif., 1977).

Chapter 5   *New trends in recreational uses of the past*

1   I. G. Simmons, *Rural Recreation in the Industrial World* (London and
    New York, 1975).

2   Isobel Cosgrove and Richard Jackson, *The Geography of Recreation
    and Leisure* (London, 1972). Especially Chapter 1.

3   J. T. Coppock and B. S. Duffield, *Recreation in the Countryside. A
    Spatial Analysis* (London, 1975); Patrick Lavery, *Recreational Geo-
    graphy. Problems in Modern Geography* (Newton Abbot, 1971).

4   Nan Fairbrother, *New Lives, New Landscapes* (Harmondsworth,
    Middx., 1972).

5   J. A. Patmore, *Land and Leisure* (Newton Abbot, 1970 and Har-
    mondsworth, Middx., 1972).

6   W. T. Alderson and S. P. Low, *Interpretation of Historic Sites* (Nash-
    ville, Tenn., 1976).

7   Art Seidenbaum, 'Angel's Flight waits for an angel', *Los Angeles
    Times*, 24 January 1977.

8   R. M. Newcomb, 'The Århus, Denmark village project: applied geo-
    graphy in the service of the municipality', *Geographical Review*, 67,
    no. 1 (1977), 86–92.

9   W. G. V. Balchin, *Cornwall* (London, 1954); Roy Millward and
    Adrian Robinson, *The South West Peninsula* (London, 1971).

10 E. C. Axford, *The Cornish Moor. A Brief Study of Bodmin Moor* (St.
    Neot, 1972 and Newton Abbot, 1975).

11 Cornwall Archaeological Society, *Newsletter,* 21 (May 1976), 5; and
    no. 24 (June 1977), pp. 4 and 5.

12 Glyn Daniel, 'Editorial', *Antiquity*, XLVIII, no. 190 (1974), 83–84.

Chapter 6   *Landscape history relics of the rural scene*

1   A. G. Brunger, 'Early settlement in contrasting areas of Peters-
    borough County, Ontario', in J. D. Wood (ed), *Perspectives on Land-*

scape and Settlement in Nineteenth Century Ontario (Toronto, 1975), 117–41.

2 Hugh Clout, *Rural Geography. An Introductory Survey* (Oxford, 1972), Fig. 1.1, p. 3.

3 Frank Emery, *The Oxfordshire Landscape* (London, 1974).

4 B. L. Young, *Rustic Canyon and the Story of the Uplifters* (Santa Monica, Calif., 1976).

5 Viggo Nielsen, 'Agerlandets historie', and Aa. H. Kampp, 'Agerlandets geografi', in Arne Nørrevang and T. J. Meyer (eds), *Danmarks Natur* (København, 1970), vol. 8, 9–34 and 35–74.

6 Viggo Hansen, 'Bebyggelsens historie', in Arne Nørrevang and T. J. Meyer (eds), *Danmarks Natur* (København, 1970), vol. 9, 9–138.

7 K.-E. Frandsen, Aa. H. Kampp and M. Mogensen, 'Starreklinte', *Kulturgeografi* 123 (1975), 117–31.

8 Aa. H. Kampp and K.-E. Frandsen, 'En gård i landsbyen', *Geografisk Tidsskrift*, 66 (1967), 198–224; 'A Danish farm in the village', *Agricultural Typology Symposium, International Geographical Union*, Hissar, India (1968).

9 State of California, Office of Planning and Research, *Historic Preservation Element Guidelines* (Sacramento, Calif., 1976).

10 Doylestown Borough Planning Commission, *Design Resources of Doylestown, Bucks County, Pennsylvania* (Doylestown, 1969).

11 Wormleighton, Warwickshire, National Grid Reference SP4453, Ordnance Survey One Inch Sheet No. 145 and Two-and-a-half Inch Sheet No. SP45.

12 W. T. Alderson and S. P. Low, *Interpretation of Historic Sites* (Nashville, Tenn., 1976).

13 H. C. Bowen, *Ancient Fields* (London, 1961; reprinted 1970); Christopher Taylor, *Fields in the English Landscape* (London 1975).

14 Joscelyne Finberg, *Exploring Villages* (London 1968); Nigel Harvey, *Fields, Hedges and Ditches* (Princes Risborough, 1976); P. H. Sawyer (ed), *Medieval Settlement* (London, 1976).

15 M. W. Beresford and J. K. S. St Joseph, *Medieval England. An Aerial Survey* (Cambridge, 1958); A. R. H. Baker and R. A. Butlin (eds), *Studies of Field Systems in the British Isles* (Cambridge, 1973); J. A. Yelling, *Common Fields and Enclosure in England 1450—1850* (London, 1977).

16 M. J. Harrison, W. R. Mead and D. J. Pannett, 'A Midland ridge-and-furrow map', *Geographical Journal*, 131, pt. 3 (1965), 366–9.

17 K. J. Allison, *Deserted Villages* (London, 1970); M. W. Beresford and J. G. Hurst (eds), *Deserted Medieval Villages: Studies* (London, 1971).

18 Harry Thorpe, 'The lost villages of Warwickshire', *Warwickshire and Worcestershire Magazine* (1959); Harry Thorpe, 'The Lord and the Landscape, illustrated through the changing fortunes of an English parish, Wormleighton', *Acta Geographica Lovaniensia*, 3 (1964), 71–126 and also in *Transactions and Proceedings, Birmingham Archaeological Society*, 80 (1965), 38–77.

19 Harry Thorpe, 'Air, ground, document', in D. R. Wilson (ed), 'Aerial reconnaissance for archaeology', *Council for British Archaeology, Research Report No. 12* (1975), 141–53.

20 E. L. Hawes, 'Living historical farms and the environmental historian', *Environmental History Newsletter*, III, no. 1 (1976), 18–40. A British example of such a recreated community is the famous, all year round experiment with an Iron Age rural settlement at the Outdoor Museum at Butser, Hampshire.

21 *ibid.*, 20–1.

22 Alderson and Low, See note 12 above.

23 Trevor Rowley and Mike Breakell (eds), *Planning and the Historic Environment* (Oxford, 1975).

24 D. N. Hall, 'Modern surveys of Medieval field systems', *Bedfordshire Archaeological Journal*, 7 (1972), 53–67.

25 Sonoma County (California) Planning Department, *Sonoma County Historic Preservation Program* (Santa Rosa, Calif., 1976), 94 pp.; Harald Uhlig and Cay Lienau, 'Types of field patterns', vol. I, *Basic Material for the Terminology of the Agricultural Landscape*. International Working-Group for the Geographical Terminology of the Agricultural Landscape. (Giessen, 1967), E1–E68.

26 W. G. Hoskins, *English Landscapes* (London, 1973).

27 R. L. Janiskee, 'City trouble, the pastoral retreat, and pioneer America: a rationale for rescuing the middle landscape', *Pioneer America*, VIII, no. 1 (1976), 1–8.

Chapter 7   *Historical remains within the urban context*

1 B. J. L. Berry, *The Human Consequences of Urbanisation* (London, 1973); Jay Vance, *This Scene of Man. The Role and Structure of the City in the Geography of Western Civilization* (New York, 1977).

2 J. H. Chambers, 'Conservation analysis', *Preservation News*, XV (May 1975).

3 Michael Aston and James Bond, *The Landscape of Towns* (London, 1976).

4 Ewart Johns, *British Townscapes* (London, 1965).

5 Lewis Mumford, *The City in History* (New York, 1961).

6 Ministry of Transport, Steering Group and Working Group, Buchanan Report, *Traffic in Towns* (London, 1963).

7 C. M. Heighway (ed), *The Erosion of History. Archaeology and Planning in Towns* (London, 1972).

8 Pamela Ward (ed), *Conservation and Development in Historic Towns and Cities* (Newcastle upon Tyne, 1969).

9 David Listokin and Peter Morris, *Neighborhood Preservation and Rehabilitation* (New Brunswick, N.J., 1975).

10 City of Tucson, Arizona, Department of Community Development, Planning Division, *Tucson's Historic Districts. Criteria for Preservation and Development* (Tucson; 3rd printing, 1974).

11 François Sorlin, Piero Gazzola and Raymond Lemaire, 'Rescue operation: the face of Europe', *Council of Europe, Committee on Monuments and Sites, Studies Series* 1 (Strasbourg, 1973), 235–47. For a good example of a detailed national programme see A. R. H. Baker, 'Keeping the past in the present: the preservation of French townscapes', *Town and Country Planning*, 37, no. 7 (1969), 308–11.

12 D. A. Hinton and David Carpenter, *Oxford Buildings From Medieval to Modern: Exteriors* (Oxford, 1972).

13 Tom Hassall, 'Oxford: an urban case study', and John Ashdown, 'The buildings of Oxford', in Trevor Rowley and Mike Breakell (eds), *Planning and the Historic Environment* (Oxford, 1975), 61–8 and 68–78; Frank Emery, *The Oxfordshire Landscape* (London, 1974), 206–15.

14 D. D. Arreola, 'Locke, California: persistence and change in the cultural landscape of a Delta Chinatown', California State University, Hayward, Department of Geography, unpublished Master's Thesis (1975); D. D. Arreola, 'The Chinese role in creating the early cultural landscape of the Sacramento-San Joaquin Delta', *The California Geographer*, XV (1975), 1–16; C. L. Yip, 'A time for bitter strength: the Chinese in Locke, California', *Landscape*, 22, no. 2 (1978), 3–14.

15 Kevin Lynch, *What Time is this Place?* (Cambridge, Mass., 1972).

16 Harry Kühnel. *Denkmalpflege und Althussanerung im Krems an der Donau. 1959—1974* (Krems an der Donau, 1974).

17 Albert Gattermann, Kurt Hinterndorfer, Herbert Rodinger and Rupert Schweiger, *Entwürfe zur Erneurung der Altstadtgebiete von Krems und Stein* (Krems an der Donau, 1975).

18 National Trust for Historic Preservation, *Historic Districts. Identification, Social Aspects and Preservation* (Washington, D.C., 1975).

19 Michael Jones and Venke Olsen (eds), *Ilsvikøra-Footdee: To Samfunn-Samme Debatt* (Trondheim, 1977).

20 Ilsvikøra, Preservation Plan. *Addresseavisen*, 2 September 1977; *Arbeider-Avisa*, 2 September 1977; and personal communication from Michael Jones, September 1977.

21 Jean-Pierre Greenlaw, *The Coral Buildings of Suakin* (Stocksfield, London, Boston, 1976).

22 Brian Goodey, 'Where we're at: interpreting the urban environment', *Urban Design Forum*, 1 (1978), 28–34; T. R. Lakshamanan and L. R. Chatterjee, 'Urbanization and environmental quality', *Association of American Geographers, Resource Papers No. 77 (1)* (Washington, D.C., 1977).

23 M. W. Barley (ed), 'The plans and topography of Medieval towns in England and Wales', *Council for British Archaeology, Research Report No. 14* (1976); L. R. Ford, 'Continuity and change in historic cities: Bath, Chester, and Norwich', *Geographical Review*, 68, no. 3 (1978), 253–74; Michael Hughes, *The Small Towns of Hampshire. The Archaeological and Historical Implications of Development* (Southampton, 1976); M. D. Lobel (ed), *Historic Towns*, vol. 1 (London and Oxford, 1969).

24 G. D. Trent (ed), *The Gentle Art of Walking* (New York, 1971).

Chapter 8   *Old landscapes bearing the imprints of industry*

1 Allan Pred, 'The external relations of cities during "Industrial Revolution" with a case study of Göteborg, Sweden: 1868–1890', *University of Chicago, Department of Geography, Research Paper No. 76* (1962).

2 E. A. Wrigley, 'A simple model of London's importance in changing

English society and economy, 1650–1750', *Past and Present*, 37 (1967), 40–70.

3   H. C. Darby (ed), *A New Historical Geography of England* (Cambridge, 1973).

4   Alan R. H. Baker and J. B. Harley (eds), *Man Made the Land; Essays in English Historical Geography, a Series from 'The Geographical Magazine'* (Newton Abbot, 1973).

5   W. G. Hoskins, *English Landscapes* (London, 1973).

6   Frank Booker, *The Industrial Archaeology of the Tamar Valley* (Newton Abbot, 1967).

7   Brian Bracegirdle, *The Archaeology of the Industrial Revolution* (London, 1973); Kenneth Hudson, *Industrial Archaeology: A New Introduction* 3rd edn. (London, 1976).

8   Kenneth Hudson and Ann Nicholls, *A Directory of Museums* (London, 1975).

9   National Trust for Historic Preservation in the United States, T. P. Wrenn and E. D. Mulloy, *America's Forgotten Architecture* (New York, 1976).

10   Arthur Raistrick, *Industrial Archaeology. An Historical Survey* (St Albans, 1973).

11   National Trust, *America's Forgotten Architecture*; David Pearce and Marcus Binney (eds), *Off the Rails: Saving Railway Architecture* (London, 1977); The Liverpool Street Station Campaign, *The London Stations* (London, 1977).

12   *The Los Angeles Times*, 'Turning point for L.A. marked', September 1976.

13   Ruth Newhall (ed), *Illustrated Historical Program Golden Spike Centennial, Lang Station, Sunday, September 5, 1976* (Saugus, Calif., 1976).

14   R. A. Buchanan, *Industrial Archaeology in Britain* (Harmondsworth, Middx., 1972).

15   Hugh Bodey, *Discovering Industrial Archaeology and History* (Princes Risborough, 1975).

16   Frank Atkinson, *Industrial Archaeology of North East England* (Newton Abbot, 1974, 2 vols.).

17   Kenneth Hudson, *A Guide to the Industrial Archaeology of Europe* (Bath, 1971).

18   Otto Norn, *En Købstads Industrialisering. Da Horsens fik Hestekræfter* (Horsens, Denmark, 1973); Gert Bech-Nielsen, J. P. Clausager, J. B. Jensen and E. B. Kallesøe, 'Horsensgruppen – en præsentation', *Industrialismens Bygninger og Boliger, 1* (København, 1975), 32–6.

19   Per Boje, 'Det industrielle miljø 1840–1940', *Industrialismens Bygninger og Boliger, Publikation nr. 10* Statens humanistiske forskningsråd og Institut for Økonomisk Historie ved Københavns Universitet (1976).

20   Knud Bidstrup, P. Bredsdorffs Tegnestue and A. Nyvig, *Nordisk Ide-Konkurrence om Horsens Fremtid. Besvarelse 27349* (Copenhagen, 1974).

21   Otto Norn, 'Arbejder-, håndværker- og industrimuseet i Horsens', *Industrialismens Bygninger og Boliger, 1* (København, 1976), 15–20;

and *Politiken Weekly*, 'Spændende museum i el-værk', (25 February–3 March, 1977), 7.
22 J. E. Koch, 'Industrial archaeology: a selected bibliography', *Council of Planning Librarians, Exchange Bibliography No. 1382* (1977).

Chapter 9 *Old landscapes bearing the imprint of the state*

1 Norman J. G. Pounds, *Political Geography* (New York, 1963).
2 N. M. Short, P. D. Lowman, Jr., S. C. Freden, and W. A. Finch, Jr., *Mission to Earth: LANDSAT Views of the World* (Washington, D.C., 1976) (see Plate 316).
3 Robert Cameron, *Above Los Angeles* (San Francisco, 1976); Emil Egli and Hans Richard Müller, *Europe from the Air* (London, 1959).
4 Personal communication from Michael Aston, Taunton, Somerset, autumn 1977.
5 Hildegard Binder Johnson, *Order Upon the Land. The US Rectangular Land Survey and the Upper Mississippi Country* (New York, 1976); Norman J. W. Thrower, *Original Survey and Land Subdivision. A Comparative Study of the Form and Effect of Contrasting Cadastral Surveys*. No. 4 in the Monograph Series of the Association of American Geographers (Chicago, 1966), 160 pp.
6 William D. Pattison, *Beginnings of the American Rectangular Land Survey System, 1784—1800*, University of Chicago, Department of Geography Research Paper No. 50, (Chicago, 1957).
7 An example of an apt monument of this kind occurs in Columbiana County, Ohio where an historic marker has been placed to commemorate the beginning of the survey of American public lands in 1785 according to the rectangular design specified by Congress in the Land Ordinance of the same year.
8 George N. Nasse, 'Historic Monuments of Albania – the City of Berat', 39th Annual Meeting, Association of Pacific Coast Geographers, Tucson, Arizona, June 1976.
9 C. P. Mountford and Ainslie Roberts, *Your Guide to Ayers Rock* (St Peters, South Australia, 1961).
10 Yigael Yadin, *Masada: Herod's fortress and the Zealot's last stand* (New York, 1966).
11 Glyn Daniel, 'Editorial', *Antiquity*, XLV, no. 177 (1971), 1–2, 4–5; P. S. Garlake, *The Ruins of Zimbabwe* (Lusaka, 1974).
12 Ben R. Finney, 'Voyaging canoes and the settlement of Polynesia', *Science*, 196, no. 4296 (1977), 1277–85; David Lewis, 'Hōkūle'a' follows the stars to Tahiti', *National Geographic*, 150, no. 4 (1976), 512–38.
13 *Los Angeles Times*, 16 September 1976. Pt. II, 3; 21 March 1977, Pt. II, 4; and 31 March 1977, Pt. II, 6.
14 David Lowenthal, 'The Bicentennial landscape: a mirror held up to the past', *Geographical Review*, 67, no. 3 (July 1977), 253–67; Kenneth Garrett, 'From Baltic To Bicentennial by square rigger', *National Geographic*, 150, no. 6 (December 1976), 824–58.
15 R. G. Collingwood, *A Guide to the Roman Wall* (Newcastle Upon

Tyne, revised 1971); G. D. B. Jones, *Hadrian's Wall from the Air* (Manchester, 1976).

16 Robin Birley, *On Hadrian's Wall Vindolanda: Roman Fort and Settlement* (London, 1977).

17 Henry A. Hartwig, Superintendent of Los Angeles National Cemetery kindly supplied this information.

18 Ruth Helkiær Jensen and Kr. Marius Jensen, *Topografisk Atlas Danmark* (København, 1976).

19 Robert M. Newcomb, 'Episodes or continuity: culture change on the landscape of Northeastern Jutland, Denmark', *Geographical Institute, University of Aarhus, Arbejdsrapport* 3 (1975).

20 Fredningsplanudvalget for Randers Amt, *Forslag til Betænkning vedrørende Naturparken 'Mols Bjerge'* (Randers, 1966).

21 The Advisory Council on Historic Preservation, *A Plan to Preserve the Historic Resources of the Gettysburg Area of the Commonwealth of Pennsylvania* (Washington, D.C., 1977).

Chapter 10 *Landscape analysis; a new tomorrow for the visible past*

1 Claire O'Kelly, *Guide to Newgrange* (Wexford, 1971).

2 Isobel Cosgrove and Richard Jackson, *The Geography of Recreation and Leisure* (London, 1972); I. M. Matley, 'The Geography of international tourism', *Association of American Geographers, Resource Paper No. 76 (1)* (1976).

3 Ministry of Land and Natural Resources, *Leisure in the Countryside — England and Wales*, Cmnd. 2928 (London,1966); J. A. Patmore, *Land and Leisure* (Harmondsworth, Middx., 1972).

4 I. G. Simmons, *Rural Recreation in the Industrial World* (London, 1975); and J. T. Coppock and B. S. Duffield, *Recreation in the Countryside. A Spatial Analysis* (London, 1975).

5 R. C. J. Burton, 'The recreation carrying capacity of the countryside: a research report presenting the methodology and results of ecological and psychological surveys of Cannock Chase, Staffordshire', *Occasional Publication* 11, Keele University Library, Staffordshire (1974).

6 Michael Aston and Trevor Rowley, *Landscape Archaeology. An Introduction to Fieldwork Techniques on Post-Roman Landscapes* (Newton Abbot, 1974); Trevor Rowley and Mike Breakell (eds), *Planning and the Historic Environment*. Papers Presented to a Conference in Oxford, 1975 (Oxford, 1975).

7 Council of Planning Librarians, Bibliographies. No. 304: J. Marsh (1972); no. 938: S. Schauman (1975); no. 1064: T. J. Nieman and R. C. Viohl (1976); and no. 1220: P. Dearden (1977), (Monticello, Ill.); and R. L. Janiskee, 'The recreational utility of rural relic landscape: a study in landscape resource perception and utilization', Ph.D. Dissertation, Department of Geography, University of Illinois (1974); J. W. Neff, 'A geographic analysis of the characteristics and development trends of the non-Metropolitan tourist-recreation industry of Southern Appalachia', Ph.D. Dissertation, Department of Geography, University of Tennessee (1975); and D. L. Stallings, 'Environmental cogni-

tion and land use controversy: an environmental image study of Seattle's Pike Place Market', Ph.D. Dissertation, Department of Geography, University of Washington (1975).

8 Historical Geography Research Group, Institute of British Geographers, *Register of Research in Historical Geography* (Belfast, 1976).
9 *Los Angeles Times*, 'Our National Parks: crisis is deepening', 26 September 1976.
10 R. S. Crofts and R. U. Cooke, 'Landscape evaluation: a comparison of techniques', *Department of Geography, University College London, Occasional Papers No. 25* (1974); Institute of British Geographers, 'Landscape Evaluation', *Transactions No. 66* (1975), 119–63; Phillip Kane, *Evaluating Landscape Attractiveness. A Review of Problems and Methods and a Technique Developed for the National Trust of South Australia.* Part of Project no. 11, National Estate Programme 1975–76 (Adelaide, 1976); E. H. Zube, R. O. Brush and J. Gy. Fabos (eds), *Landscape Assessment: Values, Perceptions and Resources* (Stroudsburg, Pa., 1975).
11 A. J. Veal, 'Environmental perception and recreation: a review and annotated bibliography', Centre for Urban and Regional Studies, University of Birmingham, *Research Memorandum, 39* (1974).
12 Vagn Rud Nielsen, 'Danish planning law: an overview', *Byplan*, 25. Årgang, Nr. 4 (1973), 105–8.
13 Fredningsplanudvalget for Frederiksborg, København og Roskilde Amter. *Fredningsplanudvalget for Frederiksborg, København og Roskilde Amter 1970* (København, 1971).
14 Fredningsplanudvalget for Ribe og Ringkjøbing Amter, *Generel landskabsplan for Ribe amt* (Ribe, 1970); Fredningsplanudvalget for Ringkjøbing Amt., *Ringkjøbing Amt. Landskabsanalyse 1972* (Ringkjøbing, 1972), English summary, 122–126.
15 The plan for Northeast Zealand, see footnote 13, contains interesting maps which illustrate settlement history and which analyze the landscape architecture of this area. An exhaustive inventory of scheduled sites was a useful publication by the North Jutland County: Fredningsplanudvalget for Nordjyllands Amt, *Nordjyllands Amt. Registrering af Fredede Arealer* (Aalborg, 1973).
16 R. M. Newcomb, 'Has the past a future in Denmark? The preservation of landscape history within the nature park', *Geoforum*, 9 (1972), 61–7.
17 Fredningsplanudvalget for Aarhus Amt og Fredningsplanudvalget for Nordjyllands Amt, *Mariager Fjord Omraadet: Landskabsplan* (Aalborg & Århus, 1974).
18 Wolfgang Framke, 'Kriterien für die Einrichtung von Naturparks', *Tagungsbericht und wissenschaftliche Abhandlungen, 40. Deutscher Geographentag Innsbruck 19. bis 25. Mai 1975* (Wiesbaden, 1976), 642–52; A. K. Primdahl and W. Framke, 'Eksperimenter i landskabsevaluering: det Midtjyske Søhøjland', *Skrifter fra Geografisk Institut ved Aarhus Universitet, Nr. 37* (1976).
19 Jens Jørgensen, 'Eksperimenter i landskabsevaluering: Perceptionsanalyse', *Skrifter fra Geografisk Institut ved Aarhus Universitet, Nr. 36* (1976).

20   Wolfgang Fieguth, 'Historical geography and the concept of the authentic past as a regional resource', *Ontario Geography*, 1 (1967), 55–60.

21   John L. Frisbee, III, 'Historic preservation and the tourist industry' (Washington, D.C., 1970).

22   US Bureau of Land Management, Department of the Interior, 'Cultural resources: one criteria for land-use planning'. *Our Public Lands*, vol. 27, no. 2 (1977), 3–6.

23   Australia, *Report of the National Estate*. Committee of Inquiry into the National Estate (Canberra, 1974).

24   Sven-Olof Lindquist, 'Kulturlandskapets miljö', *Ymer* (Årsbok, 1970), 6–28.

25   Sven-Olof Lindquist, 'Tillgänglighet och landskapsinnehåll', *Plan* (Stockholm), Årg. 27, Nr. 3 (1973), 121–39.

26   D. W. Meinig, 'The beholding eye. Ten versions of the same scene', *Landscape Architecture*, 66, no. 1 (January 1976), 47–54.

27   Geografisk Institut, Aarhus Universitet. *Landsbymiljø i Aarhus Kommune 1974* (Århus, 1975); R. M. Newcomb, 'The Århus, Denmark Village Project: applied geography in the service of the municipality', *Geographical Review*, 67, no. 1 (January 1977), 86–92.

28   V. A. Konrad and S. M. Taylor, *The Past in the Present: (Pre) Historical Resource Appraisal in the Toronto Area. A Summary Report* (Hamilton, 1977).

29   R. W. Travis, 'Regional components of the recognition of historic places', *Geography Graduate Student Association, Department of Geography, University of Illinois, Occasional Publications of the Department of Geography*, Paper no. 3 (1972).

30   Table 17 was stimulated by comments offered in the following publications: W. T. Alderson and S. P. Low, *Interpretation of Historic Sites* (Nashville, Tenn., 1976); Brian Goodey, 'Interpreting the conserved environment. Issues in planning and architecture', *Oxford Polytechnic, Department of Town Planning, Working Paper No. 29* (1977); David Lowenthal, 'Past time, present place: landscape and memory', *Geographical Review*, LXV, no. 1 (1975), 1–36; D. B. Luten, 'Parks and people', *Landscape*, 12, no. 2 (1962–63), 3–8; David Stea, 'Landscape dichotomies: pat phrases and preservation', *Landscape,* 20, no. 1 (1975), 44–8.

31   Historic Laxton village in the Midlands is an example of a feature from the past which can be preserved with both its function as an agricultural village and its form as an example of intact open field farming. By contrast, St Katharine-by-the-Tower in London represents the preservation of old forms in order that they may be put to new uses, in this case a fascinating complex of old docks and warehouses is being redeveloped to serve the commercial and recreational needs of an urban population.

32   *Aarhus Stiftstidende,* 'En ny bronzealderhøj vil koste et par millioner', by Mette Fastrup (25 November 1974), 20.

33   *Preservation News*, XVIII, no. 8 (August 1978), 1, 4, 6 and 8; and Supreme Court of the United States, *Penn Central Transportation*

Company et al., Appellants v. *City of New York et al., Opinion*, 77–444 (26 June 1978).

34   The Advisory Council on Historic Preservation, *A Plan to Preserve the Historic Resources of the Gettysburg Area of the Commonwealth of Pennsylvania*, (Washington, D.C., 1977).

35   *Preservation News*, XVIII, no. 6 (June 1978), 4; and The National Trust of Historic Preservation, *Economic Benefits of Preserving Old Buildings*. (Washington, D.C., reprinted 1978).

36   David and Ruth Whitehouse, *Archaeological Atlas of the World* (San Francisco, 1975) which lists nearly 5,000 sites; and Nick and Helna Mika, *Historic Sites of Ontario* (Belleville, 1974), which includes over 700 sites.

37   The Central Solano County Cultural Heritage Commission, *Our Lasting Heritage. An Historic and Archaeological Preservation Plan for Central Solano County* (Suisun City, 1977); and State Historical Society of Wisconsin, *Historic Preservation in Wisconsin. A Manual for Communities* (Madison, 1977).

38   City of Oakland Planning Department, *Rehab Right. How to Rehabilitate Your Oakland House Without Sacrificing Architectural Assets* (Oakland, 1978).

39   *Preservation News*, 'Training programs: a Preservation News Supplement', XVIII, no. 1 (January 1978).

40   *Bulletin of Environmental Education (BEE)*, published by the Education Unit of the Town and Country Planning Association. For examples of the use of preservation units in classroom and field, see 'Heritage education: a new dimension in environmental work', *BEE*, 85 (May 1978), and 'The Town and Country Tomorrow Competition – a symposium, from Hertfordshire teachers', *BEE*, 86 (June 1978).

41   Glyn Daniel puts it well in one of his editorials when he speaks of 'the use of the understood past by an interested and informed present', *Antiquity*, XLVIII, no. 190 (1974), 83–4.

42   Two recent publications in the field of utilitarian preservation which commend themselves by reason of their scope and attractive format are: Fredningsplanudvalget for Århus Amt, *Landskabsanalyse for Århus amt. Naturvidenskabelige, forhistoriske, historiske og undervisningsmæssige interesser* (Århus, 1977); and Illinois Department of Conservation, Division of Historic Sites, *Preservation Illinois. A Guide to State and Local Resources*. (Springfield, 1977).

Select Bibliography

Alderson, W. T. and Low, S. P., *Interpretation of Historic Sites* (Nashville, Tenn., 1976)

Århus Amt, Fredningsplanudvalget for, *Landskabs Analyse for Århus Amt.* (Århus, 1977)

Aston, M. and Rowley, T., *Landscape Archaeology* (Newton Abbot, 1974)

Aston, M. and Bond, J., *The Landscape of Towns* (1976)

Australia, Committee of Inquiry into the National Estate, *Report of the National Estate* (Canberra, 1974)

Baker, A. R. H., 'Today's studies of yesterday's geographies', *Geographical Magazine*, 43 (1970–1), 452–3

Baker, A. R. H. and Harley, J. B. (eds), *Man Made the Land. Essays in English Historical Geography* (Newton Abbot, 1973)

Baker, A. R. H. and Harley, J. B. (eds), *Man Made the Land. Essays in English Historical Geography* (Newton Abbot, 1973)

Beresford, M. W. and Hurst, J. G. (eds), *Deserted Medieval Villages: Studies* (1971)

Bidstrup, K., 'Danmark – Dit og Mit', *Dansk Byplanlaboratorium Skriftserie* Nr. 15 (København, 1977)

Binney, M. and Burman, P., *Change and Decay. The Future of Our Churches* (1977)

Booker, F., *The Industrial Archaeology of the Tamar Valley* (Newton Abbot, 1967)

Buchanan, R. A., *Industrial Archaeology in Britain* (Harmondsworth, 1974)

California, State of. Department of Parks and Recreation, The Resources Agency, *California Inventory of Historic Resources* (Sacramento, Calif., 1976)

California, State of. Office of Planning and Research, *Historic Preservation Element Guidelines* (Sacramento, Calif., 1976)

Christian, R., *Vanishing Britain* (Newton Abbot, 1977)

Cornforth, J., *Country Houses in Britain: Can They Survive?* (1974)

Cosgrove, I. and Jackson, R., *The Geography of Recreation and Leisure* (1972)

Crofts, R. S. and Cooke, R. U., 'Landscape evaluation: a comparison of techniques', *Department of Geography, University College London, Occasional Papers* no. 25 (1974)

Darby, H. C. (ed), *A New Historical Geography of England* (Cambridge, 1973)

Department of the Environment, *List of Ancient Monuments: England* (1974)

Egli, E. and Müller, H. R., *Europe from the Air* (1959)

Emery, F., *The Oxfordshire Landscape* (1974)

Fairbrother, N., *New Lives, New Landscapes* (Harmondsworth, 1972)

Falkner, A., *Without Our Past? A Handbook for the Preservation of Canada's Architectural Heritage* (Toronto, 1977)

Fawcett, J. (ed), *The Future of the Past* (New York, 1976)

Fedden, R. and Joekes, R. (eds), *The National Trust Guide* (1973)

Fieguth, W., 'Historical geography and the concept of the authentic past as a regional resource', *Ontario Geography* 1 (1967), 55–60

Ford, L. R., 'Historic preservation and the stream of time: the role of the geographer', *Historical Geography Newsletter* 5 (1975), 1–15

Framke, W., 'Kriterien für die Einrichtung von Naturparks', *Tagungsbericht und wissenschaftliche Abhandlungen* (Wiesbaden, 1976), 642–52

Fredningsplanudvalget for Aarhus Amt og Fredningsplanudvalget for *Nordjyllands Amt, Mariager Fjord Omraadet: Landskabsplan* (Aalborg & Aarhus, 1974)

Fredningsplanudvalget for Århus Amt, *Landskabsanalyse for Århus Amt. Naturvidenskabelige, forhistoriske, historiske og undervisningsmaessig interesser* (Århus, 1977)

Fredningsplanudvalget for Frederiksborg, København og Roskilde Amter, *Fredningsplanudvalget for Frederiksborg, København og Roskilde Amter 1970* (København, 1971)

Fredningsplanudvalget for Nordjyllands Amt, Sekretariatet, *Nordjyllands Amt. Registrering af Fredede Arealer* (Aalborg, 1973)

Fredningsplanudvalget for Ringkjøbing Amt, *Ringkjøbing Amt. Landskabsanalyse 1972* (Ringkjøbing, 1972)

Goodey, B., 'Interpreting the conserved environment. Issues in planning and architecture', *Oxford Polytechnic, Department of Town Planning, Working Paper* no. 29 (1977)

Hansen, P., Koester, V., and Nielsen, V., *Bygningsfredning* (København, 1975)

Hawes, E. L., 'Living historical farms and the environmental historian', *Environmental History Newsletter* III (1976), 18–40

Heighway, C. M. (ed), *The Erosion of History. Archaeology and Planning in Towns* (1972)

Hoskins, W. G. *English Landscapes. How to Read the Man-Made Scenery of England* (1973)

Hudson, K., *A Guide to the Industrial Archaeology of Europe* (Bath, 1971)

Hudson, K. and Nicholls, A., *The Directory of Museums* (1975)

Humlum, J., *Landsplanlægingsproblemer* (København, 1966)

Illinois Department of Conservation, Division of Historic Sites, *Preservation Illinois. A Guide to State and Local Resources* (Springfield, 1977)

Institute of British Geographers, 'Landscape Evaluation', *Transactions* 66 (1975), 119–63

Kennet, W., *Preservation* (1972)

Koester, V. (ed), *Bygningsbevaring* (København, 1975)

Lowenthal, D., 'Past time, present place: landscape and memory', *Geographical Review* LXV (1975), 1–36

Matley, I. M., 'The geography of international tourism', *Association of American Geographers, Resource Paper* no. 76, 1 (1976)

Meinig, D. W., 'The beholding eye. Ten versions of the same scene', *Landscape Architecture* 66 (1976), 47–54

National Geographic Society, *Visiting Our Past. America's Historylands* (Washington, D.C., 1977)

National Trust for Historic Preservation in the United States, *Historic Districts. Identification, Social Aspects and Preservation* (Washington, D.C., 1975)

National Trust for Historic Preservation in the United States and Kettler, E. L. and Reams, B. D. Jr., *Historic Preservation Law: An Annotated Bibliography* (Washington, D.C., 1976)

National Trust for Historic Preservation in the United States and Wrenn, T. P. and Mulloy, E. D., *America's Forgotten Architecture* (New York, 1976)

Newcomb, R. M., 'Geographic aspects of the planned preservation of visible history in Denmark', *Annals, Association of American Geographers* 57 (1967), 462–80

Newcomb, R. M., 'Has the past a future in Denmark? The preservation of landscape history within the nature park', *Geoforum* 9 (1972), 61–7

Nielsen, V., 'Status for den Antikvariske Lovgivning', *Fortid og Nutid* XXIV (1971), 475–98

Nieman, T. J. and Viohl, R. C., 'The description, classification and assessment of visual landscape quality', *Council of Planning Librarians, Exchange Bibliography* no. 1064 (1976)

Nørrevang, A. and Meyer, T. J. (eds), *Danmarks Natur*, 8 'Agerlandet' and 9 'Det Bebyggede land' (København, 1970)

Patmore, J. A., *Land and Leisure in England and Wales* (Harmondsworth, 1972)

Rasmussen, S. E., *København* (København, 1969)

Rasmussen, S. E., *London* (København, 1973)

Roberts, B. K., *Rural Settlement in Britain* (Folkestone, 1977)

Rowley, T. and Breakell, M. (eds), *Planning and the Historic Environment* (Oxford, 1975)

Royal Commission on the Ancient and Historical Monuments and Constructions of England, *A Matter of Time* (1960)

Simmons, I. G., *Rural Recreation in the Industrial World (1975)*

Sorlin, F., Gazzola, P. and Lemaire, R., 'Rescue operation: the face of Europe', *Council of Europe, Committee on Monuments and Sites, Study Series* no. 1 (Strasbourg, 1973)

Sparrow, C. and Peace, D., *Public Inquiries: Presenting the Conservation Case* (1971)

Stea, D., 'Landscape dichotomies: pat phrases and preservation', *Landscape* 20 (1975), 44–8

Steensberg, A., *Den Danske Landsby gennem 6000 År* (København, 1973)

Taylor, C., *The Cambridgeshire Landscape* (1973)

Taylor, C., *Fields in the English Landscape* (1975)

Taylor, R., Cox, M. and Dickins, I. (eds), *Britain's Planning Heritage* (1975)

Thorpe, H., 'Air, ground, document', in Wilson, D. R. (ed), 'Aerial reconnaissance for archaeology', *Council for British Archaeology, Research Report* no. 12 (1975), 141–53

Trent, G. D. (ed), *The Gentle Art of Walking* (New York, 1971)

Veal, A. J., 'Environmental perception and recreation. A review and annotated bibliography', *Centre for Urban and Regional Studies, University of Birmingham, Research Memorandum* no. 39 (1974)

Whitehouse, D. and Whitehouse, R., *Archaeological Atlas of the World* (1975)

Ziegler, A. P. *Historic Preservation in Inner City Areas; A Manual of Practice* (Pittsburgh, Pa., 1974)

INDEX